TALES OF
FRESH-WATER FISHING

Zane Grey

PLATE I

Tales of
FRESHWATER FISHING

by

ZANE GREY

THE DERRYDALE PRESS

LANHAM AND NEW YORK

THE DERRYDALE PRESS

Published in the United States of America
by The Derrydale Press
4720 Boston Way, Lanham, Maryland 20706

Distributed by NATIONAL BOOK NETWORK, INC.

Library of Congress Cataloging-in-Publication Data

Grey, Zane, 1872–1939.
   Tales of Freshwater Fishing / Zane Grey.
     p. cm.
  Originally published: Tales of fresh-water fishing. New York ; London:
Harper & Brothers, 1928.
   ISBN 1-58667-052-2 (pbk. : alk. paper)
   1. Fishing   I. Title

SH441 .G6 2001
799.1 ' 1—dc21   00-060140

CONTENTS

ILLUSTRATIONS

TALES OF
FRESH-WATER FISHING

A DAY ON THE DELAWARE [1]

OUR summer outing at Lackawaxen slipped by swiftly, as only such days can, and the last one arrived. As we started out in the early morning the fog was rising from the river and hung like a great gray curtain along the mountain tops; while here and there, through rifts, the bright sun shone, making the dew sparkle on the leaves. Far up the mountain-side could be heard the loud caw of a crow and the shrill screech of a blue jay. A gray squirrel barked from his safe perch in a tree by the road-side. A ruffed grouse got up from the bushes along the road, and with a great whir disappeared among the trees. The air was keen, with a suspicion of frost in it, and fragrant with pine and hemlock. This was to be our last day. We were going to improve every moment of it, and, perhaps, add more glorious achievements to memory's store, to be lived over many times in the dark, cold days of winter. I looked at Reddy and marveled at the change a month could bring. He was the color of bronze and the spring of the deer-stalker was in his rapid step.

"Well, looks as if you were not going to get that big one today," he said.

"I am afraid not," I said. "We would have had him if it had not been for your idiotic failure to land the big fellow you hooked the other day."

"I wish you would stop reminding me of that and give me a chance to forget it," he answered. "I suppose you never make any mistakes."

"But it was so careless," I insisted, "to have a four-pounder in your hands and then lose him."

"Yes, I know; but let's forget it. I hope you will hook one

[1] This story, published in Shield's Magazine, *Recreation*, May, 1902, is the first story Zane Grey ever had printed.

twice as big and that he will break your tackle and give me a chance to get a picture of you for future reference," he replied.

At the lower end of the big eddy below Westcolang Falls, the Delaware narrows, and there commences a two-mile stretch of eddies, rifts, falls, and pools that would gladden the heart of any angler.

"Now, my boy," I said, "we will toss for choice as to who takes the other side going down."

"I don't know if I would not just as willingly take this side," said Reddy, noting the swift water between him and the other shore.

"No," I answered, "that would not be fair. You know I am acquainted with the river, and the other side is the best, so here goes for the toss."

I won the toss and chose the near side, with a cheerful consciousness of my generosity, which was not in the least affected by Reddy's suspicious glances. He was game, however, and waded into the swift water without another word; and he got safely across a deep place that had baffled me many a time. I stepped into the water, which was clear and beautiful, and as cold as ice. In a little eddy below me I saw the swirl of one of those vultures of the Delaware, a black bass, as he leaped for his prey and sent a shower of little shiners out of the water, looking like bright glints of silver as they jumped frantically for dear life. It was a grand day for fishing, and the bass seized hungrily at any kind of bait I offered. They were all small, however, and as I was after big game I returned them safe to the water.

Occasionally I looked over to see what Reddy was doing. Usually he was up to his neck in the water and half the time his rod was bent double. I also noticed something that worried me considerably. It was a long, black object, and it floated from a string tied to Reddy's belt.

About noon we both made for the big stone near the middle of the river, where we rested and had our lunch. My fears were realized. That long black object was a three-pounder, a beautiful specimen of the red-eyed bronze-back of the Delaware.

"Have you been fishing, or did you come along just for com-

ZANE GREY WITH A SIX-POUND SMALL-MOUTH BLACK BASS
OF THE DELAWARE

PLATE II

REDDY GREY CATCHING BAIT

PLATE III

pany?" asked Reddy, cheerfully. I made some remark about the luck of certain people.

Reddy was satisfied to stop then; in fact, he loafed the rest of the day, but I am a hard loser and I hated to quit. Five o'clock found us at the foot of the rifts with only one more hole to fish. It was the Beer Mug, a hole so deep that it looks black, and always is covered with great patches of foam. It was a likely place for a big fellow, but I had never caught one there. Now I have memories of that hole which will never be effaced.

Reddy hooked and landed a big eel which wound the six-foot leader entirely around its slippery body. This made Reddy so tired that he said things which cannot be repeated here, and quit for the day.

I caught two small bass and a sunfish. Then I tried a hellgramite for a change. I fished the hole every way, but without success. I was reluctantly winding in my line, of which I had more than one hundred feet out, when I felt a little bite and hooked what I knew at once to be a chub. I continued to reel in my line in disgust, when suddenly it became fast on something. It felt like a water-soaked log. I pulled and pulled, but could not get the line off. I did not wish to lose fifty feet or more of good line, so I waded out and down the side of the pool to a point opposite where I thought I was fast. Imagine my surprise when I got there to find my line going slowly and steadily upstream, through water that was quite swift. I could not believe my eyes and was paralyzed for the moment. That chub was six inches long, probably, but he could never have moved the line in that manner. Reddy dropped his things and became interested in a moment, with his characteristic remark that "something must be doing."

Then I struck hard, for I knew I had hooked a heavy and powerful fish.

At the first rush he took twenty yards of line and pulled my tip under water. The reel went around so fast it burned my thumb. With one yell I settled down to business. I knew my tackle and that if the fish could be kept in that pool he was mine. He made for the head of the pool and then he went from side to side in short, furious dashes. My brother was yelling to me like a lunatic, and was running around snapping pictures of me with his camera.

I controlled the fish perfectly for the first few moments of that struggle, and then, with what seemed to me a settled purpose, he started downstream for shoal water. Below were swift and dangerous rifts for wading and I knew if he got in them I should lose him. Twice I tried to stop him, but each time I saw the wet line stretch with the heavy strain on it as he tugged doggedly; and fearing it would snap, I had to follow him. I waded downstream as fast as possible, and as I climbed over a big stone in my way I saw the fish distinctly in the shallow water below me. It was a pike, fully a yard long, and as his great yellow body flashed in the water, his head pointed toward the bottom and tail up, I groaned in spirit. He was not even tired, and there I was, in a dangerous place to wade, a five-ounce rod in my hands, and at the other end of a silken thread a monster.

Wading over a bad place I lost my balance and my thumb slipped off the reel. At that critical moment the pike made his fiercest, maddest rush. It was all over in less than a second. My reel, being a four-multiplier, overran, the wet line tangled and became fast, there was a snap, and I was looking miserably at a limp line that floated on the swift water in front of me. That was an unhappy moment.

As we walked down the winding mountain road Reddy generously forgot his wish and tried to cheer me, but without avail. I could hardly see the beauty of the setting sun, going down behind the mountains in a red blaze of glory.

FIGHTING QUALITIES OF BLACK BASS—1907

PROBABLY all fishermen, whether they know it or not, are egotists. Mark Antony was one. He could not see that Cleopatra sent a diver down to hook live fish upon his line. The genial and gentle Izaak Walton was an egotist. There is some strange spell haunting stream and lake, and it persuades most anglers to have faith in experience that they think is wisdom. As far as each individual and his contentment is concerned, experience *is* wisdom.

Besides egotism there is in nearly every fisherman a humor, a certain loquaciousness, a friendly levity, an inclination to argument, an inexplicable sense of the pleasure in idling hours along a river, and a peculiar tendency toward exaggeration which he can recognize in his companion, but is rarely capable of seeing in himself.

It is a curious fact that about the thing I love best and know most—black-bass fishing—I have written but little. Always I have observed, read, listened, yet seldom ever opened my lips except to ask questions. I do not think much of this attitude and consider it akin to the feeling I had when as a boy I would never tell where the best fishing places were.

Well, the river we fished in those bygone days was rocky and swift, and the bass we caught were both small- and large-mouth. Sometimes we got hold of a hard-fighting big-mouth bass, but not often. It is only fair for me to say that I could not champion Dilg on my experience gained in those years, nor with knowledge gained from my old comrade. And I mention him here and my past strange reluctance to write about black-bass fishing because I want to make plain that I could not approach the subject lightly.

The fighting qualities of a fish, or anything pertaining to his spirit, color, size or taste, are simply matters of environment. As

5

far as that is concerned, what any living man or creature *is* at any time in his or its life depends entirely upon hereditary influence and the shaping power of environment. That is to say, a bass will appear and fight and taste according to what the water he lives in and the food he subsists on make of him.

The fact that big-mouth bass in Eastern and Southern waters and toward the outlet of the Great Lakes are not, as a rule, worth the catching has not a great bearing on the subject. Taking fishing waters into account, those mentioned by Mr. C. might constitute one-tenth of the water where bass abound. And that one-tenth includes warm, sluggish waters, stocked waters, poor feeding waters, over-fished waters, and many other considerations not included at all in the other nine-tenths.

When Mr. C. bases his judgment upon the experience gained from Eastern and St. Lawrence waters, and the opinions of fishermen frequenting them, he is quite right in thinking as he does. But if Mr. C. will spend his summers in the Northwest and his winters in the Southeast and fish a little, he will learn by contrast.

The only men who can ever solve this problem as to the relative merits of the small- and big-mouth bass must be men with unlimited time and an insatiable desire to include all fishing waters in their experience. I have not met many such fishermen.

Mr. C. uses a term, "Carp bass." I have heard this used by a few boatmen and fishermen. It is a pure colloquialism, the same as hundreds of other local names given to different fish. He intended to cast calumny upon the big-mouth bass. To me, notwithstanding that carp are a despised fish, his remark was far from felicitous or even true. For I have hooked carp that fought like tigers. I remember one that I believed I never would bring to the boat. It took a good while to land him and he weighed only eighteen pounds.

Mr. C. brings in ridicule of the pot-bellied Florida bass, and calls them "big, flabby monsters." To be sure, the majority of Florida bass are not worth catching. But what does that prove? In northern Florida there are deep, shady, cool waters where big-mouth bass are game, and because of their size exceedingly hard on light tackle. And almost five hundred miles south of these waters, still in Florida, there is a river called Shark River. It comes down out of the Everglades and has to be entered near Cape Sable. Up at its wild headwaters this river is black, deep, swift, cool. It is full of bass—that much-despised big-mouth variety. They will bite at anything, take a fly, break water and make long, fast rushes, and they are good sport.

Again, here is another instance out of many I might put forward. Up in Sullivan County there is a lake full of bass, large- and small-mouth. The little, red-eyed bronze-backs are game to the core; the great, yellow, gaping-jawed fellows are lazy and indifferent. Now across the Delaware in Pike County, not more than twenty miles distant as a crow flies, is another lake. This lake, too, has both varieties of bass. It is a deep lake, rocky, spring-fed at the bottom, always cold. It has patches of long-stemmed lilies in thirty feet of water, right offshore. Many times I have anchored outside a little way and floated live shiners toward those lily beds. Any other kind of bait was useless. Some days were good—some bad. I always caught small-mouth bass and always they were exceedingly gamy. But—and here is the point—I have never yet been able to hold one of the great, large-mouth bass that live in that lake. I've seen enough to know that the big ones are *not* small-mouth bass. They are too heavy. I have seen them chasing shiners among the lily pads, heard them ranting and lunging around like tarpon after mullet. I did not need to see them, for the thump and roar of water was enough for me. When one of these big bass would take a bait he would start off like a cannon ball. When I hooked one he would make straight for the lily pads. If held hard he would begin to tear around and plunge just on the surface, get his head, and then go on the rampage into the lilies, generally taking tackle with him. My brother and I have always been ashamed to go after those big fish with anything but our regular light-bass tackle. But if we are ever to catch one in that place, it's got to be on heavier outfits.

I have not space to multiply examples. Suffice to say that I know that the game quality of a big-mouth bass depends entirely upon the waters in which he is found. It is not my experience that *all* big-mouth and small-mouth fight equally well when found in the same waters. But, in the main, Mr. C.'s reply to Dilg was an attack on the *species*. And as such it is wrong. Mr. C.'s experience has been limited to his own narrow field of observation.

This controversy on black-bass fishing is almost as fascinating as the actual thing. It is almost as interesting to hear or read what new fishermen think as it is to go to new fishing waters. But the way some fishermen fish is infinitely amusing to me, and the tackle they use is inexpressibly painful. Fortunately, I can also laugh at myself on occasion, and once in a while experience a severe pain at my own idiosyncrasies. Whenever I get to bragging I try to remember Cæsar's allusion to his deaf ear.

Mr. C. mentions hooking bass in the throat.

It would, of course, be unlikely for Dilg to hook a bass in the throat. And I, who am mostly a bait fisherman, would consider myself disgraced if I let a bass swallow a bait. Of late years it has been seldom that I hooked a bass below the lips, and when I did make such a fluke I was able, as I use a barbless hook, to get it out without hurting the fish and to return him safely to the water. It has been a long time since I even made a bass bleed. Dilg uses the very lightest and finest fly tackle. And I use the very lightest and finest bait tackle. This may all seem very snobbish, or æsthetic, or "classy," but it is simply the result of education. It's simply a question of tackle and fairness to fish. I have caught small tarpon in the Panuco River on tackle I once used for bass. Of course I had to use a larger reel and multiply the length of line, but in other respects I used the regular old bass tackle.

A while back, in pursuit of new knowledge, I tried those casting baits made famous by R. H. Davis. It seemed to me that all the bass were insulted and rushed savagely to attack the things. What struck me, after their peculiar luring power—which I attribute entirely to the pugnacious spirit of the fish—was the fact that a bass hooked with these gangs could not fight. He cannot break water in comparison with a bass otherwise hooked. I caught one hooked all over, mouth, head, and back, and I had to cut him to pieces to get the hooks out.

Davis is a splendid fellow and a wonderful fisherman. It will be interesting to read what he has to say in regard to the relative gameness of small- and large-mouth bass. He will take sides against Dilg, I am sure. And I regret this exceedingly, because he will be wrong, and a man with his reputation ought really to be right.

And now, in conclusion, I want to take decided exception to one remark made by Mr. C. in his reply to Dilg. I refer to his remark on fly-fishing in the Delaware. I do not intimate that this remark was intentionally misleading. Fishermen not familiar with the river would be apt to get a wrong impression.

If I know any fishing water at all it is the Delaware River. I live on it. I own nearly a thousand acres of land along it. I have fished it for ten years. I know every rapid, every eddy, almost, I might say, every stone from Callicoon to Port Jervis. This fifty-mile stretch of fast water I consider the very finest bass ground that I have fished. The mountains are heavily wooded and bold and rugged; the river is winding and picturesque and a succession of white rapids and foam-flecked eddies. The bass that grow from four to six and one-half pounds in this swift water are magnificent game fish. And that is why I am always at home in late summer when these big fish bite.

Mr. C. remarked that "thousands of bass are taken every summer with the fly on the Delaware." If it was meant seriously, I think it should have been made clear. I fancy that in his enthusiasm Mr. C. just "talked." He was not clear, deliberate, and absolutely sure of his facts.

There are black bass in the Delaware from its source down to Trenton. And at certain times during the season a few fish might rise to a fly anywhere above Milford, and very probably below in the quieter waters. The West Branch and the East Branch, joining at Hancock, are both shallow streams. Both branches furnish good fly-fishing for those who are content to catch little bass. Neither stream can be compared to the Lackawaxen River, which empties into the Delaware in front of my cottage. But I have never had a rise from a big bass in the Lackawaxen or the Delaware.

The Delaware proper only comes into existence at Hancock, and really is not a river until about Long Eddy. Cochecton Falls, five miles below Callicoon, marks the development of the best water. In ten years, during hundreds of trips between Cochecton Falls and Cedar Rapids, perhaps thirty miles of swift water and

positively the best of the river, I have never encountered a fly
fisherman. At the boarding-houses and camps I have met, in that
time, perhaps half a dozen men who had fly rods in their outfits.

The best of these fishermen, Mr. Patterson, a man of wide experience and much skill, told me he caught a good many bass. In
fact, he had sport, but he admitted the bass ran small, a two-
pounder being the largest. The bass I have caught on a fly with
few exceptions ran less than half a pound in weight. A small
gold spoon with a fly attached appeared to be more attractive,
and bass up to three pounds would take it. But for me, the real
bass, the big fellows, never batted an eye or twitched a fin at these
artificial lures. Possibly they may have done so for some better
fisherman than I am. However, I find it hard to believe. If I
saw it I would put it down as the exception that proved the rule.

I see hundreds of canoeists and fishermen come down the Delaware every summer. If they were fly fishermen I would know it.
They all stop at the hotel opposite my place. Many of them are
kind enough to pay me a little visit. Whatever style of fishermen
they were, if they caught a big bass or even made a good catch
I would be likely to find it out. Most of them, amateurs or
otherwise, had good fishing. Some were inclined to ridicule sport
on the Delaware. To these I usually told a few bass stories and
always had the pleasure of seeing them try politely to hide their
conviction of what an awful liar I was. Then I paralyzed them
by showing some twenty-six-inch mounted bass, and upon occasions a few live bass of six pounds and over; and upon one remarkable occasion I made several well-meaning but doubtful fishermen
speechless and sick. These men had fished around the hotel for
days. They were disgusted. They could not catch any bass.
Somebody sent them to me. I am sorry to state that they hurt
my feelings by asking me if I had bait to sell. That little inter-
view ended in my advising them to learn the rudiments of the
sport—to make their own flies and catch their own bait. And they
delicately implied that they did not believe there were any more
bass in the Delaware than there were brains in my head. So I
sarcastically told them to come down to the hotel float on the following evening at sunset. Next morning at daylight my brother
and I started up the river. We had *rather* a good day. At sunset

we were on time with the boat at the float. And also the disgruntled anglers were on hand. In fact, so many people crowded down on the float that it sank an inch or so under water. I wish all my readers could have heard the plunging of the big bass in my fish box as I lifted the lid. When I bent over to take out a bass I was deluged with water. But this was great! I captured a fine black fellow—about four and a half pounds—and he gaped and spread his great dorsal fin and curved his broad tail, and then savagely shook himself. I pitched him out. Souse! Then, deliberately, one after another, I lifted big bass out of this fish box under the seat of my boat and threw them into the water. Forty bass, not one under three pounds and some over four!

This is history now up along that section of the Delaware, and I am not considered so much of a liar as I used to be.

I have caught a good many Delaware bass running over six pounds, and I want to say that these long, black and bronze fellows, peculiar to the swift water of this river, are the most beautiful and gamy fish that swim. I never get tired of studying them and catching them. It took me years to learn how to catch them. Perhaps some day I shall tell how to do it. But not until I have had the pleasure of seeing Dilg and Davis and other celebrated fishermen who have not yet honored me with a visit, breaking their arms and hearts trying to induce one of these grand fish to rise to an artificial lure. Because, gentlemen, they will not do it.

Every fishing water has its secrets. A river or a lake is not a dead thing. It has beauty and wisdom and content. And to yield up these mysteries it must be fished with more than hooks and for more than fish. Strange things happen to the inquiring fisherman. Nature meets him halfway on his adventure. He must have eyes that see. One fisherman may have keener eyes than another, but no one fisherman's observation is enough.

I can learn from anyone, yet I do not stop at that, and go on trying to learn for myself. And so amazing experience and singular knowledge have become my possession. Let me close with one more word about the Delaware. In July, when the water gets low and clear, I go up the river. I build a raft and lie flat upon it and drift down. I see the bottom everywhere, except in rough water. I see the rocks, the shelves, the caverns. I see where the

big bass live. And I remember. When the time comes for me to
fish I know where the big bass are. Nevertheless, it is far from
easy to catch them. They are old and wary. I never caught one
in deep water. I never had one take hold nearer than one hundred
feet from the boat. I never use a casting rod or fish with a short
line. I never caught one on the day I first saw him. I never caught
one on any day he saw me or the boat. I never caught a very
large bass, say over five pounds, until after the beginning of the
harvest moon. Furthermore, I know that these big bass do not
feed often.

One day at a certain place I caught a small-mouth bass, next
day a large-mouth, then a *salt-water striped bass*, all out of the
same hole. They were about the same size, upward of two pounds;
none of the fish jumped and they all fought well and equally. I
could not have told the difference. This was in the Delaware, not
a mile from my home. I have seen striped bass with the shad, and
once I think I saw a sturgeon. While fishing for bass I have caught
big trout. I have had small bass bite my bare toes in the water.
I have seen bass engaged in a pitched battle with what appeared
to be some kind of order. I have seen a bass tear a water snake
to pieces. These last two instances I heard of from other fishermen
before I saw them myself.

I repeat, no one fisherman's observation or experience is enough.
We must get together or forever be at dagger's point. Hamlet
said there was much not dreamed of in Horatio's philosophy.

BLACK BASS—ARTIFICIAL LURE

THERE seems to me to be a very simple reason for black bass striking at an artificial lure. A naturalist or scientist would merely say that a bass thinks a lure is something which it is not. And whatever he thinks depends upon the individual bass.

Likewise the individuality of an angler determines his mental attitude toward black bass. I fished for bass for twenty years and always was learning. That is because Nature is infinite in her variations and mysteries. A man could go on learning forever about any fish or any wild creature, or any tame one. It is a happy pastime—an obsession for anglers, especially the black-bass type, to go on thinking, arguing, wondering all the time when they are not fishing. When they are fishing they are learning.

A bass strikes an artificial fly because he imagines it to be a live fly. It is a rather more complicated matter—his striking at a wooden-plug bait or spoon. Most certainly he sometimes shows hostility toward these hideous contraptions. I surely do not blame him for that. It is an insult to a blue-blooded bronze-back to offer him a fake wooden minnow or a queer gaudy little thing that looks exactly like what it is. During or near the spawning season both male and female bass will strike viciously at these wooden baits. And I have had them take a hellgramite or crawfish or little stone-roller catfish bait and carry it away only to spit it out. Both these actions must be instincts of self-preservation.

But I am not prepared to state that when a bass angrily strikes at a plug he is fighting it. For during my long observation of black bass I have found that they fight with their dorsal fins. It is not only a battle flag, but a weapon, and a most effective one. A fighting bass elevates that dorsal, and darts under his adversary, slitting him across the belly. I used to find many bass, suckers, carp, chubs, floating dead in the water, and all slit across the belly

13

as cleanly as if they had been cut with a knife. For years it was a mystery to me what killed these fish. And it seems to me that if a bass really regarded a plug bait as an enemy to be killed he would attack it in his fighting way. Not improbably he regards it as something queer to eat which at the same time rouses his hostility.

To tell the truth I have often wondered if bass have not an entirely different reason for attacking these hideous plug baits. The intelligence of these fish is so often insulted. Does not one of the fighting species know perfectly well that at the other end of the line dreams a triple-expansion, four-multiplying, ivory-tipped lover of the beautiful and the wild—a bug-house angler like Zane Grey? Or does he not know perfectly well that the wielder of the delicate rod, rushing madly along the shore or rowing wildly from eddy to eddy, casting nine hundred feet at every cast, is no other than a fisherman-poet who sings and lilts and carols his lays about the only fish on earth—a bass-worshiper like Will Dilg? Or that the huge cheerful loafer who lolls in a boat all day, day after day, summer after summer, idly smoking, making one magnificent cast to every cigarette, talking like an imbecile about the sunshine on yon bank, or the little birds flitting, or the wind in the flowers, thinking up terrible joke-stories to write about his angler friends, is a time-absorbing, truth-destroying, past-master bass-murderer like Bob Davis?

Is this not enough to prove why any self-respecting bass resents the indignity heaped upon him?

THE LORD OF LACKAWAXEN CREEK—1908

WINDING among the Blue Hills of Pennsylvania there is a swift amber stream that the Indians named Lack-a-wax-en. The literal translation no one seems to know, but it must mean, in mystical and imaginative Delaware, "the brown water that turns and whispers and tumbles." It is a little river hidden away under gray cliffs and hills black with ragged pines. It is full of mossy stones and rapid ripples.

All its tributaries, dashing white-sheeted over ferny cliffs, wine-brown where the whirling pools suck the stain from the hemlock roots, harbor the speckled trout. Wise in their generation, the black and red-spotted little beauties keep to their brooks; for, farther down, below the rush and fall, a newcomer is lord of the stream. He is an archenemy, a scorner of beauty and blood, the wolf-jawed, red-eyed, bronze-backed black bass.

A mile or more from its mouth the Lackawaxen leaves the shelter of the hills and seeks the open sunlight and slows down to widen into long lanes that glide reluctantly over the few last restraining barriers to the Delaware. In a curve between two of these level lanes there is a place where barefoot boys wade and fish for chubs and bask on the big boulders like turtles. It is a famous hole for chubs and bright-sided shiners and sunfish. And, perhaps because it is so known, and so shallow, so open to the sky, few fishermen ever learned that in its secret stony caverns hid a great golden-bronze treasure of a bass.

In vain had many a flimsy feathered hook been flung over his lair by fly-casters and whisked gracefully across the gliding surface of his pool. In vain had many a shiny spoon and pearly minnow reflected sun glints through the watery windows of his home. In vain had many a hellgramite and frog and grasshopper been dropped in front of his broad nose.

15

Chance plays the star part in a fisherman's luck. One still, cloudy day, when the pool glanced dark under a leaden sky, I saw a wave that reminded me of the wake of a rolling tarpon; then followed an angry swirl, the skitter of a frantically leaping chub, and a splash that ended with a sound like the deep chung of water sharply turned by an oar.

Big bass choose strange hiding-places. They should be looked for in just such holes and rifts and shallows as will cover their backs. But to corral a six-pounder in the boys' swimming-hole was a circumstance to temper a fisherman's vanity with experience.

Thrillingly conscious of the possibilities of this pool, I studied it thoughtfully. It was a wide, shallow bend in the stream, with dark channels between submerged rocks, suggestive of underlying shelves. It had a current, too, not noticeable at first glance. And this pool looked at long and carefully, colored by the certainty of its guardian, took on an aspect most alluring to an angler's spirit. It had changed from a pond girt by stony banks, to a foam-flecked running stream, clear, yet hiding its secrets, shallow, yet full of labyrinthine watercourses. It presented problems which, difficult as they were, faded in a breath before a fisherman's optimism.

I tested my leader, changed the small hook for a large one, and selecting a white shiner fully six inches long, I lightly hooked it through the side of the upper lip. A sensation never outgrown since boyhood, a familiar mingling of strange fear and joyous anticipation, made me stoop low and tread the slippery stones as if I were a stalking Indian. I knew that a glimpse of me, or a faint jar vibrating under the water, or an unnatural ripple on its surface, would be fatal to my enterprise.

I swung the lively minnow and instinctively dropped it with a splash over a dark space between two yellow sunken stones. Out of the amber depths started a broad bar of bronze, rose and flashed into gold. A little dimpling eddying circle, most fascinating of all watery forms, appeared round where the minnow had sunk. The golden moving flash went down and vanished in the greenish gloom like a tiger stealing into a jungle. The line trembled, slowly swept out and straightened. How fraught that instant with a wild yet waiting suspense, with a thrill potent and blissful!

Did the fisherman ever live who could wait in such a moment? My arms twitched involuntarily. Then I struck hard, but not half hard enough. The bass leaped out of a flying splash, shook himself in a tussle plainly audible, and slung the hook back at me like a bullet.

In such moments one never sees the fish distinctly; excitement deranges the vision, and the picture, though impressive, is dim and dream-like. But a blind man would have known this bass to be enormous, for when he fell he cut the water as a heavy stone.

The best of fishing is that a mild philosophy attends even the greatest misfortunes. To be sure this philosophy is a delusion peculiar to fishermen. It is something that goes with the game and makes a fellow fancy he is a stoic, invulnerable to the slings and arrows of outrageous fortune.

So I went on my way upstream, cheerfully, as one who minded not at all an incident of angling practice; spiritedly as one who had seen many a big bass go by the board. The wind blew softly in my face; the purple clouds, marshaled aloft in fleets, sailed away into the gray distance; the stream murmured musically; a kingfisher poised marvelously over a pool, shot downward like a streak, to rise with his quivering prey; birds sang in the willows and daisies nodded in the fields; misty veils hung low in the hollows; all those attributes of nature, poetically ascribed by anglers to be the objects of their full content, were about me.

I found myself thinking about my two brothers, Cedar and Reddy for short, both anglers of long standing and some reputation. It was a sore point with me and a stock subject for endless disputes that they just never could appreciate my superiority as a fisherman. Brothers are singularly prone to such points of view. So when I thought of them I felt the incipient stirring of a mighty plot. It occurred to me that the iron-mouthed old bass, impregnable of jaw as well as of stronghold, might be made to serve a turn. And all the afternoon the thing grew and grew in my mind.

Luck favoring me, I took home a fair string of fish, and remarked to my brothers that the conditions for fishing the stream were favorable. Thereafter morning on morning my eyes sought the heavens, appealing for a cloudy day. At last one came, and I invited Reddy to go with me. With childish pleasure, that would have caused weakness in any but an unscrupulous villain, he eagerly accepted. He looked over a great assortment of tackle, and finally selected a five-ounce Leonard bait-rod carrying a light reel and fine line. When I thought of what would happen if Reddy hooked that powerful bass an unholy glee fastened upon my soul.

We never started out that way together, swinging rods and pails, but old associations were awakened. We called up the time when we had left the imprints of bare feet on the country roads; we lived over many a boyhood adventure by a running stream. And at last we wound up on the never threadbare question as to the merit and use of tackle.

"I always claimed," said Reddy, "that a fisherman should choose tackle for a day's work after the fashion of a hunter in choosing his gun. A hunter knows what kind of game he's after, and takes a small or large caliber accordingly. Of course a fisherman has more rods than there are calibers of guns, but the rule holds. Now today I have brought this light rod and thin line because I don't need weight. I don't see why you've brought that heavy rod. Even a two-pound bass would be a great surprise up this stream."

"You're right," I replied, "but I sort of lean to possibilities. Besides, I'm fond of this rod. You know I've caught a half-dozen bass of from five to six pounds with it. I wonder what you would do if you hooked a big one on the delicate thing."

"Do?" ejaculated my brother. "I'd have a fit! I might handle a big bass in deep water with this outfit, but here in this shallow stream with its rocks and holes I couldn't. And that is the reason so few big bass are taken from the Delaware. We know they are there, great lusty fellows! Every day in season we hear some tale of woe from some fisherman. 'Hooked a big one—broke this—broke that—got under a stone.' That's why no five- or six-pound bass are taken from shallow, swift, rock-bedded streams on light tackle."

When we reached the pool I sat down and began to fumble with my leader. How generously I let Reddy have the first cast! My iniquity carried me to the extreme of bidding him steal softly and stoop low. I saw a fat chub swinging in the air; I saw it alight to disappear in a churning commotion of the water, and I heard Reddy's startled, "Gee!"

Hard upon his exclamation followed action of striking swiftness. A shrieking reel, willow wand of a rod wavering like a buggy-whip in the wind, curving splashes round a foam-lashed swell, a crack of dry wood, a sound as of a banjo string snapping, a sharp splash, then a heavy sullen souse; these, with Reddy standing voiceless, eyes glaring on a broken rod and limp trailing line, were the essentials of the tragedy.

Somehow the joke did not ring true when Reddy waded ashore calm and self-contained, with only his burning eyes to show how deeply he felt. What he said to me in a quiet voice must not, owing to family pride, go on record. It most assuredly would not be an addition to the fish literature of the day.

But he never mentioned the incident to Cedar, which omission laid the way open for my further machinations. I realized that I should have tried Cedar first. He was one of those white-duck-pants-on-a-dry-rock sort of a fisherman, anyway. And in due time I had him wading out toward the center of that pool.

I always experienced a painful sensation while watching Cedar cast. He must have gotten his style from a Delsartian school. One moment he resembled Ajax defying the lightning and the next he looked like the fellow who stood on a monument, smiling at grief. And not to mention pose, Cedar's execution was wonderful. I have seen him cast a frog a mile—but the frog had left the hook. It was remarkable to see him catch his hat, and terrifying to hear the language he used at such an ordinary angling event. It was not safe to be in his vicinity, but if this was unavoidable, the better course was to face him; because if you turned your back an instant, his flying hook would have a fiendish affinity for your trousers, and it was not beyond his powers to swing you kicking out over the stream. All of which, considering the frailties of human nature and of fishermen, could be forgiven; he had, however, one great fault impossible to overlook, and it was that he made more noise than a playful hippopotamus.

I hoped, despite all these things, that the big bass would rise to the occasion. He did rise. He must have recognized the situation of his life. He spread the waters of his shallow pool and accommodatingly hooked himself.

Cedar's next graceful move was to fall off the slippery stone on which he had been standing and to go out of sight. His hat floated downstream; the arched tip of his rod came up, then his arm, and his dripping shoulders and body. He yelled like a savage and pulled on the fish hard enough to turn a tuna in the air. The big bass leaped three times, made a long shoot with his black dorsal fin showing, and then, with a lunge, headed for some place remote from there. Cedar ploughed after him, sending the water in sheets, and then he slipped, wildly swung his arms, and fell again.

I was sinking to the ground, owing to unutterable and overpowering sensations of joy, when a yell and a commotion in the bushes heralded the appearance of Reddy.

"Hang on, Cedar! Hang on!" he cried, and began an Indian war-dance.

The few succeeding moments were somewhat blurred because of my excess of emotion. When I returned to consciousness Cedar was wading out with a hookless leader, a bloody shin, and a disposition utterly and irretrievably ruined.

"Put up a job on me!" he roared.

Thereafter during the summer each of us made solitary and sneaking expeditions, bent on the capture of the lord of the Lackawaxen. And somehow each would return to find the other two derisively speculative as to what caused his clouded brow. Leader on leader went to grace the rocks of the old bronze warrior's home. At length Cedar and Reddy gave up, leaving the pool to me. I fed more than one choice shiner to the bass and more than once he sprang into the air to return my hook.

Summer and autumn passed; winter came to lock the Lackawaxen in icy fetters; I fished under Southern skies where lagoons and moss-shaded waters teemed with great and gamy fish, but I never forgot him. I knew that when the season rolled around, when a June sun warmed the cold spring-fed Lackawaxen, he would be waiting for me.

Who was it spoke of the fleeting of time? Obviously he had never waited for the opening of the fishing season. But at last

When the Pool Glanced Dark under a Cloudy Sky

PLATE IV

I Brushed the Meadow Daisies on the
Familiar Towpath toward Home

PLATE V

the tedious time was like the water that has passed. And then I found I had another long wait. Brilliant June days without a cloud were a joy to live, but worthless for fishing. Through all that beautiful month I plodded up to the pool, only to be unrewarded. Doubt began to assail me. Might not the ice, during the spring break-up, have scared him from the shallow hole? No. I felt that not even a rolling glacier could have moved him from his subterranean home.

Often as I reached the pool I saw fishermen wading down the stream, and on these occasions I sat on the bank and lazily waited for the intruding disturbers of my peace to pass on. Once, the first time I saw them, I had an agonizing fear that one of the yellow-helmeted, khaki-coated anglers would hook my bass. The fear, of course, was groundless, but I could not help human feelings. The idea of that grand fish rising to a feathery imitation of a bug or a lank dead bait had nothing in my experience to warrant its consideration. Small, lively bass, full of play, fond of chasing their golden shadows, and belligerent and hungry, were ready to fight and eat whatever swam into their ken. But a six-pound bass, slow to reach such weight in swift-running water, was old and wise and full of years. He did not feed often, and when he did he wanted a live fish big enough for a good mouthful. So, with these facts to soothe me I rested my fears, and got to look humorously at the invasions of the summer-hotel fishers.

They came wading, slipping, splashing downstream, blowing like porpoises, slapping at the water with all kinds of artificial and dead bait. And they called to me in a humor actuated by my fishing garb and the rustic environment:

"Hey, Rube! Ketchin' any?"

I said the suckers were bitin' right pert.

"What d'you call this stream?"

I replied, giving the Indian name.

"Lack-a-what? Can't you whistle it? Lack-awhacken? You mean Lack-afishin'."

"Lack-arotten," joined in another.

"Do you live here?" questioned a third.

I modestly said yes.

"Why don't you move?" Whereupon they all laughed and

pursued the noisy tenor of their way downstream, pitching their baits around.

"Say, fellows," I shouted after them, "are you training for the casting tournament in Madison Square Garden or do you think you're playing lacrosse?"

The laugh that came back proved the joke on them, and that it would be remembered as part of the glorious time they were having.

July brought the misty, dark, lowering days. Not only did I find the old king at home on these days, but just as contemptuous of hooks and leaders as he had been the summer before. About the middle of the month he stopped giving me paralysis of the heart; that is to say, he quit rising to my tempting chubs and shiners. So I left him alone to rest, to rust out hooks and grow less suspicious.

By the time August came, the desire to call on him again was well-nigh irresistible. But I waited, and fished the Delaware, and still waited. I would get him when the harvest moon was full. Like all the old moss-backed denizens of the shady holes, he would come out then for a last range over the feeding shoals. At length a morning broke humid and warm, almost dark as twilight, with little gusts of fine rain. Of all days this was the day! I chose a stiff rod, a heavy silk line, a stout brown leader, and a large hook. From my bait box I took two five-inch red catfish, the little "stone-rollers" of the Delaware, and several long shiners. Thus equipped I sallied forth.

The walk up the towpath, along the canal with its rushes and sedges, across the meadows white with late-blooming daisies, lost nothing because of its familiarity. When I reached the pool I saw in the low water near shore several small bass scouting among the schools of minnows. I did not want these pugnacious fellows to kill my bait, so, procuring a hellgramite from under a stone, I put it on my hook and promptly caught two of them, and gave the other a scare he would not soon forget.

I decided to try the bass with one of his favorite shiners. With this trailing in the water I silently waded out, making not so much as a ripple. The old familiar oppression weighed on my breast; the old throbbing boyish excitement tingled through my blood. I made a long cast and dropped the shiner lightly. He went under and then came up to swim about on the surface. This was a sign that made my heart leap. Then the water bulged, and a black bar shot across the middle of the long shiner. He went down out of sight, the last gleams of his divided brightness fading slowly. I did not need to see the little shower of silver scales floating up to know that the black bar had been the rounded nose of the old bass and that he had taken the shiner across the middle. I struck hard, and my hook came whistling at me. I had scored a clean miss.

I waded ashore very carefully, sat down on a stone by my bait pail, and meditated. Would he rise again? I had never known him to do so twice in one day. But then there had never been occasion. I bethought me of the "stone-rollers" and thrilled with certainty. Whatever he might resist, he could not resist one of those little red catfish. Long ago, when he was only a three- or four-pounder, roaming the deep eddies and swift rapids of the Delaware, before he had isolated himself to a peaceful old age in this quiet pool, he must have poked his nose under many a stone, with red eyes keen for one of those dainty morsels.

My excitation thrilled itself out to the calm assurance of the experienced fisherman. I firmly fastened on one of the catfish and stole out into the pool. I waded farther than ever before; I was careful but confident. Then I saw the two flat rocks dimly shining. The water was dark as it rippled by, gurgling softly; it gleamed with lengthening shadows and glints of amber.

I swung the catfish. A dull flash of sunshine seemed to come up to meet him. The water swirled and broke with a splash. The broad black head of the bass just skimmed the surface; his jaws opened wide to take in the bait; he turned and flapped a huge spread tail on the water.

Then I struck with all the power the tackle would stand. I felt the hook catch solidly as if in a sunken log. Swift as flashing light the bass leaped. The drops of water hissed and the leader whizzed. But the hook held. I let out one exultant yell. He did not leap again. He dashed to the right, then the left, in bursts of surprising speed. I had hardly warmed to the work when he settled down and made for the dark channel between the yellow rocks. My triumph was to be short-lived. Where was the beautiful spectacular surface fight I expected of him? Cunning old monarch! He laid his great weight dead on the line and lunged for his sunken throne. I held him with a grim surety of the impossibility of stopping him. How I longed for deep, open water! The rod bent, the line strained and stretched. I removed my thumb and the reel sang one short shrill song. Then the bass was as still as the rock under which he had gone.

I had never dislodged a big bass from under a stone, and I saw herein further defeat; but I persevered, wading to different angles, and working all the tricks of the trade. I could not drag the fish out, nor pull the hook loose. I sat down on a stone and patiently waited for a long time, hoping he would come out of his own accord.

As a final resort, precedent to utter failure, I waded out. The water rose to my waist, then to my shoulders, my chin, and all but covered my raised face. When I reached the stone under which he had planted himself I stood in water about four feet deep. I saw my leader, and tugged upon it, and kicked under the stone, all to no good.

Then I calculated I had a chance to dislodge him if I could get my arm under the shelf. So down I went, hat, rod, and all. The current was just swift enough to lift my feet, making my task most difficult. At the third trial I got my hand on a sharp corner of stone and held fast. I ran my right hand along the leader, under the projecting slab of rock, till I touched the bass. I tried to get hold of him, but had to rise for air.

I dove again. The space was narrow, so narrow that I wondered how so large a fish could have gotten there. He had gone under sidewise, turned, and wedged his dorsal fin, fixing himself as solidly as the rock itself. I pulled frantically till I feared I would break the leader.

When I floundered up to breathe again the thought occurred to me that I could rip him with my knife and, by taking the life out of him, loosen the powerful fin so he could be dragged out. Still, much as I wanted him I could not do that. I resolved to make one more fair attempt. In a quick determined plunge I secured a more favorable hold for my left hand and reached under with my right. I felt his whole long length and I could not force a finger

UNDER THE PINES

PLATE VI

MAST HOPE BROOK IN JUNE

PLATE VII

behind him anywhere. The gill toward me was shut tight like a trap door. But I got a thumb and forefinger fastened to his lip. I tugged till a severe cramp numbed my hand; I saw red and my head whirled; a noise roared in my ears. I stayed until one more second would have made me a drowning man, then rose gasping and choking.

I broke off the leader close to the stone and waded ashore. I looked back at the pool, faintly circled by widening ripples. What a great hole and what a grand fish! I was glad I did not get him and knew I would never again disturb his peace.

So I took my rod and pail and the two little bass, and brushed the meadow daisies, and threaded the familiar green-lined tow-path toward home.

MAST HOPE BROOK IN JUNE—1910

OF THE myriad of streams that Cedar, Reddy, and I have fished in, Mast Hope Brook is the one beyond compare. It is a joy, the substance of which are low tinkle and gurgle of unseen current beneath green banks; glancing sheets of hemlock-brown water shining in the sun, rushing soft and swift around the stones; and in the distance dreamy hum of waterfall, now lulling, now deepening to mellow boom.

We left the road at the little village and took to the brook trail winding through mass-thickets of rhododendron. The buds showed ambitious glints of pink. There were weedy, swampy, grassy places, blue with violets, and cool, fragrant, dewy dells to cross before we came out into an open valley. On the hill some men were cutting timber and burning brush. Long after we had entered the forest above, the smell of wood smoke lingered with us, seeming to have penetrated our very clothes. The trees were full-foliaged, the maples blowing like billows of a green ocean. The sun was dazzlingly bright. From time to time we caught alluring glimpses of the dancing brook. Everything was bathed in the rich thick amber light of June.

We were men wearing khaki suits and wading-boots; we carried the lightest of rods, the finest of lines, the thinnest leaders, the flimsiest flies; we were equipped with all the modern paraphernalia of up-to-date anglers; but for all that we had reverted to the bare-foot days, the memorable days of cut rods and twisted threads and stubby hooks and angleworms. Moreover, our conversation could not have been considered that of expert scientific fishermen; the wildest stretch of imagination would still have left it boys' talk.

"The crick's in bully shape," said Reddy, for the tenth time. We had been there often that spring; we had always found some unfavorable condition; we had watched the lowering of the brook, the weather, the many things involved. This was the day!

"I know where my big fellow I lost last year is," added Cedar. "Mind you steer clear of me when we get to that hole."

"Wonder how many we'll ketch," I put in, all aglow with hope.

At last we reached the head of the valley and turned off the trail into the forest. It was as if we had suddenly stepped among pink-and-white patches of snow. Mountain-laurel bloomed everywhere. How fresh, exquisite were these blossoms! It was an open hardwood forest, from which the large timber had been cut, and except for a few thickets of hemlock all the underbrush was laurel. We swept aside the low bushes with our knees and buried ourselves in the tall ones, to be showered with rosy snowy petals. We were confronted by beautiful walls of green and white through which only ruthless fishermen could have crushed their way.

Strange to say, once we stood upon the bank of the brawling brook, the boyish eagerness resurging with memories of long-past pleasures gave place somewhat to the selfish zest of the battle of men. Yet, after all, it was the old, youthful, playful rivalry augmented to matured pride in achievement.

"You fellows may as well consider yourselves out of my class from the start," suggested Cedar, loftily, as he jointed his rod. "Then you won't be disappointed at the finish."

Reddy regarded his elder brother with pity and me with thoughtful scorn. "Have either of you guys any money you can afford to lose?"

If there were trout in Mast Hope Brook that could jump at a bait as quickly as we snapped at Reddy's offer, they certainly were hungry fish.

"Boys, I'll be sorry to take this money," I said. "It'll be as easy as picking blossoms from these laurels. Now, as we're ready, how shall we divide up the stream? We can't fish together."

"As usual, you'd like to go ahead and get first whack at all the pools, eh?" queried Reddy. "I've fished down a stream behind you. Not for mine! Here's an idea. I'll fish the branch. Cedar will start in here, and you go down to the little island and fish from there. We'll meet at the log bridge for lunch."

His suggestion was accepted as a capital one, and he and I were making ready to start for our respective points when Cedar whipped his rod. Naturally we waited to see the first cast. I was not very charitable in my opinion of his casting, but I had to admit that he made a wonderful picture. He jerked his line back over his head, tore off about a basketful of laurel blossoms, and completed his cast. I saw the brown hackle alight and float down and sink; then came a swirl of the water and a surge of the line. On his very first try Cedar raised and hooked a trout. The fish executed a few interesting maneuvers and then playfully leaped over a snag and fouled the leader. Cedar pulled on the line and lifted the trout clear of the water, but could not get him any farther. To our surprise, the frantically wriggling silver-sided trout proved to be a lusty broad fellow nearly twelve inches long.

"Climb down, get him, one of you!" yelled Cedar, excitedly.

"Go yourself. I'll hold your rod," replied Reddy, running back.

"Too late! All over!" I warned. . . . "That's a bad place, Cedar. Look out!"

Of course the trout wriggled off; of course Cedar slipped in, the top of one boot under water; of course he floundered out, red in the face, and inclined to a remarkable flow of unprintable language. We gathered presently that for some occult reason we were to blame for the disaster.

"I'm afraid it's a bad start," remarked Reddy, soberly. Fishermen know that when a day begins badly very seldom does it end favorably. But there is never any telling and certainty about luck.

Reddy separated from me below where the branch tumbled off the mountain into the main brook, and with a last cheery call for me to bear in mind the issue of the day he disappeared under the trees. I cut across a corner of the wooded valley, through which the stream described wide curves. My stretch of water from the island to the bridge was a long one, open to the sun, free of brush, and presented no obstacles to easy wading. The brook babbled merrily onward, yet it was in no great hurry. I flipped out my fly across a brown dimpled shallow lane and let it float downward. From then, time was annihilated, or it stood still, I did not know which. I stepped along from wet stones to dry ones, wading little coves, casting my fly into the likely places. I covered much ground and cast many times before I had a rise, and then I missed. I caught a flash of the trout as he darted away into the shady depths. The brook widened, lingering in flat reaches, and softened its rippling song. The yellow and green of willows curled over the bank; from the wet grass growing out of the trickling springs peeped long-stemmed purple violets. In places a deep gush of blue invited rest of the eye. The caw of a crow from a hillside died gradually away in the distance, and the screech of a kingfisher followed me downstream. In a long sunny channel I caught a small trout. He was by far too small to keep, so I unhooked him gently, and taking one glance at the beauty of glistening dots and black-tipped fins and wondrous blend of silver and gold, I let him go. Strikes came few and far between, but that seemed of small matter. The whole day with its possibilities, its certainties, its fulfillments, lay long ahead. Then I saw a bridge. Surely it could not be the one where I was to wait for my brothers. In bewilderment I looked up for the sun. It shone hot and white directly over my head. A vague and pleasant sense of movement, song of brook and bird and stir of breeze, one little trout, a few rises, and the hours had flown!

I climbed up the bank and lay down upon a brown needle-mat under a pine tree. The wind blew over me with fervent breath, sweet and warm and laden with the smell of pine. I was far away from the world, held drowsily still by the spell of a summer day, by the thrall of the wilderness.

Cedar and Reddy burst noisily into my solitude, and enchantment filtered out to the mountings of mingled emotions—fear that my brothers had more to tell and show than I, hope that they had each caught big ones, surprise at Reddy's clouded brow, and mirth at Cedar's wrecked rod and bedraggled clothes and flashing eyes. We were all rather uncommunicative while we ate lunch, whether from ravenous appetites or disheartening experiences and prospects, I did not know; but the pleasure of eating when hungry, the genial sunshine, and roar of the rapids in the glen below roused anew the hopes of fishermen.

"They're not rising to flies," said Reddy. "Maybe they will this afternoon."

Cedar lit his pipe and puffed clouds of smoke. His eyes lost their flame and the lines of his face softened. "I got only two strikes this morning, and that's a blamed hard stretch to fish. The second trout! Oh! Say! but he was a whale! It was this way——"

Then followed the gripping story, familiar, yet ever new: the shaded pool with its circle of foam, a brown hackle slowly floating down—a gleam of gold. Splash! Swish! Tug! Powerful fish in headlong irresistible flight—whizzing reel—slippery rocks and slippery boots. Crash!—crippled knee and broken rod—wild rush—flying water—pull, hand over hand, pull!—stretching, tangled line—agonized hope ending in despair. Snap! a trailing, limp, sagging, weightless leader!

Wisely Reddy and I let silence speak fittingly of our deep understanding of this tragedy. How many times it had been our fortune! We rested a while and then portioned off the remaining two miles of the brook. The glen just below fell to my lot and I had difficulty in repressing my gratification. My brothers strode off into the forest with the parting shot that I might just as well find a sunny spot and go to sleep.

The glen was beautiful that day. It was like a long dim hall ceiled by dark cliff shadows. Shafts of gold streaked through the black hemlocks above. Mellow hollow roar rushed at me on a damp breeze. To the swift brown torrent, to the amber moss and lacy ferns, to the huge green-stained boulders, to the golden rays of light, drifting, floating in the hazy gloom, I paid again unutterable silent tribute.

When I was well into the glen I took off my brown hackle and substituted a short, stubby, black, common fish-hook. Then stealthily looking above and below to see if by chance my brothers might be in sight, I slipped my hand into my pocket to bring forth a flat tin box. It contained a few choice common angleworms. These were the backbone of my campaign; these were the strength of my boast to my brothers; these were the secret source of my assurance. I stifled a feeling of guilt. All was fair in love, in war —why not in fishing? I acquitted Cedar and Reddy of such an underhand game, but I could not elevate myself to the heights upon which I raised them.

I passed by many good places in my hurry, and climbing over a jumble of stones in a narrow construction of the ravine I reached my pool. How my pulse danced! The brook swept down a six-foot chute between broken fragments of cliff. There was a great round pool with a lashing current on my side close to the rocky shore, a swirling, foamy back-eddy on the other. Here the sun was excluded. The shade was cool, the stones were wet with spray, the roar of the fall was deafening and filled the gorge with reverberating sound.

A perturbing thrilling portent of something about to be, rushed stirringly over me as I crouched low and crawled behind a big boulder. I had been there before. Before I had had the same presaging breathlessness that now tightened my chest. Ample reason there was for my quiver of expectation.

I cast my bait over the rushing channel into the slow-circling pool. A vicious, active, black-nosed trout broke water and spilled sparkling drops over the foam. My line swept away, then sagged. I jerked. . . . Too late! My bait was gone. I put on another, suddenly awfully aware that there were only four angleworms left. This time I cast short of the pool; my leader raced with the yellow-eyed bubbles. I was about to reel in when I got a tug. I hooked the trout and led him, fighting hard, out of the back-eddy. Once in the current he bent my rod double. I played him and reeled him out of the swift water and unskillfully lifted him to the bank. He was a fine ten-inch trout, dark blue, a silver-sided, black-spotted beauty. Crawling back behind the boulder I cast again and raised another fish and landed him. Then I caught two more in rapid succession, making four in less than as many minutes. Each time I had failed to reach the back-eddy, as I had done on the first cast.

The big hungry trout was still there and I had but one bait left. Circumstances like these make the great crises in a fisherman's experience. In that tense moment, what could have gotten from me my last angleworm? Putting him on my hook, I raised a taut arm and made a long cast.

The bait alighted perfectly in the center of the pool and slowly drifted upstream, sinking the while. . . . No rise! I felt the cold quaking sensation known only to anglers. Down, down sank my bait. How deep the pool! Suddenly there came a fierce onslaught upon my line; it nearly jerked the rod out of my hands. Loosing my thumb from the reel, I let the line play out steadily. The big trout was going deep into the depths, far under the dark shelving stone. Then the line ceased running out but did not slacken. There were little vibrations and sudden strains; I knew he had not let go; I was absolutely certain that the bait had been in his mouth long enough, too long, but I could not strike. For an instant of eternity I was bound between hope and dread.

I got up cautiously and yanked with a regular old-time boyish yank on the rod. The heavy weight of the trout, his lightning-swift movement, brought a yell to my lips. He fought deep, making me shudder as I felt the line twang from contact with stones. After that one wild outward rush he turned for his subterranean home and ploughed and tugged and plugged. It was land him quickly or not at all, that I knew; and I pulled him in a way to delight my more expert brothers, could they have been there to see. A broad bar, a dull glow, shone in the pool; then a black streak flashed into the seething white air-filled current of the chute. But he failed to make the leap over the narrow ledge, and plunged back to be swept down with the rapid, a dead weight on my line. I ran with him as far as I could go, forty, fifty feet down, and saw him swing in close to the shore, where, out of the drowning current, he began to fight again. I reeled in with all the speed at my command, and knowing it would be fatal if he once got out of that comparatively smooth little cove, I yielded to a wild impulse and began to lift. I lifted with all my strength, starting eyes fixed on the trout, yet I saw the dangerously full bend of the rod. Out of the water I lifted him, up, up, and swung him in upon the bank.

The leader snapped. He dropped to the moss and began a series of incredibly rapid flops. I bounded for him; I fell to gather him in my arms, grabbed with fingers seemingly incapable of holding anything. How infernally slippery he was! A million times I had him; a million times he slipped out of my hands. He splashed in the shallow water just as a lucky random clutch ran

The Amber-green, Pink-white Colors of the Warm Forest

PLATE VIII

Mountain Laurel along the Brook

PLATE IX

my thumb in his mouth. His teeth were sharp, but if he had been a sawfish I would have held on. With grim foreboding of possibilities I killed him. Then, washing off the dirt and slime, I laid him upon the moss and gloated over him. Fifteen inches—no—fourteen he was—a broad heavy-shouldered trout, brilliant as a rainbow, with the most delicate and rare coloring of anything in nature.

The afternoon had waned when I strode out of the forest into the open valley below. The sun rimmed fleecy clouds with rose tints and the sky was as blue as the violets underfoot. The roar of the brook receded and died away, yet lingered in my mind. In fact, my mind was full, full of the thronging sensations of this day that had passed as a dream.

Cedar and Reddy were waiting for me under a chestnut tree on the outskirts of the village. Even in the riot of my fancy the joyous certainty of victory, when my eyes were dazzled by anticipation, I seemed to see them as strangely calm and self-contained.

"Any luck?" queried Reddy.

"Great! . . . Look!" I burst out, producing my trout and laying them side by side on the grass. I waited eagerly for the acclaim due me, but it was not forthcoming.

"Pretty fair," said Cedar.

"Not so bad," said Reddy. "Did you catch those on a fly?"

"Wasn't I using a fly when we separated?" I demanded, belligerently.

"My boy, you're not one-two-six." Reddy deliberately opened his basket—I hate those baskets, for you can never tell what they will hold—and laid out upon the ground, one by one, ten beautiful trout, not one under ten inches.

I gasped weakly. "What—did you get them—on?"

"Worms," replied Reddy, smilingly.

Cedar manifested the facial agitation habitual with him when he has a fellow in a corner and can kill him at will. He began to pull something wrapped in a napkin out of his pocket, and he seemed to have difficulty. But he got it out finally. That bundle could not be a fish! I was in danger of collapse. Deliberately he laid the long white thing on the grass, slowly he put back the first fold of napkin, leisurely he turned back the second, and with many a pause, and glance at me, and calm cool smile, he unwrapped a great trout and stretched him overlappingly beside the others.

Professional pride went into eclipse; I gazed and gazed in admiration at an eighteen-inch trout, the massive many-hued monarch of Mast Hope Brook.

"Lord! You got him!" I exclaimed. "After all your bad luck—losing the other. Say! What did you catch him on?"

"My boy, he broke his back reaching for a nice big fat fishing-worm."

DEER CREEK, WASHINGTON—1918

TWO unlucky and futile trips after the famous and illusive steelhead trout had in no wise dampened R. C.'s ambition nor Lone Angler's infallible optimism nor my unquenchable ardor. Indeed I fear I have inoculated my comrades with the peculiar fever in my blood that makes me long for the unattainable. How often I find myself realizing more and more that though to catch fish is the motive of angling, it is not the all! The unattainable is not the fish. It is that beauty and spirit and life which Tagore felt when he saw the leaping fish of the Ganges River. It is what Hudson felt when he took his long, lonely, apparently objectless rides on the desert of Patagonia.

In August on our way to Vancouver we found ourselves in Seattle, with a week to devote to steelhead trout. Upon inquiring we learned that the run of steelhead was over. The recent rain was just what the fish had been waiting for. With the freshets the steelhead had gone up to the headwaters of the streams.

From several of the fishing-tackle dealers, who kindly lent us all the assistance in their power, we got vague information about the wonderful steelhead fishing in Deer Creek. Not one of them, however, had been there. They showed us Deer Creek on the map and claimed that it was almost inaccessible. But if we could get there!

R. C. and Lone Angler and I spent two days running that Deer Creek legend to earth. At length we met the best two steelhead anglers in Seattle—Hiller and Van Tassel. They vouched for the marvelous fishing we might find in Deer Creek—if we could get there. Neither of these fishermen had ever been near it. But one of their favorite steelhead pools was in the Stillaguamish at the mouth of Deer Creek. Just recently that pool had been full of steelhead. When the rains came and the creek rose these fish

35

disappeared. They had gone up the creek. This was logical, and I began to yield to my old weakness for pioneering.

Van Tassel rounded up an old G. A. R. man who fished Deer Creek and never went any other place. He showed us photographs of a mess of steelhead that made R. C. gasp, Lone Angler look queer, and me dizzy. Seventeen pounds, the smallest! Tackle-smashers! You had to have a heavy rod, line, leader, and hook to hold those Deer Creek fish. The water was deep, swift, full of rocks. In fact the old gentleman emphasized how full of rocks and fish this creek was. In about ten minutes he had us three musketeers in a state of mental aberration. Finally the practical Lone Angler asked how to get to Deer Creek.

"Wal, I ain't been thar for two years," replied our informant. "I'm gittin' too old to walk—an' you can't go any other way. Thar ain't no trail, nuther. What's wuss, them Finns have took to dynamitin' the creek."

This was like dashing a bucket of cold water in our eager faces. We thanked the old angler and repaired to a spot of seclusion where we could confer on the matter.

"Same old gag!" muttered R. C., darkly and regretfully.

"Bum steer!" added Lone Angler, tersely.

Both my comrades were for discarding the Deer Creek idea as a myth. But I was loath to give it up.

"Nothing ventured, nothing gained!" was my argument. "We miss our goal many times, but now and then we do hit it."

So again, as often before, I prevailed against the better judgment of my trail partners. Moreover, they became imbued with my enthusiasm. Over the range, far away, was something calling. We decided to motor to McMurray, a lumbering town somewhere near the headwaters of Deer Creek, and there see if we could not find some one to guide us.

Our acquaintances, Van Tassel and Hiller, were enthusiastic over this project, but they prevailed upon us to go fishing with them first. Arlington, where they wanted to take us, was on the road to McMurray.

So next morning we rode fifty miles to Arlington through country most of which was a hideous black slash left by lumbermen.

Before dawn the next morning we were on our way to the Stilla-

ALONE—CONTENT—WADING DOWNSTREAM

PLATE X

THE GLORIOUS TROUT POOL

PLATE XI

guamish River. Day broke, the sun came up, and our road led toward a great gap in a magnificent mountain range. It was a relief to get by the deforested areas and see something of Washington's thick and verdant forests. Before six o'clock we reached the Stillaguamish, a limpid little river, rushing and placid by turns. And the pool they selected to try lay at the mouth of Deer Creek.

It developed that these experts had a singular method of bait fishing. They used rather heavy fly rods with enameled silk lines, the same as those used for fly-casting; a short heavy gut leader, transparent in the water; a sinker that would roll on the bottom with the current; and very small hooks. For bait a small ball of fresh salmon eggs that hid the hook was essential. They strapped a wire or canvas basket, large as a small dishpan, to their waists. And from this strap depended also a bait box, and a long rag to do service as a towel. I was soon to learn what a mess salmon eggs make on the hands.

The use of the basket was unique. I was indeed curious about it. Van Tassel waded knee-deep into the water, put on a bait, and stripping off the reel a goodly length of line, which fell in coils into the basket, he gave his rod a long side sweep and flip and sent that bait clear across the stream. It was an admirable performance, and far from easy, as we anglers soon learned. After considerable practice I learned to master about sixty or seventy feet, which was half of Van Tassel's cast. Mostly I threw the bait off.

We fished, and our instructors fished, but not a steelhead did we raise. The fish must have left the river for the creek. We returned to Arlington, and had breakfast at noon, and afterward we drove about ten miles to McMurray. There was one street, rather forlorn and deserted; and a beautiful lake; a huge sawmill belching smoke; and all around hills denuded of trees, stark and bare.

After considerable inquiry we located a fellow named Sam Arnold. It was he who had taken the old G. A. R. angler to Deer Creek. Then we were to learn that no one else had ever fished this stream, that it was full of big rainbows and steelhead, that the distance was eleven miles over a bad trail up and down through forest.

"All right. We don't care how hard it is to get there or what it costs," I said, concisely. "We are going. Will you take us?"

It developed that scarcely a month had elapsed since Arnold had been operated upon for appendicitis, and he felt that he was hardly strong enough to undertake the trip. Furthermore, there was absolutely no one else whom we could discover that knew how to get to Deer Creek. It appeared we had come to an impasse. R. C. and Lone Angler made facetious remarks. If there was no one to take us we could not go—that was all there was to it. But I was thinking. Not for an instant did I abandon my idea of going. Deer Creek had become a haunting, compelling obstacle to overcome. Finally I suggested that he take charge of our little expedition and not do any of the work himself.

"You can ride and get some men to do the packing," I concluded

"Ride! Say, friend, there are no horses or mules in this country. If you go to Deer Creek you'll have to walk and pack your own outfit on your back."

R. C. and Lone Angler hailed this information with ill-concealed delight. It nettled me a little. Apparently it pleased them when I encountered insurmountable difficulties.

"Very well, we will walk," I replied, without the slightest hesitation. "Arnold, will you take us?"

"Guess I'll have to, seein' your heart's so set on it," he replied, with a smile I liked. "How long will you want to stay?"

"Only a few days—a week at most. We'll go light as possible. I'll give you money to buy supplies. We'll get a tent and blankets at Arlington, and be back here tomorrow morning."

"Better make it about one o'clock," he replied. "We'll ride on the lumber train to the loggin' camp. That'll save a couple of miles. An' mebbe we can hire some lumberjacks to help pack the outfit in to Deer Creek."

So then and there it was settled, and we departed. My genial and effusive comrades could not fool me. Another wild-goose chase had I planned. Maybe! But despite their laments and misgivings I knew that deep down in their hearts, where the boy still lived, they were excited and thrilled. It could not have been otherwise.

Next day at noon we arrived at McMurray with as little equipment as we could persuade ourselves was absolutely necessary. We brought no tent because there was none at Arlington, and only a few blankets which a kindly merchant lent us. Van Tassel came with us.

Arnold was on hand to meet us, having with him four boys to pack the outfit. One of these was a sturdy fellow who carried an Alaskan pack-board to sling on his back. He had packed his own outfit over Chilcoot Pass.

While waiting for the lumber train we talked somewhat of the difficulties of getting to Deer Creek, but mostly of the alluring possibilities. It is that unknown element of chance, of adventure, of luck that makes wild expeditions so thrilling.

When I saw the lumber train I wondered where we would ride. The cars were merely frames on trucks, with huge iron spikes to hold the logs. It did not look at all safe. Lone Angler reversed his familiar speech. "We got here first, but I wish it'd been last and we'd missed this Pullman."

The train was long, and the longer it grew the more my doubts augmented. There was a caboose, however, and we threw our baggage into it and climbed aboard. Several other passengers were bound for the logging camp. This camp was about seven miles away, but we had to travel twice that distance to get there.

The moment I climbed aboard I knew things were going to happen. They did, and they began at once. The engineer of the train knew, of course, that he had some new passengers, and he undoubtedly intended that we should remember the ride. He started off smoothly and evenly. R. C. and I went out on the back platform of the caboose. I was facing the door, looking in, while holding on to the brake wheel with both hands. R. C., too, faced forward, but he did not have hold of anything. He was admiring the scenery. We were leaving McMurray and running rather fast, for a log train, when suddenly the engineer threw on the brakes. The caboose gave a terrific jerk. I thought there was a wreck. Every one inside went plunging head over heels. I saw Lone Angler

Wiborn fall from the back end to the front end, and turn upside down in a corner, and drop like a sack of potatoes. Everybody howled. R. C. suffered a catapultic slam against the side of the caboose. His face appeared pasted against the wood, and as he drew it away, in rage and pain, I saw a big bruise appear high on his cheek. Then he furiously arraigned me for leading him on this log train. Really, the way some people's minds work is beyond comprehension. As it turned out, R. C.'s hurt could not be compared with Wiborn's, and with those of others inside the caboose.

The next happening was the advent of a loquacious brakeman who related hair-breadth escapes of the train crew while on duty. Never took a round trip without jumping the track, ditching a car, or piling up logs!

"Aw, we don't mind shake-ups, onless when we're crossin' trestles," he averred, nonchalantly. "Some of them trestles is high an' on curves."

The first trestle was bad enough for me. It was long and on a curve, and it rattled and creaked and shook under the log train. If it did this under an empty train what would it do under a loaded one? I could only conjecture. My Deer Creek enterprise began to lose something of its allurement. We passed over the lowlands, and climbed the foothills, and then began to cross trestles, some of which spanned the heads of canyons over a hundred feet deep. I saw deep cuts on the railroad ties and woodwork where cars had run off the track. Moreover, these high trestles wabbled so that my hair started to rise stiff on my head.

About half a dozen miles up in these foothills the sixth car in front of the caboose jumped the track. What a fearful lurch it gave us! The engineer stopped the train in less than a car-length. Dust rose in a cloud. We all climbed down to find the rear wheels of the derailed car two feet off the track.

"Huh! We started out on a walking tour and I reckon we'll walk back to McMurray," grunted R. C.

But it turned out presently that such accidents were trivial to the resourceful train crew. They placed a heavy triangular piece of iron against the wheels, and then the engineer, starting slowly ahead, pulled the dislodged car back on the track. The opera-

A Still, Dark, Curving Pool of Beautiful Deer Creek

PLATE XII

WHERE THE BIG STEELHEAD LAY

PLATE XIII

tion did not consume five minutes. We rode on without further mishap, around the slopes of denuded hills, and eventually arrived at the logging camp.

A great black and brown slash in the forest, a hideous clearing of stumps and burned tree trunks, surrounded a number of buildings, large and small, all constructed of new yellow lumber. Railroad tracks ran here and there. This logging camp was owned and operated by an English company, and we were told that it was a model up-to-date camp in every particular. Verily it did appear so. Store, restaurant, billiard hall, reading room, mess house, bunk houses, all were spick and span. These lumberjacks had a chef, electric lights, hot and cold water, a doctor, and all possible conveniences.

While Arnold was endeavoring to hire more men to pack us in to Deer Creek I climbed an adjacent hill where the lumbering was in progress. There were several crews of men at work in that vicinity. I saw an engine they called the "donkey" mounted upon a huge log sled, pull itself through the forest, over logs and stumps. I saw another in actual operation. By means of a thick wire cable this engine pulled huge logs eight feet thick and a hundred long fully a quarter of a mile uphill, to load them on the steel-spiked trucks. What they called the spar tree was most interesting of all to me. It was one that dominated a central point on a hill, and had been shorn of branches and top, and braced by wire cables on all sides. The running cable from the "donkey" was attached high up this spar tree on a pulley, and it swung monarchs of the forest with incredible ease. The most astounding feat was to see a lumberjack prepare one of these trees for a spar. He wore long-spiked tree-climbers, and he had a rope looped round tree and himself. He gave the loop a hitch upward, and then holding the rope he jammed his spikes into the bark and walked up several steps. Ax and saw dangled below him on a cord. Arriving at the first branch, he leaned back in the loop of the rope, pulled up his ax, and in a few strokes chopped off the branch. Up and up he scaled, cutting branch after branch, and when perhaps two hundred feet from the ground he discarded ax for saw and sawed the trees through at that point. A fifth of the huge cedar fell with a crash. The trunk swayed to and fro under the shock. Yet the lumberjack held his position securely and safely.

Men like this lumberjack and the flag-pole painters on the city skyscrapers and the construction workers of steel buildings are all of the same breed, men, heroic and daring, forgetful of self.

All around me sounded the crash of the falling giants of the woods. In that sound I heard the death knell of the magnificent cedars of Washington, of the towering beautiful firs of Oregon, of the grand redwoods of California. The speed of the juggernaut appalled me.

Upon returning to the water tank where I had left my party I found them almost packed and ready to start. Arnold had succeeded in hiring four lumberjacks to help us. This made ten men, counting Arnold and my chauffeur. Arnold insisted on carrying a pack. And as for R. C. and Wiborn and myself, we had a load that I grimly realized would grow heavy.

Our guide led off on an old abandoned railroad track that soon left the camp and wound into the forest. All of a sudden I strode out of a ghastly naked blot on the earth, out of the hot glaring sunlight, into what seemed long arched temples of green and amber, dark, shady, cool, and fragrant. The forest primeval! How high the towers of lacy fringed foliage! These cedars were huge, round, straight, smooth-barked, brownish-gray in hue, with branches far aloft.

We left the camp at four o'clock. With all our load we could not tarry and rest, and our guide kept up a good pace. Once Lone Angler remarked: "If that guide hadn't been operated on lately he'd be running through the woods. We're sure lucky."

Half a mile out the railroad ended and we took to a trail. It was one seldom used. For the most part it appeared so covered by the underbrush meeting overhead that we could scarcely see the forest trees, and nothing of the sky. Vines, ferns, flowers, grass, damp and luxuriant, with the fragrance of the forest, brushed us softly as we passed. The walking over a soft springy duff was easy, and for a mile or more it was level. Then we began to climb. Soon the trail opened into a forest like a park, and ground, logs, and trees appeared to take on an amber-green cast. Every fallen tree was a long mound of moss, fringed with exquisite tiny ferns.

We labored up and down through this forest, and the sunlight began to fail. About six o'clock we descended another heavily wooded slope, and at the foot of it came upon a dark body of water—Cavanaugh Lake.

There was scarcely open space enough for a camp. But as darkness was not far away I thought we had better make a halt. Across the lake a big black mountain loomed up, forbidding in the dusk.

We pitched camp as best we could. There was no dry firewood, and the expected cheerful hour was here comfortless and gloomy. The day had been long and arduous. My comrades were tired and somewhat dejected. My usual spirit seemed ebbing. Sleep seemed the only solution.

We were up at dawn, in the cool dark dampness of the forest, packing before we had breakfast. And when we left that camp the sun was just silvering the fog over the lake. Fresh and rested, we did not feel daunted at the prospect of a six-mile tramp to Deer Creek. But right off we struck an uphill trail, and soon realized what it meant to pack heavy burdens. Our packers rested every quarter of a mile, but we seldom passed them. It took an hour to climb that wooded ridge.

Here we entered a denser forest, and one strikingly beautiful and strange. I looked as I trudged along, although there were many places where the trail led over windfalls and deep narrow gorges spanned by fallen trees, and here I needed my eyes for careful stepping. The great cedars predominated, some of which were apparently ten feet or more thick at the base and towered straight and true so high that I had to crane my neck to see their tips. And then these tips seemed lost in a green spreading canopy pierced by shafts of golden sunlight and flecked with spots of blue sky. Underbrush was scant and very low, in remarkable contrast with the Vancouver forests. The green mantle of moss covered the ground and everything upon it, as completely as a heavy snow might have. Not a speck of bare earth or stone revealed itself to my searching gaze. The trail was like many layers of the softest Persian rugs. It gave forth not the slightest sound. This made walking easy. In some of the huge fallen trees notches had been cut for steps. It was a novel experience to take five or six steps to get over one log. Walking the many logs over narrow gullies and ditches was thrilling, though not conducive to enjoyment. They were slippery with wet moss. The beauty of this forest consisted of gray somber tree trunks rising out of a wonderful dark green, to disappear in a spreading roof of lighter green, pierced by arrows of golden sunshine.

The reason for the strangeness of it, however, did not readily come to me. At last I analyzed it as a solemn dead silence and a total absence of life. Not a sound! Not a stir of leaf or rustle of brush! There was not a bird or a squirrel or an insect, or any living creature to cross my sight or utter sound to hear. Moreover, I could not find a single track in the trail. For that matter, there were but few places where any wild creature would have left tracks. Melancholy, lonely, silent as a grave, this forest began to have a depressing effect on me. What a damp, sodden green maze! I contrasted it most unfavorably with the dry, sweet open pine forests of Arizona, with their golden aspen glades and their flaming maple thickets, where the elk bugled and deer rustled the leaves, and turkeys called, and squirrels and birds chattered all day long.

At the end of two hours of climbing and plodding, packing more than I should have carried, I just about hated that forest. It developed, however, that I had no time for self-indulgence. At a fork in the trail the lumberjacks mutinied. Arnold could not change them. They wanted to quit then and there. By dint of persuasion and offer of extra money I got them to go on.

Soon after that we reached the brow of the mountain and started down. R. C.'s quick ear, keen as an Indian's, first caught the low mellow roar of running water. It came from deep down in that green-choked abyss, and gradually grew stronger. What a relief to start downhill, even if it was steep and falling and sliding seemed the order of travel!

Our guide evidently knew where he was heading, but he certainly got off the trail, if there was one. And he led us down places that filled me with vague distress. How would we ever climb back? But getting out was not yet the issue. Deer Creek sent up a deep roar of rushing waters. That was a spur. As we descended farther into this canyon, the underbrush, mostly maple, grew high and thick, shutting out the light. Windfalls were so intricate and immense that they simply had to be climbed over, and as all this was at an angle of forty-five degrees, our labor and hazard were considerable. Once R. C. slipped and fell into what appeared to be a green hole. I was much concerned and called lustily. No answer! I fell all over myself getting to this place, and looked down. He had slid into a hole under a windfall, and had found an easy exit below. The rascal did not answer me because he wanted me to think he had been killed. And I heard Lone Angler say to him: "Say, what's the Chief bawlin' about? Do you think he's just right in his head?"

At last we descended to a point where, from under the giant cedars, we could look down upon Deer Creek. A beautiful green-and-white stream, shining here, dark and gleaming there, wound through a steep-walled canyon. It was worth working for. What struck me at once was the wonderful transparency of the water and the multitude of boulders, some of them huge.

Here everyone except myself appeared to want to rest. The men wiped their moist red faces. Arnold, however, looked pale, despite his smile, and I feared he had overexerted himself.

"Deer Creek, all right," he said, "an' I just saw a jack-salmon going up the shallows. But the water looks pretty low—too low. This has been the dryest season for years."

"We got here first and no low water is going to queer us," averred Lone Angler.

"What bothers me, now we're here, is how'n h— we'll ever get out," replied the realistic, romance-killing R. C.

"Sufficient unto the day is the trouble thereof!" I exclaimed. "Let's get down to the creek, and across somehow."

The last descent into the bed of that canyon was performed with considerable rapidity and ease—we ran down a mossy incline, slid down a steep gravel bank, and fell the rest of the way in soft clay. Then we walked down to the rocks, and unpacking our rubber boots we waded after the men across to a sandy level on the opposite side. I paid the lumberjacks and dismissed them. Arnold and his boys I kept to do our camp work and help us get back. I calculated we would have considerably less to pack back, and in case we could not take all the outfit these boys could make another trip in. Indeed, I gave scant thought to our return trip.

We were here on Deer Creek. Van Tassel, however, seemed immensely disappointed in Deer Creek. It was too low and the steelhead were not there. Incongruous indeed it seemed that this little creek could be full of big fish. But I refused to entertain any other idea.

We made camp with our limited outfit, as best we could, and then while the men busied themselves cooking a meal we anglers rigged up our tackles. Van Tassel found that the salmon eggs we had packed for bait had grown stale, and to him this appeared a grievous misfortune.

Right above camp there was a riffle and below that a deep pool. Arnold informed us he had seen fish in it, but could not be certain they were steelhead. R. C. fished it carefully, after our method of trout fishing, without getting a strike. Van Tassel had no better luck. Lone Angler slipped off up the creek by himself, and I went downstream. Pools appeared to be scarce. Half a mile below camp I came upon a jumble of immense boulders, some as large as houses, that blocked the whole canyon bed, and through the labyrinthine passages the creek foamed and eddied and babbled in a most bewildering network of waterways. I climbed up on boulders, and leaped fissures, and leisurely clambered this way and that, dropping my bait in likely places. Small trout took my bait off persistently, but that was all I had in the way of bites. I sat on one huge rock and then on another, content, absorbed in the music of the stream, the strange conformations of the smooth boulders, the color and current of the water, the sense of the overshadowing mighty cedars. Deer Creek was the most beautiful trout water I had ever seen. Clear as crystal, cold as ice, it spoke eloquently of the pure springs of the mountain fastnesses. Under the water the rocks were amber-colored, and along the banks they were green with moss and gray with lichen.

Van Tassel passed along the bank and worked on down the creek out of sight. In an hour or so he came back carrying a six-pound salmon. He had not seen a steelhead nor had a strike from one, and considered the fact most damaging to our hopes. He had found one large pool where steelhead should have been if they were anywhere in Deer Creek. We returned to camp. R. C. reported only numerous small trout. We hoped for better from

Lone Angler. But about sunset, when we were ready for supper, he returned without a fish.

"Saw some thundering big fish up above. Wonderful pools up there," he said. "But I couldn't get a strike or class the fish."

"Reckon they're salmon an' steelhead," said Arnold. "You see, the creek is low an' these big fish are wary. They have enemies. You must keep out of sight. Every pool ought to give you one strike a day. Mornin' is best. You'll ketch some steelhead an' hook some big ones."

His assurance was cheering and satisfying, and I replied that we were not difficult to please. A little went a long way with us.

After supper I was tired, and enjoyed a rest. Likewise did Wiborn. But R. C. took his rod and slipped off downstream to the pool just above the jumble of huge boulders. A big cedar tree had fallen across the creek and lay a few feet above the water. The current had cut a deep long narrow hole close to the right bank, and it shoaled gradually almost to where the tree crossed. I had fished it and remarked what a likely place it looked.

Presently we were all roused by a ringing yell from R. C. Jumping up, I looked to see him hanging on to a bent wagging rod. We all started to run to see the fun, and I, having on light rubber shoes, made better time over the boulder-strewn shore. I reached the fallen tree and, leaping upon it, ran out over the shoal water.

"What—you—got?" I queried, out of breath, as I looked at R. C.

He stood over to my left, nearly fifty yards, and judging from his face and the way he was working that tackle I anticipated much.

"Don't know what he is," he replied, "but I never had a fish nail a bait so hard. He went like a flash, down there. Thought it sure was good night. He's got most of my line, but think he's coming back."

I had seen R. C. reeling frantically, and next I made the astonishing discovery that his line ran right under the log upon which I was standing. Suddenly a fish swam into my sight—a trout—gray-green, and of gamy shape, two feet long. For an instant I did not connect him with R. C. Then I saw the leader curved in front of him. I yelled and waved. The trout shot into deep water out of sight. By this time the rest of our contingent had arrived, to become interested spectators of the fight. I saw the fish twice after that, once when he leaped, and again when he flashed rose and silver at the lower end of the pool. Van Tassel saw him too and assured R. C. that he was a steelhead, and advised very gentle handling. Eventually R. C. led the tired fish out of deep water, through the little channels among the rocks, and slipped him into a safe place where he lay gasping.

Not only was this the first steelhead we had ever captured, but the first we had ever seen. It was a strikingly beautiful fish, graceful, symmetrical, powerfully built, with great broad tail and blunt, pugnacious nose. The faint pinkish color, almost a glow, shone from a background of silver and green.

R. C. was very proud of his first steelhead. "You never could have made me believe he didn't weigh twice four pounds. Some fish!"

Then, wetting his hands, R. C. carefully unhooked the steelhead and gently slipped him back into the stream, which action greatly pleased Lone Angler and myself.

That night round a real camp fire Arnold told us some interesting facts about fish. One of them particularly struck me as worthy of recording.

"Both Chinook salmon an' steelhead have gone up the creek," he said. "I know, because the jack-salmon, the kind Mr. Van caught, always follow them. They eat the salmon eggs. I've watched a big fat salmon spawning in shallow water, an' I've seen a jack ram her—bump her in the side hard an' bust out her eggs. Then that jack would drop back in the current an' eat the eggs. I've seen it done."

The reward of all watchers of the trails and streams is that sometime they see a rare and marvelous phenomenon of nature. All observers do not see the same, for nature is vast and inexhaustibly rich in its strange habits of self-preservation and evolution.

We went to bed, to discover that away from the camp fire the air was full of tiny invisible gnats. They annoyed us, bit severely, but in spite of them we fell asleep and had a restful night. R. C. was the first of us up. He fished the pool in front of camp before he washed his face. While the others were dallying over a bountiful breakfast I made off upstream as fast as I could travel over the slippery rocks.

How cool and fresh and shady and redolent of cedar that deep canyon! How melodious with murmur and gurgle and roar of water! Then the beauty of this Deer Creek and its environment gave me a sense of sheer, wild, exquisite joy.

I passed a number of likely-looking pools that I left for my comrades. But presently I came to one that resembled the pool of an angler's dream. Above rushed a narrow fast rapid, white and foamy, and it ended in a deep dark lane between two rocks, and below widened out, and at last shoaled to a sand bar on the left and a shallow channel of rocks on the right.

I kept out of sight, and going round this pool, I came down behind the big rock on my side, and dropped my bait into the swift water. As it sank and floated down I certainly trembled. And scarcely had it gotten beyond the rock when a fish took it with a violent jerk and ran. What a thrill tingled along my veins! The days of my boyhood danced in my very bones. I hooked that fish.

Then came a solid pull, a screech of the reel, and a heavy splash. The fish had leaped behind the rock. As I ran up on this boulder my line was going out so fast that I wished for anything but a fly reel. Besides, there were only forty yards of line.

A dark gleam shot into the shallow water. How swift! Then it changed to a silver flash with glints of red. I saw a big fish swoop up and then come clear out into the air—a steelhead, savage and beautiful, fight in every line of his curved body. Then he plunged back to dart toward me. Slack line! There were yards of it. I could not reel it in, and he ran past me, pulling a bagged line after him, and ran up into the white swift water. Instantly he turned back and ran the length of the pool. But I did not see him then. On his second run upstream, which was slower, I got the line tight and kept it so. He repeated his dash into the swift water and then darted again for the end of the pool. Evidently this time he meant to go down into the rapids below, but he miscalculated and got into the shallow water and over the sand bar.

At this juncture I leaped off the rock and ran along the pool, beyond the shoal place, and then I had him at a disadvantage. He made surges here and there, stirring up the mud, and splashing like a crippled duck, but when he essayed to cross the bar back into the pool I held him. And so we fought it out there until he was vanquished. I put him on a string before I weighed him. Six and one half pounds! Then I tied the string to a root and let him recover and swim around, as I used to do with sunfish and bass when I was a boy. Van Tassel came along and warmly congratulated me on my good fortune. R. C. and Wiborn next hove in sight, slipping over the boulders, and they had lots to say. We saw a dozen long gray wavering fish shapes deep in the lower end of that pool—big steelhead—but we could not induce them to bite. Then we separated.

I wandered off up the creek, passing on my way the most wonderful pool I ever saw in my life. Heroically I left that for my comrades and departed upstream. In the next mile and a half I found some likely places and saw some fish, but did not have another strike. The water was too low and clear. Perhaps I was gone several hours, and when, on my return, I reached the wonderful pool, my three companions were there, talking across the creek, rods idle, lazily sunning themselves.

"Some whales in here," said R. C. "No good. They won't bite. Come over and look. Make you sick!"

"If we had fresh bait we'd catch one," added Van Tassel, who was on my side of the creek. R. C. and Lone Angler sat perched upon an enormous boulder, fully twenty feet above the pool. I made facetious remarks anent their lack of persistence and skill, and I looked for a place to cross. At the head of this pool ran a wide rapid of white water difficult to ford. I made it just by an inch. Then I scrambled down the shore, and climbed a bank, and labored over a huge pile of driftwood, and at last reached a point where I could jump on to the rock. Joining my comrades, I looked down where they pointed.

Deep in the limpid eddying water I saw many fish shapes, some of them so large as to seem in that comparatively small stream an exaggeration of the sight. But this particular pool could have harbored a swordfish. It held a great deal of water. And these fish were steelhead. I wondered why they would not bite. Then in a sort of helpless exasperated admiration I gazed from fish to pool. What a place for fish!

The enormous boulder projected far out into the pool. Just at the point where I stood it was narrowest, and the water appeared fifteen feet deep, gradually shoaling below, and widening into a broad space full of rocks and channels. But for thirty yards it was the tail end of a quiet pool, and I could see the amber bottom and little trout with startling clearness. In front where the steelhead lay the deep part began and ran up into the other half of the pool, black and swirling, with rock-lined banks, constricting to the swift water where I had crossed. What futile and thrilling conjecture as to how many fish lay unseen in that shadowy depth! Overhead towered the giant firs and cedars, so that only at this hour of noon did the sun shine here.

My brain conjured up days and tricks of my boyhood. Surely one of these steelhead could be caught, by hook or crook. R. C. and Lone Angler were talking about Santa Cruz Island, from which the latest mail had brought them news of a run of swordfish. They did not pay any attention to me. And on the other shore Van Tassel appeared asleep.

At the last pool above I had put on a little spinner to try, and it occurred to me now to twist off the small shiny spoon, leaving the tiny triangular gang of three hooks. Above this I slipped on a heavier lead, and then, half in earnest and half to deceive my comrades, I put on a small lump of salmon eggs. Thus equipped I stepped to the brink of the rock and cast out over the shadowy steelhead, and let my lead go to the bottom. My comrades took my move as an insult to their skill.

"Say, what're you going to do?" testily queried R. C.

When I did not vouchsafe any reply Lone Angler spoke up, "We fished this hole."

They both looked at me with lazy supreme scorn. But I paid little heed. I had an idea that, unless I had forgotten the skill of my boyhood, presently something would happen. When I saw the big steelhead paid no attention to my line, I knew positively there would be a startling surprise for my lofty companions.

Very cautiously I drew my line toward me. I could feel the lead dragging on the bottom. I could see my line stretching down and beyond the big steelhead on the outside. I expected to have a little fun, yet instinctively there was more than that in my thrill. You never can tell! Then I jerked hard.

My hooks caught. My rod bent. It quivered. Then suddenly sped upstream and off my reel. The screech of that reel galvanized my comrades. It did more to me. Actually I had hooked that big steelhead. I yelled with the sheer fun of it. The boys sprang up, amazed, open-mouthed, to watch my rod and line. Such a run! That fish took all the line off, and up there in the fast white water he leaped into the air.

R. C. saw that greyhound leap. So did Lone Angler. They yelled lustily. The steelhead looked enormous. As for me, that fierce run, and then the great size of the fish—these were my undoing. From jest I passed to dreadful earnest. A flash of reason crossed my mind—I would get just what I deserved. But that never changed me one whit. I was charged with uttermost longing and determination.

The steelhead hung up in the white water. I thought he had fouled my line. No! I felt the wavering of him to and fro. He had every inch of the line out, and it stretched as tight as a wire. I went to the extreme edge of the rock and extended the rod as far as possible. Suddenly the fish turned and came back, not swiftly, so that I was able to reel in the slack line. Slowly he swam toward me, deep, about in the middle of the channel. He passed the rock, out of the dark water, into plain sight.

"Oh! Oh!" exclaimed R. C. in mingled amaze, consternation, and delight.

"Look at that trout!" added Lone Angler.

I saw, but I could not express my feelings. I felt like a lost man. Retribution had overtaken me! Yet—it was possible to land this fish. He swam easily, then made a run that for sheer speed and vigor completely dazzled me. I thumbed the reel— the line. But he came to the surface and smashed the water white. Then he bored in three feet of water, and knocked his head against the rocks, and scared me stiff. If he kept on downstream all was over! But he came back upstream, holding along the bottom. Slowly he passed out of sight, and steadily my line

THE FIGHT WITH THE BIG STEELHEAD (Plates xiv to xviii)

PLATE XIV

PLATE XV

PLATE XVI

PLATE XVII

PLATE XVIII

My First Steelhead

PLATE XIX

went up the pool, to its deepest, blackest center, and there it stopped as if snagged.

For a long time he sulked on the bottom, during which I worked all I dared. Next he swam to and fro, and around, up and down, and then ran up into the swift water to hang there as if anchored. He stayed there what seemed a long time. But the steady strain I put on him gradually drew him out of the current. Down he came.

This time he headed for the dark shelving hole under the rock. I saw the dim shapes of snags and sunken logs. How he plugged! But I risked losing him and held hard. The rod bent under the rock in my effort to pull and lead him. There was a bad snag on the surface of the water, lodged against the rock. R. C. tried to climb down to move it while Wiborn went ashore, and by dint of strenuous work they pulled it out of the way.

My fish went down into the shoal place below us, and there in plain sight he swam two feet under the surface. R. C. and I gloated over that sight. He was getting tired. There was indeed a chance of vanquishing him. He swam around directly under us, and then we had our clearest sight of him. How long, thick, heavy! He had shoulders like a bonefish. His back was dark green, covered with black dots. When I pulled hard enough he turned on his side, and that moment was indescribable. Half a foot broad! A wide flare of deep rose color and silver! His fins waved like aspen leaves in a gentle wind. His huge mouth gaped, and then shut.

"What'll—he—weigh?" I panted.

"Twelve pounds—oh, maybe more," replied my brother. "This is awful. But you'll get him."

"Look at him, R. C.," I burst out. "Just look—so you'll never —forget. He'll go all of fifteen pounds. And I'll never hold him."

All this while I heard Van Tassel yelling at me, advice no doubt, but I never distinguished a word. My fish worked around the rock, and up the pool again.

"Can't you get across, on the other side?" queried R. C. "Then you could keep him away from these snags under the rock."

It was fully a ten-foot jump down to a log behind the rock,

and more than that to the ground. When the steelhead got well upstream I essayed to go around with him. When Wiborn saw my intention he yelled. "Don't try it. That's how I broke my leg!"

Nevertheless I made the bank in two jumps, holding my rod up in both hands. Then as luck would have it the steelhead took a notion to go back, and this time he went fast. My line went round and over the rock. I had to get back. How I accomplished it I never knew, but I climbed straight up to R. C.'s outstretched hands. The contrary steelhead fooled around, swam back, and suddenly, without giving Wiborn any chance to get ready to photograph a leap, he came up and out, fully six feet into the air, a most prodigious performance, something unequaled in my experience of a beautiful and wonderful sight. But Wiborn was not ready. The steelhead plunged back. I believed that last effort had used him up.

Accordingly, when he headed slowly up the pool toward the swift water I jumped down on to the log, thence to the ground again, and ran over the rocks, reeling as fast as I could; and I all but fell several times.

I passed Wiborn and got even with where the steelhead hung. I could see him in the foamy water, wagging wearily. I leaped from the shore to a submerged rock, and then I was so close over the fish I could have kicked him. My rod described a circle. I plunged in ahead of him and waded in swift water up to my waist across a place I never would have dared in a calm moment. When I got across the boys whooped.

Whereupon I led my fish downstream, through the deep water of the pool, below to the place where the shoal began. Here I got his head under control, and half led, half dragged him into six inches of water. He was almost spent. Lazily he flopped.

"Scoop him out!" yelled R. C. to Van Tassel.

"Yes, yes," I joined in. "Get behind him—pitch him out on the sand."

"Aw no, you'll lose him," replied Van Tassel, in consternation. That was a trying situation for him. He was afraid to take the risk. But I knew as my fish began to slip and work out of that favorable place that we had lost our opportunity.

"Try it again," shouted R. C. "Then hand your rod to Van—and take the chance yourself."

This appeared the best of advice. I attempted it. The steelhead got his head and swam away, very wearily and ponderously. He could just wag his tail. But he was so heavy that I dared not check him entirely. I eased up, let him go a little, then pulled carefully to turn him. More than once I had his head coming round. I reeled in the line he had taken. Slowly he floated, tail toward us, gradually yielding. His broad tail waved. His great mouth gaped. He turned on his side, flashing pink and silver in the sunlight, and just when I realized he was a vanquished fish, most beautiful and desirable in the moment of surrender, the hooks tore out. For another moment he did not realize he was free. Then he righted himself and swam off very slowly, his great shape gradually growing dim, until he vanished in the depths of the pool.

TYEE SALMON—1919

THE Pacific salmon belongs to the genus *Oncorhynchus* and is closely allied to the Atlantic salmon. It has not been studied and written about by anglers and naturalists as has its Eastern brother. Nor has it appeared to hold equality with the Atlantic salmon for beauty and game qualities. I am not yet prepared to defend some species of the Pacific salmon to this extent, but I do not believe justice has been done them.

There are six species peculiar to the north Pacific: the quinnat, tyee, sockeye, humpback, cohoe, and dog salmon. Few if any of these fish survive their first spawning season in the rivers of Oregon, Washington, British Columbia, and Alaska.

For more years than I can remember I have been hearing wonderful fish stories about Campbell River, Vancouver Island. At the mouth of this river was the most famous English angling resort; and compared by many English writers to Long Key, Florida, and Tampico, Mexico, and Avalon, California.

According to these angling writers the tyee salmon was the equal of the tarpon and the tuna. This was interesting to me, but not convincing, for I could find no record of tyee larger than eighty pounds. An English authority on fishing-tackle for Canadian waters advocates heavy rods and twenty-one-thread lines for tyee. An international club man and sportsman, in a privately printed book on his fishing experiences, puts himself on record as claiming that the heaviest of tackle is necessary for tyee. He warns the light-tackle anglers that they would spend their time mending broken outfits or buying new ones.

This made me more curious than ever about tyee salmon and decided me to go to Campbell River.

To that end I left off fishing for broadbill swordfish at Cata-

56

FISHING FOR TYEE SALMON

PLATE XX

A Totem Pole at Campbell River, Vancouver Island

PLATE XXI

lina on August 15th—an unfortunate move, judging from the run
of broadbills at the close of the season—and accompanied by my
faithful and long-suffering comrades of the open, R. C. and Lone
Angler Wiborn, engaged passage north by steamer and train.

We left Vancouver by steamship *Princess Pat* and had a hard
time getting our car and baggage aboard. So much red tape!
The channel was like a swift green river, with big black timbered
mountains on each side. Once out in the open water of Puget
Sound the steamer took on more speed and crossed to Vancouver
Island in two and one half hours. Our landing point was Nanaimo,
a quaint little old English town. Here we tried to buy fishing
licenses, but could not. So I had to console myself by buying
woolen socks to take home to the youngsters.

Then we started north for Campbell River, one hundred and
twenty miles, at two o'clock. We discovered at once that the
individual who was hauling our baggage by motor truck could
not make more than six miles an hour. It took three hours to get
to a little hamlet where we got rid of him and hired a fellow who
ran so fast we could not keep him in sight.

The country was mountainous and the timber had been cut. We
saw only a few habitations and passed two little hamlets. Logging
and mining appeared to comprise all the industry in sight. Everywhere were blackened burned-over timber slashes hideous to me.
Now and then we would get a view of the Sound, or rather Inside
Passage to Alaska, and that was fine. But we ran into cloudy
weather and rain, off and on. We crossed some clear beautiful
streams and could see the dark slopes of lofty mountains running
up into the clouds.

About fifty miles out we left the cut-over areas and rode into
the forest. It was thick, dark, green, wet, with enormous trees,
firs and cedars, so high I could not see their tops. We ran twenty
miles or more through forest, now and then crossing open places,
and finally came to a beautiful river. From the bridge we saw
thousands of salmon running upstream in the shallow water. They
appeared to be from two to three feet in length, rather dark gray
on the back, and quite plump, with a sharp nose. Under the
bridge the water was shallow and we could see the salmon climbing the little riffles and sliding over the rocks. At first they came

steadily, but presently when they saw us they dropped back to the deeper still water below. Whereupon I crossed the bridge and went down along the wooded bank of the river to a place where I could watch unseen. It was a beautiful river, about a hundred yards wide, and perhaps three feet deep, with the most wonderfully clear water. And this area as far as I could see up and down was full of salmon. Dark purple patches showed where the fish were massed. Everywhere they were breaking water on the surface and leaping out. I could see where the river ran out into the strait, and I calculated there was a steady stream of salmon coming in.

Upon returning to the bridge I met a native who said the fish were humpback salmon and good for nothing. Nevertheless, that place was hard to leave.

Before dark we ran into a storm. The new driver ditched his car. It jumped about nine feet. I yelled, "Good-by, tackle." But we did not lose anything except time.

Then we ran into a forest, and it was hard to keep up with our new driver. He was a war veteran, and had driven an airplane or something in the war. How black the forest was!

But we kept in the road somehow, and got to Campbell River at ten-thirty.

Next morning disclosed a sullen gray sky, stiff wind, a swift rough channel of sea between Vancouver Island and another island, where the ships run. Alaska was not far distant. And it felt like Alaska.

There was a settlement—a few French Canadians and Indians, a tavern, and some weather-beaten houses. I did not know how it would look in sunlight, but this day it was bleak and dreary. We drove up to a lake that might have been beautiful on a sunny day. The forest was magnificent, the richest, greenest, most verdant I had ever seen. The cedars and firs, massive and straight, stood far apart, and towered over the jungle of underbrush which consisted largely of broad-leaved maples. It seemed impenetrable. How wet and glistening and darkly green! This was a country of rain, of fertility. Vines and creepers matted the underbrush.

In the heart of this woodland, a few miles up from the settlement, the Campbell River plunged into a canyon, making a waterfall that matched the beauty of the surroundings.

All that afternoon we worked over the light tackle with which we intended to catch tyee. Our genial host, a French Canadian, had been there for many years, and had seen the time when Campbell River was a famous fishing resort. But he had never seen any fishing-tackle like ours. Plain it was that he was too well-bred and considerate to ridicule our beautiful six-ounce tips and nine-thread lines. The English are a sport-loving people, and they make a few reels and lines and rods suitable for fly-fishing for salmon and trout, but they had then no salt-water tackle that an expert American angler would use.

There were several fishermen at the tavern, one of whom was from New York. He had visited Campbell River before. He had caught a few small tyee the preceding August, but this season he had not caught any.

"Fished out long ago," he said, of Campbell River. "The net boats have ruined what was once the greatest fishing in British Columbia."

That was discouraging for us. Our host said we had come to Vancouver fifteen years too late. He was nothing if not candid, and I liked him for telling us the truth. But the Indians caught tyee every day, he said, and we might catch some, if we could hold them on our rigs.

We listened to a good many fish stories. The record tyee had been caught by an Indian, on a hand line, and it had towed his canoe across the straits and eight miles farther before being subdued. This fish weighed eighty-five pounds. There was a sixty-seven-pounder mounted in the lobby of the tavern, indeed a wonderful-looking fish, built for speed, strength, and endurance. But neither sight of it, nor the stories of the difficult capture of big tyee, nor the skepticism of the New York angler, nor the tackle recommended by the British sporting stores, nor even the damning evidence in the international club man's privately printed book dampened our ardor or shook our confidence in the little light tackle. They were not *too* light.

R. C. eyed that sixty-seven-pound tyee on the wall, and finally he said, "If I couldn't lick a fish like that in thirty minutes I'd eat him!"

Lone Angler Wiborn more than backed up R. C.'s statement.

"Nothing to it," he said, tersely. "These fellows don't know. It is only of late years that anglers have become expert with light tackle. Mark what I say—we'll pull the heads off these tyee."

I did not say much. After a long series of lessons I was learning restraint. Often I spoke through feeling rather than knowledge. But R. C. and Lone Angler, for all their ideals and high standards, were practical realists in matters pertaining to the open. They did not make many mistakes, and they had about convinced me when one of the Indian boatmen came in. His name was Jim and he hailed from Cape Mudge, across the strait. He was a fine, stalwart, dark-faced Indian, and spoke English well.

I showed him my tackle and asked, "How long will this hold a tyee?"

Very curiously and interestedly did he handle that rod and reel, and how skeptically he fingered the thin linen line.

"About two minutes," he replied, with a frank smile.

I liked that smile. "Jim, I don't want to take your money or I'd bet you. But I'll hire you and your boat—and if I don't surprise you I'll make you a present."

We engaged Jim and another Siwash Indian, and cheerfully consented to be roused at four-thirty in the morning. The dark lowering clouds and the fitful wind with gusts of rain did not promise happily for the morrow. Surely the best virtue of fishermen is their hopefulness.

The watchman called us promptly at four-thirty. It was dark and cold. I could hear the rush of the swift water. This channel was not a river. Campbell River ran into it.

At five o'clock we were out on the dock waiting for our Indian guides. And in this instance the city white men waited for the dusky citizens of the wilds. They came at five-thirty, when it was clear daylight. My boat was a dinky, punky little dory, canoe-shaped, with a box-like cabin forward, and a deep cockpit. It had a tiny engine, one cylinder, and it sounded as if the next beat would be its last. My courage began to ooze at the thought of trusting myself in it out on that swift dark channel. The clouds hung low, scudding northward, and the shores were lined with a gloomy, mysterious fringe of forest. By way of more discouragement it began to rain. Cold, pelting, heavy drops! Before we

reached the mouth of the river the rain ceased and the clouds broke
eastward to show silvery light. All around, however, were masses
of purple cloud, stormy and sullen.

The wide river appeared to slide out of the forest between two
dark capes of forestland. Ducks were everywhere, and small salmon were leaping. The larger type tyee salmon showed only occasionally, making a heavy break on the surface or showing a broad
tail. They had a gamy look and gave me thrills.

The method of fishing for tyee salmon was to troll with a spe-
cially made spoon that in size, silver color, and motion resembled
a herring. This spoon trolled on its edge and imparted a singularly
life-like motion.

The morning air was cold and damp. My hands began to freeze,
and likewise my feet. Clouds of mist shrouded the fir trees. No
mountains could be seen. But as fish were breaking all around me
and the environment bore a wild and primitive aspect, I was able
to endure.

With my light tackle, the regulation Tuna Club outfit, I was
rather embarrassed by the heavy lead necessary to sink the spoon
deep.

The native fishermen as they passed us in canoes and skiffs all
eyed our light tackle askance, and some of them showed ridicule. I
had my doubts as to the justice of their convictions. Jim said the
Canadians, the Englishmen, and anglers who just happened there
used hand lines for these tyee salmon, or eleven-and-one-half-foot
rods, with twenty-one-thread lines, and heavy wire leaders. But
in spite of such information R. C. and Lone Angler and I could
not bring ourselves to such rigging for what we called small fish.

My greatest trouble was to keep the heavy lead from pulling me
overboard, and to wind in to clean the grass and seaweed off my
spoon. But I persevered under most trying conditions, and in
about half an hour had a strike. A good hard strike of a game
fish! I hooked him, and I fully expected to be wrecked. He went
off on a light drag, giving sudden quick jerks that were new to
me, and swerving here and there so that at times I could not feel
his weight and imagined he had gotten free. But it turned out that
I still had him. And it did not take me long to realize that in
spite of tactics new to me I would not have a great deal of trouble.

He broke water once, and showed a broad dark tail. Again he headed for some drifting kelp and I was hard put to it to hold him. I just managed to keep him free of it.

After a while I had him close enough to see him, and that was indeed compensation for much. He shone dull green-silver and appeared to be speckled like a trout. He looked big. I landed him without considerable trouble or effort, and he proved to be a fair-sized fish, long and broad and thick, mottled green on the back, dull silver underneath, with full square tail and the typical salmon head, small and thoroughbred.

The event preceded more cloud and rain, and I fished in a storm, and grew thoroughly wet and chilled. That squall passed over, and in the ensuing hour I caught a spring salmon, about five pounds, a cohoe of about the same weight, and a good-sized cod-fish. These furnished a little exercise and considerable amuse-ment, especially the cod. I could not imagine what I had hooked. It moved, certainly, but that was about all. When I saw a huge yellow wavering fish come slowly up out of the depths I was amazed. Its size was unbelievable, considering its lack of spirit. When the Indian lifted it aboard I saw a large long fish, brown of back, with enormous mouth, and gills that gaped to resemble the spread ears of an elephant. Withal it bore some semblance to codfish caught off Atlantic City.

Then I struck another tyee, a larger one, manifestly, and had a few hard jerks from him before he threw the hook. That jerk of the head worked in this instance. He got away. After that incident there was more cold and rain, until I was all but frozen. But I stuck it out and at the end of that storm I hooked another tyee. This one performed differently, running on the surface, and splashing and cutting capers generally. I held him gingerly and played him skillfully, to the delight of the Indian, who man-ifestly had been won over to my way of angling. I landed this tyee in fifteen minutes and it proved to be a larger and a brighter, more striking-looking fish.

Several more hours of trolling in the rain was about all I wanted, so we went back to the dock. R. C. and Lone Angler had not done anything, except break a leader, one of the flimsy contraptions sold in Vancouver to anglers ignorant of what was needed. After this we made our own leaders. My catch proved a source of surprise and wonder, the natives especially being curious.

We sought a warm fire and some breakfast, after which we talked fish. We could learn nothing from the Indians, and little from the natives. What a strange, ancient, worn-out place, this Campbell River! And once it had been the most famous of English fishing resorts.

It rained on and off all day, but at four o'clock we ventured out again. As luck would have it the rain ceased and the clouds broke to a wonderful panorama. I had real enjoyment out of this hour, though the fish did not strike. I saw a good many tyee rolling on the surface like tarpon, and always there were other salmon and fish breaking. Fish hawks were at work, and ducks winged swift flight up and down the channel. Toward sunset the lights changed and there were a few moments of exquisite beauty. A vivid sundog gleamed among the creamy white clouds of the south. It was a strange mixture of colors, rose and gold-green, and faint purple, and lesser hues. Then a rainbow appeared to the east, a high thin arch, unlike rainbows I had seen. But the sunset in the gap of the mountains held my gaze. It was a bright open space in all the angry mass of cumulus clouds, a stormy flare of fire and gold against white clouds like rolling smoke. These colors were intense, and seemed moving, changing. In a few moments this effect changed and died into dull gray.

Next morning I was again on the river at five o'clock. The sky was overcast, but not so threateningly, and there was some prospect of sunshine.

The few moments of sunrise were reward for the effort to come out into the cold gray dawn. A magnificent mountain range showed under a curtain of cloud, and the sun lighted up snow peaks and glaciers and rugged black domes of rock. Then indeed I realized I was in British Columbia and not far from Alaska.

During the next hour I saw many tyee rolling, and had one strike. There were five Indians fishing and they failed also. Their method was to troll from their canoe-shaped dug-out boats. These were hollowed out from tree trunks, and were evidently propelled by paddles before the white man's method of using oars was copied.

One of the most striking features at Campbell River was the sound of the water out in the channel. It must have been a rip tide. All I could see was a roughened line of tiny whitecaps. But the sound was menacing. It did not resemble the moaning of the sea across a bar, nor the low sullen roar of river rapids, but it gave me a deep and haunting thrill. Nearly all the time, and especially at night, I was aware of this strange, weird murmur of chafing waters. It held a cold note of the northland. It suggested the contending tides of the dark green Arctic seas. Not a welcome sound for an angler!

This day I had rigged my heavy leads to break from my line when I had a strike. Of course I would lose them, but that was no matter. What I wanted was to be free of their cumbersome weight when I had hooked a tyee. And I began to be afraid I would not have the pleasure and gratification of trying out my little trick. Our host had frankly told us that the rainy season had arrived, and the tyee fishing was over for the year. So I persevered with the patience born of long endurance. Also I watched R. C. and Lone Angler in the other boat, hoping to see them hook a fish. But no such luck! I did see, however, one of the Indians playing a tyee on a hand line. His skill was worthy of a better method. The canoe was low in the water and light. The fish pulled it here and there. I was sure the Indian had a lead sinker that would weigh two pounds. This tyee did not jump or thresh on the surface. Gradually the Indian drew it closer, until he could lift its nose out of the water. Then he whacked it with a short heavy club. I saw him slide the big broad silvery salmon into his canoe, and the sight inspired me to more persistence.

R. C. and Lone Angler at last drifted out of sight round the bend, on their way back to the settlement. All but one of the Indians quit fishing, and I was about to give up when I had a powerful, electrifying strike. So quick, so heavy was it, that I experienced an exultant thrill.

That tyee hooked himself, and in a second had freed the line of the heavy leads. For once I did not call the boatman. His engine was barely working and the boat scarcely moved. As that tyee raced off I put on the light drag and shut down on the reel with my thumb. The sudden strain almost jerked the rod away

A Fine Chinook—22 Pounds

PLATE XXII

Two Tyee Salmon, 32 and 38 Pounds

PLATE XXIII

from me. But the line held and checked that rush. Up came the salmon to make a magnificent break on the surface, half out, showing his noble proportions, and the dark green silvery colors. With his head in the air, mouth shut tight, he gave that peculiar jerk I had noted in the others. Indeed, it was a tackle-smasher, but when he performed it I saw that he did not have a tight line or strain to pull against. Before he disappeared I estimated his weight to be over fifty pounds. My largest tyee had weighed thirty-eight pounds, a goodly fish, but not heavy enough to prove our theory as to the light tackle.

This tyee I now had on was one of the big fellows. In the next two moments he made one long and one short run, both of which I stopped at will. Then I pumped him close to the boat. He tried to go down to the bottom—a favorite pastime of tyee, I was told—and I held him easily. Indeed, I held him much tighter than I usually hold a heavy fish, and I did it because I had a grim desire to try out the light tackle and see how quickly I could land him.

Just then the Indian poked his head out of the little cabin, to see what I was doing. He was amazed. A grin appeared on his face. He threw out the clutch.

"Tyee?" he asked.

"He sure is, Jim, and you can get out here with your gaff," I replied.

"That pole's bendin'," he added.

Assuredly it was. But nothing to compare with the way it had bent while holding a tuna. That very rod had stood a five-hour fight with a yellow-fin tuna. I was no longer fearful of the light tackle. Scarcely three minutes had passed and I knew I had this tyee whipped. I could stop him any time. Then in my misguided ambition I took a chance of his being well hooked and began long lifts with the rod, reeling hard. He was strong. He was game. Resenting that treatment, he rushed to the surface and began to surge and thresh. Swiftly I reeled in the slack, and holding hard I tried to lead him closer. The hook tore out.

Too late I realized my hurry and mistake. How I regretted it! I did not mind the tyee getting free so much as I did my foolish haste. But I had done enough to know that the Tuna Club light tackle was ideal for tyee salmon. On the way back to the dock I did not begrudge a tribute to this great northern fish. He is a magnificent, versatile fighter, strong, fast, enduring, and upon the fitting light tackle will call forth all the excitement, skill, and work any angler could ask. But I should add—the tyee, unless the netting is stopped, will soon be a memory. Like the sockeye, he is fast disappearing in the track of commercialism. Before that time comes I intend to journey northward, far beyond Vancouver, and find a river where tyee run large and many, and there fish for him and study him to my satisfaction.

In my mind's eye I can see what that place will look like—a broad swift river, sliding out of a dark forest into a green channel, with glancing, shining cold lights from the setting sun, with shadows of the bold, wild mountains, and in the eddying tide where fresh and salt water meet, the riffle and splash and surge of the beautiful green-backed tyee.

AT THE MOUTH OF THE KLAMATH

UPON arriving in Seattle from Vancouver Island we sent our Tuna Club light tackles home by express, reserving only the fly rods and casting rods we expected to use on steelhead trout in Oregon. And this circumstance seems wholly accountable for the most extraordinary fishing adventure I ever had, up to that time. It happened on our way home, after the beautiful Rogue River, with its incomparable steelhead, had captivated us and utterly defeated us, and when we had given up for this trip.

Leaving Grants Pass, Oregon, we visited the remarkable caves west of there, and then journeyed on over the Cascades to Crescent City, on the coast. I have no space here to tell of that beautiful ride and of the magnificent forests of redwoods still intact in northern California.

Some miles below Crescent City we came to a quaint little village called Requa. All we knew of it was that it was the place where we had to ferry across the Klamath River. The town perched upon a bluff, high over the wide river, and appeared to have one street. A long low white tavern, old and weather-beaten, faced the sea, and the few stores and houses were characteristic of a fishing village. Indeed, the place smelled fishy. I saw Indians lolling around on the board walks, and as we drove down under the bluff toward the ferryboat I espied numerous Indian canoes and long net boats, sharp fore and aft.

We had to wait for the ferryboat to come across. While watching the wide expanse of river, more like a bay, I saw fish breaking water, some of them good heavy ones. Next I heard two young men, who were behind us in a Ford, talking about fish. Whereupon I got out and questioned them. Fish! Why, Requa was the greatest place to fish on the coast! In justification of their claim they showed me three Chinook salmon, averaging thirty pounds, and several large steelhead, all caught that morning in less than an hour.

"What'd you catch them with?" I inquired.

"Hand lines and spoons," was the reply.

Then I went back to our car and said to the driver, who was about to start for the ferryboat:

"Back out of here somehow. We're going to stay."

R. C. and Lone Angler Wiborn eyed me with slow-dawning comprehension. They were tired. The trip had been long and hard. The drive over that dangerous road of a thousand sharp curves had not been conducive to comfort or happiness. And on the whole they had been very much disappointed in our fishing. The end of September was close at hand, and we were due to arrive in Flagstaff, Arizona, on the 29th for our hunt in the wilds of the Tonto. I appreciated their feelings and felt sorry, and rather annoyed with myself. But obviously the thing to do was to take a chance on Requa.

"Only one day, boys," I added, apologetically.

"What for?" queried R. C.

"Why, to fish, of course," I replied.

"Ahuh!" he exclaimed, with a note of grim acquiescence.

Lone Angler's face was perfectly expressionless, calm as a mask. He looked at R. C.

"Sure we're going to stop. I knew that all the time. I was just waiting until the Chief smelled fish."

"But we haven't any tackle," protested R. C.

I had forgotten that. Assuredly our trout tackles were not fitted for Chinook salmon.

"Maybe we can buy some tackle," I said. "Anyway, we're going to wet some lines."

Whereupon we went back to the inn, engaged rooms, got our baggage and tackle out of the car, and after lunch proceeded to investigate Requa in reference to things piscatorial.

Verily it turned out to be a fishing village, and the most picturesque and interesting one I ever visited. But all the tackle we could discover in the several stores were the large spoons and hand lines which were used there. We purchased some of the spoons, but the hand lines we passed by. Next we got one of the

"WHAT DO YOU KNOW ABOUT THIS?"

PLATE XXIV

CRATER LAKE

PLATE XXV

storekeepers to engage a launch and two skiffs, and men to operate them for us, and somewhere around three o'clock we were out on the water.

I drew a long flat-bottom net boat, which was a great deal easier to handle than one would suppose from looking at it; and the young man who rowed it was employed in the canning factory. He did not appear to be communicative, but he did say that the tide was going out and that the morning incoming tide was best.

The day was not propitious. With the sky overcast, dark, and gloomy, and little fine gusts of rain flying, the air cold, and the wind keen, it did not appear a favorable or opportune enterprise. I regretted subjecting R. C. and Lone Angler to more privation, discomfort, and work. Not that they were not cheerful! Two gamer comrades never pulled on wet boots in the dark of dawn! As for myself, I did not really care—the thing to do was to try— no one ever could tell what might happen. So we made ready to troll around that bay.

Lone Angler had found a steel rod, which he equipped with a trout reel full of light line, and he waved that at me with these enigmatical words: "Now fish, you Indian! We got here first!"

R. C. and I had found two green Leonard bait rods that had been made for me some years before and had never been used. They were about nine feet long, slender and light, but remarkably stiff, and really unknown quantities. I had ordered them to try on bonefish, but had never used them. For bass they would have been ideal. I had a good-sized reel half full of No. 6 linen line, and to this I tied the end of two hundred yards of braided silk bass line. For a leader I used one purchased at Campbell River for tyee salmon, and selected a moderate-sized steelhead spoon with two hooks. Thus equipped, and with misgivings and almost a contempt at my own incomprehensible assurance, I began to fish. I did not look to see what R. C. put on his rod. I knew he was doomed to catastrophe, so it did not matter.

My boatman rowed me down the bay, not, however, very near the mouth of the river. But I could see that the bay constricted, with a high rocky bluff, almost a mountain, on one side, and a wide sand bar on the other. Evidently the mouth of the river was narrow I heard the boom of surf and the scream of sea fowl.

There were several other boats out with fishermen dragging hand lines behind them. Here and there on the yellow, rather muddy surface, fish were breaking. I trolled up and down and around that bay until I was thoroughly cold and tired and discouraged, without a strike. R. C. and Wiborn had no better luck. We went back to the inn, where a warm fire and good supper were most welcome.

After supper I went over to talk with the storekeeper. He struck me as being part Indian, and I had confidence in him. I have Indian blood in me. I told him of our luck. He advised me to stay on and try the incoming tide, early in the morning. He said the outgoing tide was no good for fishing. So after considerable argument with myself I decided to stay.

"Boys, go to bed early," I said. "Tomorrow we'll try again."

Next morning was clear. I saw the sun rise. What a difference it made! The air was crisp and clear, invigorating, and the day promised to be one of Indian summer. We got to the boats early, before anyone else was down. The man with the launch had not arrived. Lone Angler said he would wait for him, while R. C. and I took out one of the long skiffs. I found it very easy to row.

Requa and the mouth of the Klamath did not seem the same place as yesterday. All the way down the bay I marveled at the difference. Could it have been wholly one of spirit? The sun was bright on the dancing waves. Fish were breaking everywhere. Pelicans were soaring and swooping and smashing the water. Myriads of sea gulls were flying and screaming over the long sand bar. Low and clear came the sound of the surf.

I rowed straight for the mouth of the river to get into that narrow channel, where my adviser had earnestly solicited me to go. Before we got down to it I was struck with the singular beauty of the place. Huge cliffs, all broken and ragged and colored, loomed over the west shore of the channel, and on the eastern side the long bar ran down to a point where I could see the surf breaking white.

"Say, some place!" exclaimed R. C., as he turned to look ahead. His eyes lightened with enthusiasm. "Fish, too. . . . Gee! look at that splash!"

When we got to the channel we found it to be several hundred yards long, and perhaps a hundred wide at the narrowest part. It was not straight, having a decided curve. A swift current of dark green sea water was running in, to be checked by the pale yellowish muddy water of the river. There was a distinct irregular line extending across the channel, the line of demarcation where the fresh water contended against the incoming tide of salt water. There was indeed a contest, and the sea was slowly conquering, driving the river back. In this boiling, seething maelstrom salmon and steelhead and cohoes were breaking water. On the point of sand a flock of sea gulls were gathered, very active and noisy. They were flying, wading, standing around, some of them fighting, and all of them screaming. Black cormorants were diving for small fish, and every time one came up with his prey in his bill several of the gulls would charge him and fight for his prize.

I took everything in with quick appreciative glances. How glad I was I had elected to try this morning! The charm of the place suddenly dawned upon me. Looking out toward the sea I saw the breakers curl green and sunlit, and fall with a heavy boom. Along the rocky point of the channel there was a line of white water, turbulent and changing, the restless chafing of the waves. And that river of dark ocean water, rushing in, swelling in the center, swirling along the rocks, and running over the sandy bar, assuredly looked as dangerous as it was beautiful.

"New sort of a place for us, hey?" inquired R. C., gazing around. "Never saw the like. What do you make of it?"

"Great!" I exclaimed. "I'll bet we break some tackle here."

I rowed to and fro along the edge of the incoming tide several times without R. C. getting a strike. Then I said: "I'm going to get out into that tide. You let your spoon down to where the salt and fresh water meet."

R. C. looked dubiously at the swelling green current, as if he thought it would be hard to row against, and perhaps not safe. I had found that the big skiff moved easily, and I had no trouble getting out fifty yards or more right into the middle of the channel.

Almost immediately R. C. yelled: "Strike!—Missed!" Inside of a minute he had another, and hooked the fish. It began to leap.

"Steelhead, by Jove!" he shouted. I rowed out of the current, back into the river water, and watched as pretty an exhibition of leaping fish as one would want to see. This steelhead cleared the water eight times and fought savagely. R. C. handled him rather severely. After he had landed the steelhead I rowed back into the channel and R. C. let his spoon down into that frothy mêlée of waters.

"This won't be much fun for you," asserted my brother.

"Fish!" I yelled. It was not easy to hold the boat in one place. Only by rowing hard could I keep even with a certain point. R. C. had two strikes, one of which was very heavy, but both fish missed the hook. Then he connected with one, a fish that kept low down and pulled hard. I rowed with all my might, holding the boat in the current while R. C. fought his fish. But I gave out and had to drift back into the dammed-up river water, where my brother soon landed a cohoe.

"Let's try anchoring out there," suggested R. C. "Maybe we won't stick. But we can't drift out to sea, that's certain."

This was a good idea. Promptly rowing back to the same position, and then twenty yards farther, I dropped the oars, and scrambling to the bow threw over the anchor. It caught and held in perhaps twenty feet of water. The boat swung down current, and straightening, rode there as easily as a cork. We were amazed and delighted. R. C. let out his spoon, down into that eddying, fluttering rip tide, while I took up my own tackle to get it ready. This was a moment of full content. No hurry to fish! I gazed around me, at every aspect of this fascinating place, as if to absorb it with all senses. I saw that the attractive features were all increasing. The sun was higher and brighter. The sky had grown deeply blue. Thousands of sea fowl were now congregated on the sand bar, and their piercing cries sounded incessantly. There the sea could not be forgotten for a moment. How the green billows rose higher and higher, to turn white and spread on the strand! The surf was beating harder, the tide coming in stronger. Foot by foot the yellow water receded before the onslaught of the green. How strange that was! These waters did not mix. Music and movement and color and life! Every time a rosy, shining steelhead leaped near the boat I had a thrill. I felt grateful to him for showing the joy of life, the need of a fish to play and have a fleeting moment out of his natural element. Yet I also wanted to catch him! This was not right and I knew it, but the boy in me survived still and was stronger than all the ethical acquisitions.

"Wow!" yelled R. C., jumping up with his green rod wagging. I heard his reel whiz. "Did you see that son-of-a-gun? . . . Good-by to your green rod!"

This fish broke water on the surface, but he did not come clear out. I saw the pink color of him and part of his back.

"Big steelhead. Pull him up to the boat," I said.

"Aw!" That protest was all R. C. made. Perhaps he wanted to save his breath. For he certainly had all he could handle in that swift water. The steelhead did not jump or run; he just stayed down at the end of that mill race and defied R. C.

Fifteen minutes had passed when I inquired of my brother if he intended to land that fish so I could put my line overboard. No reply, but he risked my rod a little more! Meanwhile I saw the queer flat launch with Wiborn coming down the bay, and after it half a dozen skiffs. R. C. paid no attention to them. He was intent on landing his steelhead. I did not think he ever would do so. What a terrific strain he put on the slender green rod! It bent double and more. Gradually R. C. worked that stubborn fish close to the boat, and there we had our trouble, for when, by dint of effort, he got the steelhead nearly within reach of my gaff, the swift current swept it away. Naturally I grew excited and absorbed in our fight with him, and did not look up again until we finally captured him—not a steelhead, after all, but a ten-pound cohoe.

When we had him in the boat we looked up to see the launch close at hand, and a fleet of eight or ten skiffs anchoring or about to anchor right in front of us. For all we could see, there was only one rod in that formidable crowd, and that was a long flimsy buggy-whip sort of pole in the hands of a girl. Her boatman was a young fellow who could not row, that was certain. They looked like tourists, bride and groom, perhaps. I hoped they would hook a good-sized salmon, but I knew if they did they would never catch it. Several of the skiffs kept coming on, and actually got in front of us, ready to let anchors down where R. C.'s spoon was twirling. This was terrible. R. C. and I were trained in a school where an angler respects the rights of others. Besides, to use Lone Angler's favorite expression, "We got here first!"

R. C. yelled at them, and finally they reluctantly rowed out of direct line with us and let their anchors down somewhat to our right. Next my driver and his man, who had brought us down from Seattle, came splashing along in another skiff, and they anchored even with our position, not twenty feet distant. Lone Angler, coming in the launch on the other side, laughed at us. "Ha! Ha! You'll have a fine time—if you hook a salmon."

R. C. looked at me and I looked at him with the same thought in our minds—that here was a perfectly wonderful morning spoiled almost at its very beginning. Only a matter of twenty yards of the channel lay open, and that was to our left under the cliffs. All the space to the right was covered by skiffs with anchors and heavy hand lines down. What chance now had we to catch a fish? There were Indians in these boats and white natives of Requa, all probably fishing for their livelihood. We could see that they regarded us with friendly amusement, as if they would soon have some fun at our expense. Soon see the delicate little rods smashed!

"Reckon we're up against it," said R. C. soberly. "Hard luck, though. What a grand place to fish, if those ginks weren't here!"

"If we hooked a heavy fish now we'd not have one chance in a thousand, would we?" I queried, hopelessly.

"I should say not," replied my brother. Then suddenly he called out: "Look! Lone Angler has snagged on to something. Gee!"

Thus directed, I saw Wiborn frantically hanging on to his little black rod. The launch was below us to our left. The fish he had hooked—most manifestly a big one—was running fast across the channel straight for the anchored skiffs. Plain it was to us how our comrade was suffering. Usually a skillful and graceful angler, here he was bent out of position, hanging on to his rod with both hands, obviously thumbing the reel with all his might, in an effort to turn that fish. In vain! The rod nodded, bent down, straightened—then the line broke, and Lone Angler fell backward into the cockpit of the launch. R. C. and I had to laugh. We could not help it. Humor is mostly founded on mishaps to others! Lone Angler rose from his undignified position and seemed divided between anger and sheepishness. What a disgrace! When he saw us waving our arms he waved back at us.

"He was a whale!"

R. C. and I were next attracted by the commotion in the skiff nearest to us. My driver was a Greek named Pappas, and fishing was new to him. His companion must have known still less. From the yelling and rocking of the skiff, and wild action, I gathered both of them had hooked fish at the same time. At any rate, they were frantically hauling on their hand lines. The lines became tangled, but the boys kept on pulling. They got in each other's way. Something broke or loosened. Pappas nearly fell overboard and his friend, stupidly holding his limp hand line, made no offer of assistance. Finally scrambling back to safety, Pappas entered into a hot argument with his companion, and they almost came to blows.

Next, one of the natives in a skiff hauled in a good-sized salmon, and others had strikes. Then suddenly the girl angler with the buggy-whip rod had a strike that nearly jerked her overboard. She screamed. The rod went down, and evidently under and around the boat. The fair angler did not seem to want to catch the fish, but to get rid of the rod. Her escort took it, holding an oar at the same time, and when he managed to stand up the fish was gone.

"What do you know about that?" queried R. C., ruefully. Manifestly it was no unusual occurrence to hook big fish at the mouth of the Klamath.

For answer I let my spoon drift down into the place where the salt tide was more and more damming back the fresh water. No sooner had it reached the spot when a heavy fish hit and began to run off with my line.

"Pull up anchor and grab the oars," I yelled. "We'll follow this bird."

R. C. lost no time, and before the fish had half my line off the reel we were following him. He swam straight through the narrow opening between the cliff and the anchored boats, out into the wide waters of the bay. There, by careful handling of the light tackle, I brought this fish to gaff in twenty minutes. It proved to be a Chinook salmon weighing twenty-two pounds, the first of that species I had ever caught, and certainly large enough to inspire and lure me back to try again.

As we rowed back past the skiffs some of the natives called to ask us to show our fish. R. C. lifted it up. They were outspoken and fine-spirited in their tribute to the little tackle. We anchored again in the same place. Conditions were perceptibly changed. The current ran swifter, fuller, with more of a bulge in the center. It lifted our skiff, and I knew that soon the anchor would drag. The sea was booming heavier behind us, and the swell of the waves now rolled into the channel. All the lower end of the sand bar was covered with water. Yet still the black cormorants and the white gulls contended for the little fish. Their screams now were almost drowned by the crash and wash and splash of threshing waters. Still farther back had the dark-green tide forced the yellow river. There was a mist in the air.

R. C. and I let out our spoons together. This time they drifted and sank, down to the margin of the tide. Something hit my spoon, but missed the hooks. I was about to tell R. C. when an irresistibly powerful fish ponderously attached himself to my spoon and made straight for the skiffs with their network of anchors and hand lines.

"Oh, look at him!" I wailed, as I tried to thumb my reel. It burned too severely.

"Good night! I knew it was coming. But stay with him till your hair falls out!" cried my brother, as he swiftly reeled in, and then jumped to heave the anchor and get to the oars.

When he had done so and was backing the skiff down the channel all the two hundred yards of silk line was gone off the reel, and the green linen line was going. My fish ran straight for the boats, and then apparently began to zigzag. Not the slightest hope had I of saving either fish or line. It was fun, excitement, even if no hope offered. R. C. had risen to the occasion. If my line had been round a hundred anchors he would not have quit. Lone Angler appeared beyond the skiffs and he was watching.

"Whatever you do you must be quick," was R. C.'s advice.

The whizzing of my reel began to lessen. I calculated that was because the line had become fouled on some of the anchor ropes. We cleared the first skiff. My line stretched between the anchor rope of the second skiff and the skiff itself. I had to pass my rod between skiff and rope. It went under water. I heard my reel handle splashing round. Both natives and Indians were helpful, both in advice and with their efforts. They all pulled in their hand lines, the nearest of which was wound round my line. What a marvel it seemed that my fish apparently stopped pulling while we untangled my line from the big lead sinker and spoon on that hand line! But so it actually was. The next skiff had out a long slack anchor rope. It appeared that my line had fouled this deep under the water. I put my tip down, tried to feel the line, then dipped my rod under the rope and lifted it out on the other side. Wrong! I had only made a loop around the rope. I had to laugh. How futile! Yet I did keep on—did not surrender. I dipped the rod back again, and then the second time. The line came free. It began to run off my reel, faster and faster. There was only an inch of thickness left on the spool.

"I'm a son-of-a-gun if I don't believe we'll get clear," said R. C., giving in to excitement.

I had not yet awakened to any new sensation. Foregone conclusion had it been that I would lose this fish.

But I stood up and looked ahead. To my amaze my line was out of the water for a long distance ahead of my rod. Then I saw a man in the last skiff, standing up, holding my line high. It was slipping through his fingers.

"I got you free of my line. You're all clear now. He's on—and he's a whopper," called this fellow.

Impossible to believe my eyes and ears! I saw this fisherman, a big brawny man, bronzed by exposure. His face bore an expression of good will and pleasure and admiration that I will never forget. Somehow in a flash it electrified me with the idea that I might catch this fish.

"Look out, you'll fall overboard!" warningly shouted R. C. "Brace your knees on the seat. I'll catch up with that son-of-a-gun!"

R. C. began to row fast, and fortunate indeed was it that he had grasped the situation. For as he got into action, I glanced at my reel to see only a very few laps of the green line round the spindle. I turned cold. For an instant my right hand seemed paralyzed. Then I began to reel in readily. With sinking heart I watched it, sure, painfully and dreadfully sure, that my fish had gotten away. Why had I given credence to a futile hope? Why had I been so foolish as to surrender to a wild dream? He was gone. Then the line suddenly came so taut that the reel handle slipped out of my fingers and knocked on my knuckles.

"He's on yet. Row fast. If I can only get back to the silk line!" I called.

R. C. saved me there, and very soon I had all the green line on my reel. With the stronger silk line to rely upon now I had more and more irresistible hopes. I could not help them. To hook that tremendous fish, whatever it was, to get safely through that maze of skiffs, anchors, and hand lines, to feel the silk line slipping on my reel—it was unbelievable, too good to be true.

R. C. rowed perhaps three hundred yards beyond the last skiff before I could get enough line in to feel safe. Then we took it more easily, and gradually I got so much line back that I knew the fish was close. In fact it soon transpired that he was directly under us, swimming slowly. This was good, and I could not have asked for more. But when he turned and swam back toward the skiffs—that was another matter. It made me sick. It began to worry R. C.

More and more I thumbed the reel. The rod bent in a curve so that I had great difficulty in keeping the tip up. I did not dare look often at the rod, because when I did I would release the strain and the fish would take line. At times it would be nip and tuck. Then when I held him a little too hard he would make off toward the skiffs and the channel. In time he led us back to within fifty yards of the danger zone.

"Hold him here or lose him," said R. C., sharply. "No use to follow him farther. . . . Be awfully careful, but hold him. That rod's a wonder or it would have broken long ago."

I stepped up on the stern seat and desperately strained every nerve to perform the most difficult task ever given me in an angling experience. To hold that fish, to check him, turn him and lead him without breaking rod or line, seemed an impossible achievement.

I elevated the rod and shut down on the reel. Slowly the arch of the rod descended, the line twanged like a banjo string, and just as something was about to break I released the pressure of my thumb and let the fish have a few feet of line. Then I repeated the action. Again!

"Row just as slowly as possible," I admonished R. C. "Not back, but across, quartering the current. Maybe that will turn him."

R. C. had no answer for me then. He rowed with great caution. And the fish gradually worked down toward the other skiffs at the same time that our boat was moving across the current. I could see all the other fishermen watching intently. We were close enough for them to see clearly our every move. From somewhere came Lone Angler's call of encouragement.

For me those moments were long, acute, and fraught with strained suspense. How many times I closed down on the reel I never counted, but they were many. My efforts to continue this method could not have lasted long. My arms ached and my right hand became almost numb. I grew breathless, hot, and wet with sweat, and when my eyes began to dim from the strain of nerve and muscle I knew the issue was short.

My fish had just about reached the zone of the anchored skiffs when almost imperceptibly he began to sheer to the right. Not a minute too soon! R. C. let out a pent-up whoop.

"We're leading him," he said. "Careful now. Only a little more and we'll be out of danger."

I had stood about all I could stand of that strain, so that even if the fish did come with us a little it was not easy for me. Gradually we worked him across the outlet of the river, behind the rocky bluff into wide placid waters. There I let him swim around until I rested my aching arms and cramped hands. Soon I felt equal to the task again and began to work on him. In the deep still water I soon began to tire him, and in half an hour more he came to the surface and wearily leaped out, a huge Chinook salmon. Eventually he gave up and we lifted him aboard.

Then I was indeed a proud and tired angler.

"Good Lord! Look at that fish—to catch on a bass tackle!" exclaimed R. C.

Broad and long and heavy, silvery and white, with faint spots and specks, and a delicate shimmering luster, with the great sweep of tail and the cruel wide beaked jaws, he was indeed a wonderful fish.

We rowed back to the point to exhibit him to the interested spectators, and then we went ashore on the sand bar to take pictures. It was all I could do to lift him high enough. Fifty-seven pounds! That was not an excessive weight to lift with one hand, but I was exhausted.

R. C. and Lone Angler refused to compete with me any more that day. I heard R. C. speak in an undertone to Lone Angler, and what he said sounded something like, "Hope he's got enough this trip!"

This I pretended not to hear, and I told my companions to take a last look at the most thrilling and fascinating place to fish I had ever seen. The world is wide and there must be innumerable wild beautiful places yet unexplored that await the hunter and fisherman. Of these I am always dreaming and creating mental pictures. Yet the waters a fisherman learns to love always call him back.

Requa, the fishing hamlet, quaint and old-fashioned, picturesque and isolated, stood out on the bluff above the Klamath, and faced the sea apprehensively. By the sea it lived. And its weather-beaten features seemed to question the vast heaving blue.

Down under the bluff the river was damming against the encroachment of the sea, and now the green water was slowly receding before the yellow. Ebb tide! The salmon and steelhead had ceased playing on the surface. But the glancing ripples were still there, the swooping pelicans and the screaming gulls, and the haunting sound of the surf.

CRATER LAKE

IT WAS along toward the end of June, 1919, when we left the little mountain resort of Prospect, Oregon, and headed for Crater Lake. The weather was hot, which fact made us welcome the dense shade of the magnificent forest. To me traveling by auto is not so attractive as other means. You go so fast you cannot see anything distinctly, let alone remember it. And dust raised by a car is somehow different from dust raised by a horse. Oregon is too beautiful to travel through swiftly and in discomfort.

The road gradually climbed for thirty miles or more until we got out of the thick timber. At the entrance of Crater Lake National Park we were informed that the road up to the lake was not yet open. We could ride a few more miles, until we came to the snow, and then we would have to walk. As it was already afternoon, we decided to spend the night at the camp there and in the morning get an early start for the lake.

The place was interesting enough, aside from the scenery, which was superb. A number of people, tourists and otherwise, appeared to be going to and fro. They all talked much about what they called the excellent rainbow-trout fishing in Crater Lake. But I did not see any fish and no one I spoke to had gotten any more than a look at the lake. I did meet an old fellow, a road-mender, who labored under a good deal of excitement owing to the fact that a huge grizzly bear had interfered with his labors, and —— But this is a fish story. We slept that night in tents, and I also could tell an interesting number of details about the Oregon wind and the cold, and strange animal prowlers.

Next morning was bright, keen as a whip, and nipping cold. A breath of the mountain air was exhilarating. We rode out a couple of miles, through a park-like, sparsely timbered country, until the snowdrifts blocked further progress. A number of workmen were cutting a road through deep snow as hard packed as ice. They told us to follow the trail up to the summit.

That walk, or rather climb, was pleasant despite its difficulties. Giant brown-barked fir trees stood majestically out of the snow-drifts, and their soft green foliage shone beautifully against the background of white. The fragrance of these great Oregon pines was so cold and sweet. Mrs. Grey and I rather lagged behind my brother and the rest of our party. The altitude was hard on my wife, not to mention the steep parts of the icy trail. We rested a good many times and profited by that in our enjoyment of the white-and-green forest, and the occasional glimpse through the timber out over the wild range. Toward the summit, where the ascent grew steeper, we were hard put to it to make headway. Mrs. Grey is wonderfully mathematical, and she said often, between panting breaths, "If we—slip back—two steps—for almost—every step up—when shall we—get there?"

Finally we reached level ground from which the snow had melted. Evidently there was a considerable strip of this ground between where we stood and the rim of the crater. I could not see the lake. To our right a jagged range of snowy rock rose high and appeared to circle away toward the north. To our left bare ground and green grass led up to a stone house which evidently was a hotel.

Crossing this strip, we soon stood upon the rim, with Crater Lake far beneath us.

I expected something remarkable, but was not prepared for a scene of such wonder and beauty. Crater Lake was a large body of water set down deep in the pit of an extinct volcano. It seemed a blue gulf. Nowhere else had I ever seen such a shade of blue. This color was not azure blue or sea blue. How exquisite, rare, unreal! After a moment I seemed to think that it resembled the blue of heaven seen from the peak of a high mountain. This rare blue is not of the earth. Crater Lake had more similarity to an amethyst than any jewel I knew. An amethyst in which tints of lavender and heliotrope were dominated by blue! The color, then, of this wonderful lake was its most striking feature.

The shores were precipitous, in some places sheer bold bluffs of red rock, in others steep slopes of ash-colored talus, with patches of snow everywhere. Prominent in the foreground was a cone-shaped island, evidently cinders or lava, and it was quite abundantly timbered with fir or pine. The slope at my feet looked almost like the Grand Canyon in winter, so snowy and steep was it. I could see a trail over the snow slanting away to the right and going down under the rim. It did not look inviting, but it showed that some persons had dared to venture down into the crater at this season.

While the others of my party gazed spellbound, I broke away from the scene and went in search of information. The hotel was not open. I found a couple of campers busy at their meal, but they could not speak English and I could not speak the language manifestly theirs, so I could not learn anything from them. I met a workman who gave me but scant notice. At length I ran into a fellow who said he was employed there, and he concluded his reply to my query by asking me what I wanted. I guess I did look rather disreputable. At least I had on very old and very rough clothes, and could not have been mistaken for a tourist. My brother was carrying my fishing-tackle.

"I want to fish," I replied.

"Too early," replied the man.

"Why? Won't the trout bite?"

"Yes, they'll bite all right. Some of the boys have been down an' caught messes. Big ones, too. But the trail ain't open."

"I saw a trail going down over the snow. Is that where they went down?"

"Yes. But it ain't no boullevard."

"Will the trout rise to a fly?" I went on, nothing daunted by his disparaging tone.

"No. Only spinners, an' they gotta be big."

"Any boats down there?"

"No. They was all smashed by snow-slides."

"Much obliged," I concluded, and turned away.

"Say, I reckon if you start down you'll get down quicker'n you'll climb up," was the departing sally of my informant.

What an asinine speech, I thought! I pondered a little. Usually I am wary of these dry natives of a place. But where fish are concerned I am not much given to reflection. In this case, if I had not been so thrillingly eager to fish in that beautiful blue lake, I might have spared myself considerable perturbation. Instead, however, I went at once in search of R. C. and began to elaborate on the size and number of rainbow trout in Crater Lake. My wife interrupted my eloquent advance.

"But, my dear, you wouldn't think of going down here—down this awful steep slope—*over the ice!*" she remonstrated.

"Sure. It'll be exciting. Something new—climbing down over the ice to catch trout!" I declared.

"Zane, permit me to correct you," remarked R. C., ironically, as with keen dark eye he surveyed the long slant of crusted snow. "You mean sliding down. But not for me! Do you take me for a Swiss ski-runner?"

The old story! From time out of mind—from earliest boyhood —I have had to persuade or coax or bribe or force my brother R. C. to go with me upon venturesome quests. I am generous. I always want to share my adventures. And R. C. has had most wonderful adventures that he never would have dreamed of but for me. Yet always when there is a new one, R. C., instead of being more and more eager to go, grows harder and harder to persuade. In this case, after I had about exhausted myself, the issue seemed lost. But suddenly I had an inspiration. I turned to my wife.

"I don't like to go down alone. For I'm not so careful when I'm by myself. You know R. C. is slow and sure on bad trails."

I might have said more, but it was not needed. My brother did not wait to hear the importunities of the ladies. "Aw, come on!" he exclaimed, in scornful resignation. "Here goes. Stunt number sixteen hundred and seventy-three! . . . You go first. If you start to slide and I don't see you any more I'll come back."

I meant to be funny and so did he, but somehow it really was not funny. Rather soberly I took my tackle and knapsack and started down over the little stretch of bare ground to where the trail began on the snow. This trail was merely the boot-tracks of men made when the snow was soft. At this hour of the morning, before the sun had risen high enough to strike over the rim, the snow was as solid and slippery as ice. In fact, a dozen steps from the edge it was ice and it had the pale-green color of glacial ice.

57 Pounds!

PLATE XXVI

The Bears on the Way to Crater Lake—Tame, but Not Very!

PLATE XXVII

The trail led away to the right, gradually descending under the rim, but it was not yet steep or difficult. At least it did not seem to be the latter. I kept my eyes upon my feet and the next place to step, so did not see anything else. I heard R. C. close behind me.

We must have come down a hundred yards before either of us spoke.

"We'd better go back before we get in bad," said R. C., sharply.

"I admit—it's a little ticklish," I replied, "but let's stick to it."

"Stick on!" declared my brother, grimly.

We continued down fifty yards or more. If anything, the trail became a little steeper. Surely the boot-tracks grew farther apart and shallower and icier. I found myself stepping with less confidence. I did not slip, but I feared I would. My knapsack encumbered my shoulders. As I bent down it flopped around, bothering me. I carried my tackle in my left hand, and used my right to hold on to the snow-crust. Its surface was hard and smooth. It gave me a feeling of security that really was false. I kept on. The going grew worse. I could not risk walking slowly, so I went fast. Then I came to a bad place. All ice and not level! I passed it, reached a jump-off or break of several feet in the slope, where I had secure footing. Here I paused to rest. I was panting and sweating. My hand shook a little. This was more than exciting.

"We ought to have brought a couple of sharp sticks," I said.

"Yes," replied R. C. His voice sounded queer. I looked ahead and suddenly was amazed and frightened. We were now down upon the wide, white, steep slope. The trail was merely tracks of ice, very narrow, and it slanted. To the left of the trail the slope was so steep that it looked almost straight down. I could see a long way, yet could not see where it ended. It glistened, and was as smooth and hard as ice. I realized instantly then that a misstep on the trail, a slip, meant catastrophe. My enthusiasm died a violent death. I grew a little sick.

"Red, we'd better go back," I said, quickly.

"I can't—turn," he replied, and his voice was not steady.

I wheeled to see him on that icy dangerous place. His usual ruddy color was gone. It flashed over me that all in a moment, seemingly, we had gotten into a perilous situation.

"Come on—come quick and sure," I called. It was the only thing to be done. Another moment of hesitation might have been fatal. Down ahead of me about forty or fifty feet was a bush standing out of the snow. It looked strong. It stood near the trail. Alert and tense, with swift steps I went down, made a lunge for the bush and caught it. When I looked back R. C. had reached the safe foothold I had vacated.

"Are you all right?" he called, sharply.

"Yes—all right so far."

R. C. whistled, and wiped the sweat from his face. I expected him to taunt me with the predicament into which I had led him, but he did not. I guess the situation was too serious.

"Now what?" he queried. "We can't go back now. When the sun softens this snow it'll be easy getting up. But that'll be hours. We can't stick here. We have to go on."

I had been studying the lay of the trail beyond my position. There was still a little hazardous place to descend. But this did not frighten me as did the fifty feet between where I held on and R. C. stood.

"Reddy, it's easy from where I am," I said. "Just a few steps—and see—if I did slip I'd slide down to that line of brush."

"Yes, I see," he replied. "You're about out of the woods. But I don't like this . . ."

He abruptly broke off, closing his lips tight. I could see his jaw bulge. Instantly he had recognized the need of action. He saw the place—realized the danger—knew that what he must do would be the better for instant action. This is what men learn in the open. I think it was a great deal harder for me than for him. As he started with swift light steps my hair stood up stiff and I shook all over. I held to the bush with one hand and with the other extended my tackle toward him as far as I could reach. He did not slip once. When he grasped my rod, then my hand, and at last the bush, it surely was none too soon for me. It took me a moment to get my nerve back. Then I faced down the trail again. When I had passed that part of the trail still hazardous, I drew a deep breath of relief. Next I slipped on a place that was not bad at all, made a frantic effort to recover my balance, fell, and slid like a flash down a dozen yards into the line of brush at the edge of the snow. Here at least I was safe. R. C. came on down without mishap. We waved our hands to the watchers far above and then sat down to rest.

"Some place—that!" ejaculated my brother. "I was scared at first. Then I got sore. And what do you think? On that last bad place all I thought of was the time when we were kids—coasting down Maple Hill—and my sled went over the bank—breaking my arm in two places. Do you remember? Funny what a fellow thinks of!"

Yes, it is strange, surpassing strange. I was reminded of more then, and it was that, whatever R. C. might lack in enthusiasm at the outset of an adventure, he always made up in nerve when he really was launched upon it. He was cool, logical, and had a kind of grim humor.

We rested there a little while, and then resumed our descent of the trail, finding it easy by reason of the brush. It did not take long to get out of sight of the rim. We found breaks in the snow slope, and there were places we had to climb down, but we did not encounter any more risks. To be sure, some of the rocky slides were hard to stick on. We had glimpses of the lake down through the firs, and each one seemed more picturesque. The closer we came to the water the bluer grew the color. There was a singular contrast between the white sliding snow-bank, which was really a glacier, and the green of firs and blue of lake. It resembled a scene in the Alps rather than the Rockies. The last part of our descent led through rocks and brush and bare earth. The avalanche of snow, however, stretched down clear to the water and at the edge of the lake was perhaps three hundred yards wide. We reached a bluff overhanging the lake, from which vantage point we took stock of our possibilities.

We would have to go down across the last of the snow-bank to the rock-lined shore. There appeared to be only a limited section of this shore line that we could fish. Precipitous banks confined us to this one short stretch. Wading in that icy water would have been a foolish procedure. The shallow water near the shore was a bright green, with a golden or amber tint. The rocks looked gilded. This shelf of rock extended out a few rods to the edge of what seemed a bottomless blue gulf. The jump-off into the pit of the volcano looked straight down, and it must have been the extreme depth of the lake that gave the water such an exquisite shade of blue.

"Look!" yelled R. C. in my ear. He pointed down to the right, along the shallow strip of green. There I was thrilled to see a number of very large trout swimming aimlessly around in less than two feet of water. I counted them, and each one looked larger as I enumerated it.

"Nine! That's a sight worth sliding down the snow to see, hey? . . . Now, I just wonder—will they bite? I'll just about bet they won't."

"Well, we'll snag a couple, then," declared R. C., reverting to the days of boyhood pursuits when the achievement, the capture, was all in all. "Say, are they rainbows?"

"Why, yes, they look like rainbows. What else could they be?"

"Search me. Look at that big black fellow. He'll weigh— what?"

"Six or eight pounds," I replied, trying to be conservative.

"They're all lunkers. But they don't look like the same kind of trout to me."

Indeed, there was a great dissimilarity. The huge black trout formed a class by himself; there were several brown; one a pale yellow, with something of the amber tint of the rocks about him; and three or four that looked to have a bluish cast.

"Ha! Look who's here!" exclaimed R. C., and he pointed to another bunch of trout coming along the shore from the opposite direction. "Come on."

R. C. strode down the snow-bank toward the rock-strewn shore. I would have liked to watch and study those trout for a while, but my brother was going to fish for them. That was too much for me. In a few moments we were down on the bare rocks. Trout were passing to and fro. If I know anything of the nature of trout, these certainly saw us. But they showed no fear.

"You try a fly. I'll use a spinner," said R. C. "You go upshore and I'll go down. If you get a bite, yell!"

One of our practices, learned when we first began to fish, was to tell each other in case of a strike, or a hooked fish, or, in fact, anything that occurred in the way of excitement or encouragement.

Specimen of Crater Lake Rainbow Trout

PLATE XXVIII

THE GREAT WHITE PELICANS WITH BLACK-TIPPED WINGS

PLATE XXIX

I strongly suspect, however, that the secret of this was that I would rather see R. C. start something then do it myself, and he had exactly the same sentiment. Fishing keeps men boys longer than any other pursuit!

I rigged my tackle with flies and began to cast here and there over the passing trout, in front and behind them, and all around. They would not rise to any of my casts. Then I changed my flies and tried again, warming to the work, and casting to the best of my ability. No good! I cast till I was tired.

Suddenly from down the shore pealed a yell. I looked. R. C. stood on a rock with his rod bent. I saw a wave; a splash. He stepped inshore, pulled his rod around, bent down, and came up with a big trout in his hand.

"Punk! No pep! He was a dead one!" yelled my brother.

"How big?" I called.

"Oh, four pounds! Whale of a trout! But he had no more fight than a sucker!"

"Try again," I replied, and sat down to change my flies for a spinner. I selected the largest and gaudiest I had. While I rigged this on I saw R. C. catch another trout, a smaller one, that appeared to be landed in short order. By this time I was curious about these Crater Lake rainbows. They acted and looked rather queer to me.

Then I got up to try my hand again. All I succeeded in doing was to scare away the bunch of trout in that particular spot. I moved upshore. More or less all the time trout would be passing up or down, some in close, others far out. As they did not seem to mind me, I got over trying to be careful, to keep out of sight. I stepped out boldly. And I cast that spinner in nine hundred different ways. No good! I heard R. C. yell, and then I heard him yell again. I was too busy and mad to watch him catch fish.

Presently along came a fine big speckled trout in about a foot of water. I made an atrocious cast and in trying to recover the line I pulled the spinner by the trout. He turned to follow it. I had my rod pretty well up and back, and I kept dragging the spinner toward me, more to get it away from the trout than anything else. Well, he followed it almost to the rock I stood on and the faster the spinner came in the swifter the trout swam. Finally he struck it, not three feet from me. I was hopelessly out of position with the rod 'way down behind me, and a mile of slack line waving around my head. I could not jerk. But the trout turned around with my spinner in his mouth, swam off, and hooked himself. It was ridiculous that this should be thrilling to the point of excitement, but it was so. That trout made two or three little runs and then flopped over on his side and let me lead him to the bank. He never kicked once. It was a rainbow of about three pounds weight, of a singular bluish-bronze color on the back, pale silver underneath, with dark flecks, and a bar of rainbow tints down the sides. The fish was in poor condition, almost as flat as a flounder. I killed it and cut it open, expecting to find evidence of recent spawn. But I could not find any indication of it, nor was there food of any kind in its stomach. Thereupon I packed the fish in the snow-bank and went back to casting, more curious than ever.

It developed that by accident I had learned a cast which attracted these fish. I could make them follow the spinner and run in to take it. I caught the limit allowed, and all of these trout together, one of which weighed five pounds, did not show any gameness or speed or fight or endurance. I hooked a still larger one that leaped and freed himself, but even so he did not show any of the vicious and pugnacious qualities common to trout. The fishing, then, was a total surprise and disappointment. A novel feature about the adventure was that, when I had caught a fish, I had only to walk a few steps to pack it in snow as cold as ice. The sun had come out hot, softening the snow, and I enjoyed reaching out for a nice cool snowball whenever I was thirsty.

I dressed all these trout, and not in one of them did I find any trace of food. I went along the shore and studied the water and rocks and bottom, but I could not find any sign of life. Not a minnow or little trout or bug or worm or fly! This was in the latter part of June. It did not prove that the rainbow trout were actually starving in Crater Lake, but they were in bad condition and I claim it was a result of lack of sufficient nourishment.

Presently R. C. showed up, dragging trout that under normal fishing conditions would have made my eyes bulge. We exchanged views. He had arrived at my conclusions, and he added that he did not believe the crater of an extinct volcano was a natural environment for trout.

Climbing out was hard, because it was almost straight up and we were burdened by the weight of the fish. But we took our time and rested every few steps. I certainly enjoyed the ascent more than the descent. I had leisure to look about me. A breeze had rippled and ruffled the surface of the lake, somehow marvelously transforming the color of the water. Great white clouds sailed in the sky and were reflected in the lake. The wind sang in the fir trees. I did not see a bird or an animal of any species.

When we reached the danger zone where it was necessary to cross and climb, we found that the softened snow made safe travel. We did not care how laborious it was. We were nearly two hours in climbing out, part of which time, of course, we had rested. On the whole it was an adventure well worth experiencing. The kingdom of Adventure is within us. A trip or a fishing jaunt or a climb upon the hills is successful and happy only as we possess in our hearts the things we go out to seek.

I rested and lingered on the rim of Crater Lake long after the others had started down toward camp. I seemed to wait for something I had not yet gained. The feeling is difficult to describe. Nevertheless, the superb panorama of snow-covered peaks, the black-timbered slopes between, the westering of the sun behind huge columnar white clouds, and the lake of heavenly blue, deep-set, like a rare gem in bronze—these would leave me rich enough with impressions, even though I did not gain the haunting one I craved.

Then, like magic, it came. The most wonderful and beautiful of nature's transformations must be watched for patiently. I saw a breeze rippling the waters of the lake. It changed the color; it darkened the blue. I thought a shadow of cloud had fallen. But, no, it was just a melting change of color. It seemed that some marvelous medium had dissolved under the gentle breeze and was moving across the lake, merging and mushrooming like smoke, dominating the blue. It seemed too beautiful, too exquisite to be real. It was a nameless tint. It resembled the rare color of the wild lilac of the Oregon forests—a purple lilac; and even as I looked it vanished, like the color of a dream.

PELICAN BAY

NEW places to fish and hunt and explore have always had a perennial fascination for me. I often catch myself dreaming of strange, beautiful waters teeming with fish, and verdant woodlands where wild animals roam undisturbed. How many lonely crags where the eagles perch and scream—how many open mountain ridges where the elk bugles his siren whistle to his mate —how many grassy hill-tops, high above the sounding sea—how many windy heights of the desert—how many miles of ocean lanes, full of great marine fishes—and how many dark, cool pools where the trout lurk hidden—how many, how infinite the number of new, strange, wonderful places in the world that I can never see! It is a melancholy thought. Yet it is happiness to know there are such places.

Old familiar places haunt me more than the new ones. Camps and streams and lakes and shores, with long acquaintance, become dear. The thought of saying farewell to them hurts, even though another visit some day is sure. And to say good-by forever—that is losing something beloved. I am always divided between the thrilling call of the new places and the haunting memory of the old.

Pelican Bay lies at the extreme head of Upper Klamath Lake, Oregon. More like a river than a bay, it winds under the shadow of vast black-timbered slopes that rise to glistening peaks of white snow, pure and noble against the blue sky. Cold streams pour down from the mountain crags, and the courses of these waterways are shaded by Oregon forests and choked by wild lilac. Of all wild flowers these are the sweetest and most exquisitely beautiful. Both leaf and blossom of this wild plant are more delicate and smaller than those of the cultivated species. I have seen five varieties of color—white, lilac, lavender, a rarest of rare purple, and lastly a shade of pink that is nameless. The fragrance is faint, but as exquisite as the flower.

The waters of Pelican Bay are amber-colored, a rich, deep amber that gleams like gold. And verily, I believe, in the black, cool depths of these waters the rainbow trout are so abundant that they must lie on the bottom, side by side, like pickets of a fence. This may seem a remarkable statement, but my story of fish, when I come to it, will lend strength to my conviction.

Anyone who visits Rocky Point Camp at the head of this lake cannot but be pleasantly struck with the felicity of its name. Pelican Bay! In spring and summer and fall a great flock of pelicans live there. For many years I have been acquainted with pelicans, but never had I seen such wonderful birds as these. Twice the size of ordinary pelicans, white as snow, with black-tipped wings, they assuredly are the eagles of their species. Indeed, they remind me of eagles. They have a habit, never observed by me in other pelicans, of soaring high in the air and sailing round and round, up and up, until they are out of sight. I never tired of watching them.

All birds, as well as animals, have remarkable habits that are well worth studying. Some of the things done in nature are incredible. Only long association with wild creatures in the open can bring a naturalist to rational acceptance of the marvels of life.

In the spring when the waters of Pelican Bay are high, flushed by the melting snow, and when the great white birds have returned from some unknown winter quarters in the south, they have been observed to collect in a huge flock and swim out over the inundated marshland. Here they form a compact line, like that of warriors about to charge an enemy encampment, and spreading to a circle they begin a flapping, swimming commotion in the water, and proceed to drive the fish inshore. This circling attack resembles the work of fishermen with a drag-net. Probably it is just as efficient. When the pelicans get a school of small fish on the run they close in around them, driving, flapping, striking, until they corral the frantic victims in the shallow waters close to shore, and there follows a veritable massacre. The big ludicrous bills wag in the air and shake the little fish like terriers with rats; the pouches under these bills seem ever distended. Large pelicans have a large capacity. They swim inshore, flap and bob and splash, all the time narrowing and thickening their line of offense, until the luckless school of small fish has been devoured.

And then they—but there are other things to tell about concerning Pelican Bay—the ducks and herons and bitterns that were everywhere; the black-and-white and blue-gray terns, more wonderful fishers than the kingfisher; the snipe concealed in the tule rushes, strange birds that made a low, humming, melodious sound; and not to forget the big, swift-leaping, hard-fighting rainbow trout.

We trolled from a rowboat, using a spinner. I had an ordinary bass tackle, rather light, but with good-sized reel and plenty of line. The large rainbows do not rise to a fly, so we left our fly-fishing until later. On the way to the dock of the little camp we had encountered a youngster getting out of a skiff. He had a burlap sack over his shoulder and a dinky little rod in his hand. The sack looked bulky, and it made me curious.

"Say, sonny, what have you in that sack?" I asked. "Looks like cabbage."

"Nope. I ketched a few. Was only out about two hours. They ain't bitin' good," he replied, and lowering the obviously heavy sack, he opened it and let us look in. R. C. peeped in first. He started, then put his head almost inside the sack.

"Jiminy!" he ejaculated.

Whereupon I pushed him aside and looked in myself. I saw a pile of rainbow trout, some of them alive, curling their fins, and colored like the rainbow from which they derive their name. There must have been about a dozen, running from four to six pounds.

"How many?" I asked, faintly.

"Reckon I ain't counted them yet," replied the lad, and shouldering the heavy sack, he trudged away.

"What do you know about that!" exclaimed R. C.

We were both flabbergasted. "This is Oregon, you know," I said, "and it's wild country up here."

We got into the rowboat selected for us, and with me plying the oars, we went round the bend of the narrow bay, and soon reached the half-mile stretch of amber water where we had been told to fish. It certainly was a beautiful place. On our right lay the marshland with green tule and flags, and on our left the forest of fir and pine sloped dark green up to the white-capped peaks. We headed down the middle of the bay, with R. C. trolling a hundred feet back. He had a five-ounce rod, a fly-rod at that. The time was about five in the afternoon, with sun westering behind the mountains. How cool and dark and deep the water looked! Everywhere we saw little waves and widening rings and ripples, showing where trout had stirred the surface. White pelicans, graceful as swans, were swimming ahead of us, leaving long wakes behind them. I heard the screech of a kingfisher and the strange hoarse croak of a bittern. Herons winged lumbering flight along the marshy shore.

Not any boat in sight! What I had taken for a boat turned out to be a log upon which were squatting a row of white pelicans. All except one were asleep, and he evidently was a sentinel. It was hard to row and watch R. C.'s line, and at the same time attend to all going on around me, but I tried to do it. We expected, of course, to get a strike every moment. This, however, did not happen. It never does happen for R. C. and me. We have to work for fish. I saw the wave of a trout that must have been half as long as one of the oars, more or less. But nothing happened in the way of a strike. We passed the mouth of an estuary that marked the end of our fishing ground, and I turned the boat, making closer for the marshy shore. The mouth of this estuary was full of floating moss and great pond-lilies, with dark deep channels between. I saw a crane standing like a statue on a snag. He was so interesting that I watched him and so did not observe R. C. lean over and rise and jerk. But his motion startled me and I pulled rather sharply on the oars. That gave the boat a lurch just as R. C. got to his feet. Alas! He fell all the way from the stern to my seat and landed on me like a thousand bricks. Wonderful to relate, he held his rod up free, and I saw it bend double at the same instant a rainbow shot out of the water. He looked black, with gleams of pink. Down he soused and up he flashed, to shake himself so that I plainly heard it. By this time I had stopped the boat and R. C. was on his feet. Neither of us had said a word. In fact, I was so scared I could not speak. If I had been minding my business R. C. would not have had that tumble. Fishing from a boat in this fashion is being at home for us, in spite of the awkwardness. How different that rainbow acted from the rainbows of Crater Lake! This fellow bounced out of the water as fast as he fell back into it. When he took to plugging he was strong and stubborn for a three-pound fish. Presently R. C. led him alongside and I slipped a net under him. The rich, dark, many-hued beauty of this rainbow brought forth my unqualified admiration. Like the water, he was amber-colored, and his sides had broad bars of faint rose and pink and opal and mother-of-pearl, all faintly spotted with exquisite dots.

Our agreement was that we would each row for the other until each caught a fish. So with my turn at the rod I began full of expectancy and thrills. But nothing happened at the end of my line. Several futile trips up and down the stretch convinced me that I was unlucky. So I persuaded R. C. to change places with me. I told him that he did not know where to row to find the fish.

During the next half-hour, with me at the oars, R. C. ruined the five-ounce fly-rod on seven trout hooked and three landed. Two of them would weigh about six pounds each. They made that rod wabble like a buggy-whip, and the last one bent a ferrule. So R. C. had then to take the oars and let the unlucky fisherman have his innings.

The sun was setting behind the snow-clad peak, burnishing the white into a wonderful rose. Wild fowl were winging rapid flight across the lake, perhaps toward their night quarters. How golden the water seemed!

I asked R. C. to row me along close to the tule. This species of swamp vegetation resembles an extremely large cat-tail plant without the tail. They grow in deep water, and here the shore was evidently quite a goodly distance in through the tule. Aquatic birds were plentiful in that dark covert. I could hear them splashing. By peering keenly I saw a bittern on a reed watching me with uncanny eyes. He was gray and dull blue.

I trolled so close to the tule that I had to use a short line. Here I had seen some big waves made by fish. We glided along noise-lessly, without a ripple or splash, and we covered the whole length of that particular stretch without any luck. A stake, about thirty feet from the tule, marked the end of this course, or a shallow

The Author's Wife Screamed: "You Keep Still! You'll Make Us Lose Him!"

PLATE XXX

DOLLY GREY'S ANSWER TO THE DOUBT THAT
WOMEN CAN ENTER THE FRATERNITY OF FISHERMEN

PLATE XXXI

place. At any rate, R. C. turned here, just inside the stake, and on that turn, as I reeled my spinner closer, I saw a flash of red-silver, a swirl on the water, and then a sousing splash. Almost instantly, after the hard, heavy strike, a huge trout leaped out high, shaking his head like a dog. I heard the spinner jingle! He was the largest trout I ever saw, and he made a leap that almost robbed me of sense enough to hold my rod. At that he nearly jerked it overboard.

Down he soused, and R. C. made a Herculean lunge on the oars. My back was turned. I could not understand. "Hold him! Hold him hard! Don't give him an inch!" bawled R. C. And the force of his command set me to thumbing the reel. I lifted on the rod. The trout pulled it down. Up he leaped! He was black and red. His broad side, his stiff fins, his curved tail, all his quivering body, caught the gleam of the setting sun. I saw him, but not clearly. I was too wildly excited to see anything clearly. On his next leap he actually hit the stake I had noticed before. He fell back, and on the right side. Then I realized why R. C. had been rowing so hard and yelling so loud. If he had not done both, the trout would have gone inside that stake, and that, of course, would have meant loss. My pang of dread, then, was really suffered after the reason for it no longer existed.

"He's a lunker!" yelled my brother. "Let him run. I'll follow him."

New and strange indeed was it for me to have a trout run out line. He did not go straight. He tumbled out about every ten yards, and I think he must have leaped half a dozen times before R. C., rowing powerfully, got well out into deep water. Then he stopped the boat and I stood up to fight him. I really had done nothing but hang on to the rod somehow. But now I began to show that rainbow something. Indeed, I showed him a good deal. Part of it was how to crack a rod! He made a threshing, zigzaggy fight close to the surface, but did not leap again. Fortunately the rod held, and after some minutes of grim trepidation on my part, and sundry short dashes on his, I finally got him within reach of R. C. and the landing-net. Whoop I certainly did when I spread him out, and whoop I did again when I lifted him. He weighed eight pounds. He was a dark, speckled trout, with only faint rainbow tracings of color.

On another day R. C. had his battle with a big rainbow trout. Most certainly, assuredly, and inevitably it had to be larger than mine. Really, if he did not beat me of his own accord a larger fish than mine would be sure to jump into the boat!

This day we reverted to the old style of using live minnows for bait. That is the boyhood method for bass as well as trout, and because it is a habit of boy fishing, some day I intend to prove that it awakens more pleasant memories and stirs more wild thrills, and that it is therefore the best sport.

We did not land any rainbows, however, while using minnows for bait. I hooked a heavy creature of some kind that moved out sluggishly toward the middle of the lake. I could not stop him. The situation was just awakening to some excitement when the hook tore out. If that fish was a rainbow he was one of the old granddaddys said to inhabit the lake. Eighteen-pound rainbow trout have been caught there, and many seen larger than that.

Toward sunset that day we went back to using spinners. There was quite a breeze blowing, rippling the water, and presently trout began to rise all around us. We could not troll fifty yards without a strike. In short order I ruined another light rod. I found out that evening how difficult it was to let four- and five-pound rainbow trout go free.

Then, with me at the oars, R. C. had a smashing strike.

"Wow! . . . Some trout!" he yelled, standing up. His rod curved, the line zipped, the reel sang. "Back water! Back water!"

The boat was a heavy old scow. I plunged the oars deep and heaved with all my might against that breeze. I backed water all right, but I did not back the boat. If anything, we drifted a little.

"Back water!" yelled R. C., stridently. "Don't you see how he's taking line. He'll break it. Back water—harder!"

I backed until I nearly pushed and heaved myself lame. Then, the right oar slipped out of the rowlock and I plunged forward with great momentum, banging my head, skinning my knuckles, and bruising my arm. Marvelous to behold, R. C. maintained his equilibrium. But he did not keep his temper. He used very rude and undecorous language. I could have stood that, but, as I manfully breasted the wind again, he scornfully accused me of trying to make him lose his fish because it was bigger than my eight-pounder. More than once before I have averred that fishermen, on occasions, become little boys again.

"I'm doing my part—you do yours," I yelled. "I'll turn round. . . . Look out!"

It must be confessed that I gave a prodigious pull on the right oar before I yelled a warning. The boat wheeled around. But incredibly, R. C. never lost his balance. Just then he could have tiptoed on a tight rope.

"Now wind up your line," I shouted, and began to row desperately. This way I made the boat fly through the water.

"Fine! Now you're getting there," declared R. C. as he wound the reel. At every stroke of the oars he would sway back. He had his knees braced against the stern seat.

"You'll fall out," I called once, as he staggered.

"Big trout! I'm getting line now. Gee! he had out a mile. Nearly all of it. . . . Slow up a little. We're close to him. . . . There! Now keep rowing easy and we'll follow him."

"Has he jumped yet?" I queried.

"No. But he's a rainbow. I saw the red and silver on him. Some fish, believe me."

Presently the fish changed his course and swam alongside the boat, about even with the stern where R. C. stood, and there he stayed, vigorously plugging just under the surface. I could see his wake, then a swirl and now a gleam of color. He made a short, solid, thumping splash, went down, and sheered off. We followed him, caught up with him. This time he saw the boat, and he shot away in a beautiful run. Once I thought he would leap. But he did not. We chased him, followed him, drifted with him, and humored him for I do not know how long. R. C. did not make any blunders in handling that fish. At last we drifted gently broadside with the breeze, and the big trout followed us. He was about vanquished. But R. C. led him up to the boat several times before he would trust the use of the landing-net.

"Say when," I said, as I leaned over with the net.

No wonder R. C. was careful! The rainbow curled and curved on the surface, a great trout as long as my arm, gasping and rolling, with his brilliant colors so exquisite against the dark amber-hued water.

"Now!" called R. C., sharply.

No more careful and dexterous could I have been if my life had depended upon that issue. This rainbow trout weighed seven pounds. For me the climax of this angling experience came when I broke in upon R. C.'s raptures. I told him how and what he had yelled at me while I was almost killing myself trying to back water against the wind. He astounded me by appearing grieved and hurt that I should so misunderstand him!

Another afternoon the trout would not rise at all. We grew tired rowing the boat. I ran the bow into the moss and lily-pads at the mouth of the estuary, and R. C. prepared his cushions in the stern for a nap, while I settled myself comfortably to pass an hour or so until a little breeze would come or the trout begin to rise.

How still and beautiful the summer day! Great white clouds, as white as the snowy peaks, sailed in the blue sky. The atmosphere was rich and thick with an amber light, as if it caught a reflection or tinge from the lake. Scarcely a ripple showed on the water. Warm golden sunshine varied with mellow shadow, according to the pleasure of the drifting clouds. How still and dreamy the scene! The fragrance was of mountain air, scented with dry pine and fir, wafted down to mingle with the rank, damp, reedy odor of the marshland. I wanted to surrender to the drowsy lull, to this spell of the lotus-eater.

A kingfisher screeching by stimulated me to the opportunity at hand. To see, to hear, to feel, to smell out in the wild open, in a beautiful place like Pelican Bay, was equal to the enchantment of dreams. So I decided to forego the nap.

The next sound to thrill my intent ear was the low, soft, strange hum of a jacksnipe. I could not locate him. He seemed near, then the next time I heard him he seemed far. Then I got the

LADIES' DAY AT PELICAN BAY

PLATE XXXII

OVER THE BARS THE ROLLING WATERS GO

PLATE XXXIII

impression that there were two snipe. No sound I ever was familiar with had any resemblance to this. I listened and listened. A hum, then a mellow trill, then a low, hollow whirring, then a strange, deep, faint concatenation of exquisite notes! How impossible to believe that it was made by wings! But it fitted the lonely, languorous marshland.

Next I was attracted by sight of a couple of terns close at hand. They were fishing at the mouth of the estuary. One was dark gray and the other almost white. They were slender, shapely birds, almost as large as a pigeon, only with sharp-pointed wings and tails. Their motion was swift, irregular, darting, until they poised in the air, like a sparrow hawk, fluttering motionless in one spot. I could see the keen heads pointed down and the peering intentness of these fishers. Suddenly one shot down like a plummet. Splash! He went clear out of sight. Then he emerged, rising buoyantly, with a wiggling minnow in his bill. It did not have a chance to wiggle long, however. Next, the other tern flashed down, and he, too, came up with a tiny fish. For some time after that I watched them at their feeding. It seemed to me that they darted down into the water a good many times without catching a minnow. Here was remarkable contrast to the birds of prey of the desert— the shrike or road-runner or hawk. These desert murderers never miss their prey! Food is scarce and life is fierce in the desert. In the marshland, on the contrary, birds do not have a difficult task in procuring food, and hence are not so highly developed.

When the terns went on their way out of my sight, I gazed out into the lake, and was pleased to see that a number of great white pelicans had come into view. One was asleep, with his head twisted round upon his back, and he drifted with the lazy current. While in this position no particle of the black markings on his wings showed. Several others were swimming along, rather aimlessly. Those that interested me most were the ones in the air. First I counted five sailing along, wide wings outstretched, with their breasts scarcely a few inches above the water. They sailed as one bird. How swift, how wonderful, how beautiful that flight! Without movement of a feather, so far as I could see, they sailed a hundred, two hundred yards, and more, before bending their wings. Then, with powerful sweep, up and up they flew, forty or fifty feet above the lake, suddenly to straighten those wide wings again and swoop down like thunderbolts, to repeat the marvelous performance of sailing close to the water. They passed out of sight. Next, a lone pelican came flying high above those on the lake, and he began to circle down—around and down till he made a long swift slant, lowering his feet into the water, and sliding with long splash to a graceful settling. He did not close his wings until his momentum had ceased. For some reason beyond my understanding the nearest pelican resented this newcomer, and lumberingly launched himself into the air. But once he got up he showed what command he had of those tremendous wings. The newcomer gave chase, and both pelicans flew over me, perhaps fifty feet above the lake. How they cut the air! I plainly heard the rushing sound, as of stiff feathers cutting against the wind. The enormous size of these pelicans struck me forcibly. They passed on out of sight over the marsh. Others came sailing along on the opposite side, and at one time they resembled a long white ribbon with knots tied in it. They alighted near a log that stuck out of the tule. One by one they climbed up on it. This appeared to be a signal or an invitation for those swimming around, for they headed that way. In ten minutes more all the pelicans in sight—eleven, to be exact—were perched on that log, flapping their wings, picking themselves, or settling down into round balls of white.

Fly-fishing in Pelican Bay was just as remarkable as trolling, though the trout, of course, did not run so large.

Above the camp a dark limpid stream poured its cold waters into the bay. At twilight, below the mouth of this stream, rainbows of two and three pounds would rise to a little fly of brown or gray. We rowed a boat up here and let it drift along about thirty yards from the shore. For that matter, the current was so sluggish that the boat scarcely drifted at all. The stillness of the evening was broken now and then by the heavy splash of a big trout chasing minnows, and by the hoarse croak of a bittern. All over the pale gleaming mirror of water could be seen little waves and widening rings, disturbances made by rising trout. Casting inshore, whenever we accomplished a skillful presentation of the flies, we would get a strike. Not always did we achieve this, so that it took a good many casts to drop the lure deftly and softly. Then the trout made the water boil. On light tackle these rainbows leaped and fought gallantly, deserving the freedom most of them received at our hands. It did not seem to make any difference how much disturbance a fighting trout made in the water, for immediately afterward in the same spot a clever cast would raise a fish. Once R. C. hooked a big one that leaped high, showing his big curved black body against the pale gleam of water, and he shook himself convulsively, making a sharp, wrestling sound, and threw the hook.

As darkness came on the trout rose less and less readily. But R. C. was loath to leave that enchanting spot. So was I. And for me the fish were only incidental. Night awoke the denizens of the marshland. Insects began to hum; frogs opened up with long melodious trill and now and then a deep raucous rumble; the bitterns boomed; and over all rose the strange wild humming sound of the jacksnipe. It seemed that the world had been left to these night criers and to darkness and to us. R. C. must have felt the charm of the lonely hour, for he gave up casting and sat down to listen. Old sweet sensations welled up from the depths of my being, making this hour familiar with long ago. Somewhere, thousands of years before, the spirit that was in me had lived such an hour, and now claimed my heart and rested upon it an aching melancholy happiness.

The best of a fishing experience does not always happen last, but in a story it should always be given the climax of the end. The end of everything should be the best—even the end of life. So I will close this sketch of Pelican Bay with the exceedingly remarkable, not to say funny, experience that befell my wife and her companion.

R. C. and I had dutifully taken them out upon several occasions, and rowed the boats for them, and saw that they hooked trout; and we patiently bore with the atrocious and deplorable bungles they made, and when they did well we were certainly not lacking in praise. But for some unaccountable feminine reason they were not satisfied. They said they wanted some *fun*. They decided to go out alone, row their own boat, troll, and handle fish for themselves. As the day was calm and the boats perfectly safe, I consented, with a word of caution, to let them go.

When R. C. and I turned the bend in the river-like bay and got out where the ducks were paddling round, and the pelicans were sailing like white streaks, and the trout were raising winged ripples upon the water, then we forgot all about the ladies.

A couple of hours later, while I was rowing along close to the tule and behind a green point of marshland, we heard screams. We were alarmed. I began to row with all my might. Suppose the girls had upset their rowboat—or one had fallen overboard in that deep water—or—anything! My blood ran cold. I rowed so hard I lifted the bow out of water at every stroke.

Then we rounded the point of tule.

"They're all right!" yelled R. C. "Don't kill yourself! . . . But, Gee!—there's something doing! What do you know about that?"

My relief and thankfulness were so great that the reaction gave me sort of a momentary collapse. I sagged in my seat. But I heard shrill cries of excited women. Then I looked.

Mrs. Z. G. and her companion, whom we playfully called Dalrymple, were not fifty yards from us. Their boat appeared all right, only it acted strangely. Dal was puddling with the oars, and Mrs. Grey was pulling frantically on a fishing-rod, the tip of which was under water.

"Say, Doc, she's hooked to a lunker!" exclaimed R. C. "Wow! Look at that splash. . . . By George! he's gone under the boat!"

Then, quite naturally, R. C. and I in unison began to yell advice, warning, and command at the ladies. Moreover, I rowed our boat closer. I happened to remember my camera.

Suddenly my wife screamed at us: "Never you mind! You just—go away! . . . It's my fish! . . . We'll catch him—all by ourselves—or die!"

"All right, we'll stay away," I called, as I stopped rowing. "But, my dear, I'm afraid you'll die."

R. C. was red in the face and looked as if he might burst any instant.

"Say, he's under your boat," he shouted, waving his arms. "Pull him round—to the right—to the right. . . . Dal, row hard—left

Where the Melodious Roar of River——

PLATE XXXIV

Fred Burnham, the Great Fly-fisherman, Essaying to Teach the Author the Art of Casting

PLATE XXXV

oar—left oar! . . . No—no, don't pull on both oars. . . . For Heaven's sake, can't you turn the boat?"

"I *can't* row—darned old boat!" cried Dalrymple, half in rage and half in tears. "Never—rowed boat—before!"

"Well, anybody could see that," declared R. C. "But do as I tell you. Pull on your left. . . . Aw!"

She presented the most awkwardly animated object of a feminine boatman that I had ever seen. She could not handle the oars. They were long and heavy. The handles got stuck, and when she pulled one by the other, then she failed in her stroke because she bumped her knees. And once, when she did get a free pull, the blade of the oar skittered out of the water. Of course she slid off her seat.

But if Dalrymple was funny, she was not to be compared with her companion. My wife had a light rod, and it bent double. It should have broken half a dozen times. But she hauled away on it with all her might without doing any damage, and also without any appreciable effect upon the fish. For an ordinary angler that fish would have gotten away long ago. Once I thought he was gone. But I made a mistake. When Dal sprawled back upon the seat and grasped at the oars, she dipped one deep, and lifted it under the tip of Mrs. Grey's rod. Then the tip did come up out of water. My wife yelled. I could not distinguish what she said, but I could vouch for her lung power. The line fouled on the end of the oar. "Good night!" cheerfully called R. C. But, lo and behold! nothing broke; the line slipped free; the fish made a heavy splash. Then Dalrymple executed a wonderful maneuver with the oars and the boat began to go round as on a pivot. Mrs. Grey had to pass her rod over her head to clear the end of the boat. Next, Dal managed to stop the boat in its mad revolutions, but at the wrong time, for it left Mrs. Grey with the rod bent back over her head. The fish pulled hard. I leaped up to snap some pictures of this situation, and perhaps I lost sight of some of the best of it. R. C. began again to yell directions. My wife yelled back at him: "You keep still! You'll make us lose him!"

At that R. C. fell back in the stern and roared. Never before had he laughed like that! And I, unable to contain myself longer, also gave up to mirth. When a few moments later I raised myself and cleared my blurred eyes, I was amazed and delighted to see that Dal made a lunge with the landing-net, and then, by dint of much effort, lifted and lifted until the fish came on board. I heard it flop on the floor of the boat.

"Say, Doc, that fish was yellow," declared R. C. "It wasn't a trout."

As I took up the oars pandemonium broke out in the other boat. Dal screamed wildly: "It's no fish! . . . Eel—snake—reptile! Oooo! don't let it near me!" She scrambled back on the stern seat until I was sure she would fall overboard.

"Hey there!" I yelled. "Look out! Don't fall over!"

Mrs. Grey screamed also, but presently I descried that it was with laughter. Then the fish began to flop all over the boat. I realized that if I did not hurry, both my wife and Dal would fall overboard. When I had brought my boat alongside theirs, what did I see but a big yellow sucker, nearly three feet long, hooked in the tail. My wife had snagged him with the spinner. I thought R. C. would have hysterics, and my own strength was gone. The ugly-looking sucker flopped again, then lay still.

"Hit him with—your gaff-handle," I said, trying to talk while I choked.

"Dal, you do it," begged my wife.

"Never! . . . Oooo! there he's beginning again!" wailed that young lady.

"Soak him, Dolly," croaked R. C., who was now quite purple in the face.

"Go ahead, my dear. Hit him," I added. "I can't reach over there. If you don't he'll chase you out of the boat."

Thus directed, my wife, with slow, fearful hesitation, picked up the gaff, and poising it over the luckless fish she wavered, and then gave him an exceedingly gentle tap that would not have hurt a mosquito.

"There! He's dead!" she barely whispered, in awe and horror at her brutality.

By this time I was beyond speech. The sucker evidently selected this moment for one last mighty effort, and he made a great flop, landing on the gunwale. The line caught on the oarlock and pulled the spinner loose. With a dash of freedom the fish jumped out, splashed down, and was gone.

"Oh yes, he's dead! he's dead!" howled R. C. "Haw! Haw! Haw!"

WHERE ROLLS THE ROGUE

THE happiest lot of any angler would be to live somewhere along the banks of the Rogue River, most beautiful stream of Oregon. Then, if he kept close watch on conditions, he could be ready on the spot when the run of steelhead began.

This peculiar and little-studied trout travels up streams and rivers flowing into the Pacific, all the way from northern California to British Columbia. During the run, which occurs at varying seasons according to locality, the steelhead are caught in abundance, on bait, salmon eggs, spinners, and spoons. But so far as I can learn they will rise to a fly in only two rivers, the Eel and the Rogue, particularly the latter. The Rogue is probably the outlet of Crater Lake, and is the coldest, swiftest, deepest stream I ever fished.

The singular difference in steelhead of different localities is probably a matter of water. The steelhead that runs up the Klamath, which is a stream of rather warm, yellow, muggy water, is less brilliantly colored than the Rogue steelhead, and certainly not to be compared with him as a game fish. Many anglers claim that rainbow trout and steelhead trout are one and the same species. My own theory is that the rainbow is a steelhead which cannot get to the sea. He is landlocked. And a steelhead is a rainbow that lives in the salt water and runs up fresh-water streams to spawn. Once the whole western part of the continent was submerged. As the land became more and more elevated through the upward thrust of the earth the salt water receded, landlocking fish in lakes and streams. The rainbow might be a species that survived.

The relation of the two fish has never been satisfactorily established. But one thing seems assured—to fly fishermen who know the Rogue River, the steelhead is the most wonderful of all fish.

I first heard of steelhead through Mr. Lester, a salmon fisherman of long experience. He was visiting Long Key, Florida, and happened to tell me of his trip to Oregon and his adventure on the Rogue. He said he could not hold these steelhead—that when they were hooked they began to leap downstream through the rapids, and had to be followed. The big ones all got away. They smashed his tackle. Now this information from a noted salmon angler was exceedingly interesting. That happened six years ago. I made a trip to Oregon and found the Rogue beautiful beyond compare, but there seemed to be no fish in it. Two years ago R. C. and I ventured again, along about the end of June. Forked-tail trout and Chinook salmon had begun to appear, but no steelhead. They were expected any time. R. C. and I could not catch even the less desirable fish that had already come. We persevered, but all to no purpose.

The summer, 1922, recorded a different story. Upon our return from Vancouver and Washington we reached Grants Pass, Oregon, just when the run of steelhead was on. This was in September, and Lone Angler Wiborn had accompanied us. Fishermen friends we had made there assured us that we had struck it just right and were in for the sport of our lives. Fred Burnham, of California, surely one of the greatest of fly fishermen, was there, and he, in company with several of the native experts, kindly took upon themselves the burden of showing us how and where.

We had the finest of tackle, but only two fly-rods in the collection that would do for steelhead. Too light! And not one of our fly-reels would hold a third enough line. There were no reels of American manufacture that would do for this great fish. We had to have English reels that would hold a hundred yards of linen line besides the thirty or forty yards of casting line. These steelhead ran, we were told. All our flies were too small. Number fours and sixes were used, and Royal Coachman, Professor, Brown Hackle were advised as a start. I had a very old Kosmic fly-rod, nine and a half feet, eight ounces, that took the eye of these gentlemen anglers. Burnham had a hundred rods, but said he would cheerfully steal my Kosmic if I did not sleep with it. We rigged up seven-ounce Hardy rods for R. C. and Lone Angler. All this fuss and care and deliberation over a lot of fishing-tackle seems to many people an evidence of narrow, finicky minds. It is nothing of the kind. It is unalloyed joy of anticipation, and half the pleasure. If anyone should claim it a remarkably expensive procedure, I could not gainsay that.

Next morning we got up in the dark, and had breakfast at five o'clock in a little all-night restaurant, and were on the way up the river to Pierce Riffle before daylight. The morning was cool and gray. Forest fires were burning in the mountains and the fragrant odor of pine filled the air. Gradually the day broke, and when we turned off the road and ran down to the river the red of sunrise tipped the timbered peaks. A fringe of trees bordered the river and hid it from sight until we penetrated them.

The roar of swift, heavy waters greeted me before I saw the long green-and-white rapid that bore the name Pierce Riffle. Upstream the broad river glided round a wooded curve, and hurrying and constricting its current slid into a narrow channel with a mellow roar. A long flat bar of gravel led down to the water, and on the other shore the current rushed deep and strong, chafing at a rocky willow-skirted bank. The whole disturbance of water was perhaps a quarter of a mile long. Below the riffle opened out a magnificent broad stretch of river. The white water poured into it. There was a swift current, and dancing waves for a hundred yards, after which the water quieted and glided smoothly on toward the curve where the river disappeared. A faint violet light glimmered over the river. Most striking of all, however, were the significant widening circles and agitated spots of the placid surface upstream, and the hard splashes in the swift current before us, and below at the head of the big pool the sight of many fish breaking water, frequently several at once, trout of varying size, and steelhead that showed their beautiful colors, and occasionally a huge salmon. Certain it was that, what with trying to see all this and rig my tackle at the same time, I missed threading my line through at least two guides on my rod.

Lone Angler, true to his instincts, slipped off alone downstream; R. C. headed for the middle of the riffle, while Wharton led me up to the wide sweep of water where the river glided into the rapids. I had only hip boots and could not wade far out. Wharton wore waders and went in above his waist. Then he began to cast his fly, reaching fifty, sixty, and even seventy feet. Out there in the middle and beyond was where the steelhead lay. Even had I been able to wade out there I could not have cast far enough. At once I saw the very high degree of skill required. My spirits and hopes suffered a shock, and straightway I felt discouraged. Nevertheless, for a while I divided my time between trying to cast my fly afar and watching Wharton at work. He claimed he was not a fine fly-caster, although he could reach the distance. But that morning the steelhead were not striking. After long patient efforts he tried one of the tiny brass spinners, without any better success. Eventually the sun grew hot and the fish stopped breaking and playing on the surface. R. C. and Lone Angler had found no luck. We gave up and started back to town. Wharton advised us to try it in the afternoon, from four o'clock until dark.

The day grew very hot and oppressive. The mountains appeared shrouded in smoke. Oregon was in the grip of a very severe hot, dry spell of weather, and was sadly in need of rain.

By two o'clock we were on our way up the river, and this time we strolled beyond Pierce Riffle to see an irrigation dam where, we had heard, salmon and steelhead congregated in great numbers and were visible. The concrete structure was indeed a fine piece of work, but we hardly more than glanced at it.

A board walk crossed the river on top of this dam. From the road, high up, we could see the fish leaping, and we ran over one another to get down on that bridge. Water was streaming through cracks in the gates. Evidently this dam had been built across a rocky formation in the river bed. Below stood up narrow ridges of rocks, and between two of these ran a channel of swift water, dropping every few rods over a ledge. This channel was alive with steelhead. First we saw them leaping up the white foamy falls; then we found them in corners and eddies of the channel, and lastly we stood right over a place where we could see hundreds of these wonderful fish. Not more than thirty feet below us! Shallow swift water ran over smooth rock, and swirled in a deep eddying pool, and then rushed on to take the first fall. Here had congregated the mass of steelhead. They had gone the wrong side of the dam to get up, for the fish ladder was at the other shore of the river. Every moment a steelhead would dart up the swift water and leap against the concrete wall, to fall back. The average weight of these fish appeared to be about six to seven pounds, but we saw many of ten and twelve pounds, and a few larger still. They were of different colors, some dark-backed, others yellow, most of them speckled gray-green. Whenever one turned on his side, then we caught the beautiful pink and silver gleam.

We crossed the river to find on the other side a wide deep pool below the apron of the dam, and up out of this led the zigzag fish ladder, an admirable waterway of many little steps, whereby the fish could get up over the dam. By watching sharply, we were able now and then to see the dark flash of a fish in the white water. Hovering and wavering in the pool were large purple shadows, big salmon waiting for night to take their turn at the fish ladder. Occasionally one of these huge salmon would swoop up in the current, and lazily expose his back to the sun and to our fascinated gaze. One would have weighed more than sixty pounds. As he loomed up he gleamed purple, then darker, shading to brown, and when he came out into the light he seemed to have a greenish-black back covered with dots, and his tail looked a foot wide.

"Say, if we could only drop a line to him!" ejaculated R. C.

Speech was inadequate to express what I felt. Almost I regretted the law and the huge white sign which forbade fishing within four hundred feet of this dam. We idled there watching, and then we went back across the dam to where the steelhead were leaping and splashing. At last R. C. and Wiborn had to drag me away from there.

Five o'clock was it instead of four when we arrived at Pierce Riffle. Dusky and hot lay the somber smoky glare over the river. But the water would be like ice.

No fish appeared to be breaking. Possibly the steelhead had moved upstream. We were told that they arrived in schools, tarried at a riffle or rapid, and passed on during the night. But any day might bring a new and fresher school.

We were on our own hook, so to speak, this afternoon, and therefore more leisurely, more independent, and less keyed up. R. C. was at the head of the riffle in less time than it takes to tell it;

Mr. Carlon, the Portland Expert, Patiently Helped Me to Raise My First Steelhead on a Fly

PLATE XXXVI

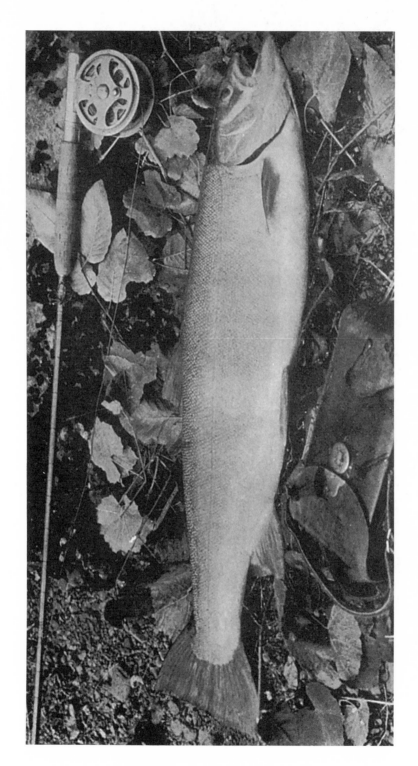

HERE HE IS!

PLATE XXXVII

Lone Angler took a long while to get into new waders; and I wasted a good deal of time over my tackle. This afternoon I wore hobnailed shoes over heavy stockings, dispensing altogether with rubber, and I was rather loath to enter that ice-cold water. Still the day had been so hot that I should have welcomed the coldest of water. My brother started out with a spinner, and he had not made a dozen casts before he raised a fish.

We did not need his yell to gather that he had apparently hooked a moving avalanche underwater. His rod jerked down and shook like a buggy-whip swinging a heavy lead. I could not hear his reel, but I did not have to hear it to know his line was flying off. Floundering out with great strides, he began to run down the gravelly shore. Right even with us then we saw a black threshing fish split the white water and disappear. R. C.'s rod sprang up like a released sapling. Gone! He waved a sorrowful hand at us and began to reel in. R. C. waded back as far as he dared into the swift heavy current, and began again to cast, quartering across the river, so that his line bagged and drifted down the current, dragging the spinner.

Lone Angler and I waded in at the head of the great pool. Industriously I plied my fly, cast after cast, sometimes executing a good one, until in half an hour I grew tired and discouraged. Steelhead began to leap in the shadow of the willow bank just opposite me. I waded in to my hips, until I had difficulty in keeping my balance in that swift current, and I cast desperately to reach the coveted distance. But always I fell short several yards.

Presently a newcomer appeared on the scene, a little man in farmer garb, with an old straw hat and a pointed beard. He had a cane pole fully twenty feet long. At the butt he had a reel attached, and I saw the big shiny spinner dangling from his line. Some rods above us he labored out on a rocky point, and thrust the enormous pole out over the river. It seemed as though it might reach across. The spinner floated down the length of line he had out, about as long as his pole, and sank from sight. Then this native fisherman stood motionless like Ajax defying the lightning. I wondered skeptically and disdainfully what he imagined he was going to catch. Then in about two minutes he gave a jerk and his long pole bent. Something was pulling mighty hard on his line. But he made short shift of that fish, dragged it ashore and up on the bank, a steelhead of about five pounds. Again he thrust the huge telegraph pole out over the river. Fascinated, I watched him. Just as I feared, pretty soon he had another strike. I saw the pole jerk and curve. This fish was heavier and a fighter. I saw it smash the current and scoot through the water like an arrow. The native endeavored to be as ruthless and violent as with his first fish. He tried literally to drag the steelhead out. I had hard work to control myself, to keep from yelling to him to play the fish. But he bent the huge pole double, dragged a big white tumbling fish in among the rocks in shallow water, and floundered after it. Disaster attended his awkward and uncouth attempt. The steelhead broke the line and got away. Then the old Oregonian exhibited some peevishness. He looked and acted as if a shabby trick had been played upon him. I was tickled, and could almost hear him mutter: "Wal, by Jiminy! I'd 'a' hed thet one if he hedn't busted my line."

He disappeared in the willows and I went back to my own fishing. But presently I heard a sousing splash near me, and looked around to see another native standing in the water above me, holding out a cane pole fully as long as the other fellow's. What was more and worse, that pole was bent. This native had hooked a fish. Suddenly I felt the line rub along my legs. Amazed and angry, I waded back. Then I heard the well-known swish of a taut line cutting water. The man waded down and back, lifted his line over my head, and went ashore. He followed that fish along the shore, and presently pulled it out on the sand, a fine steelhead. Then he approached his former position. I saw him stick some kind of bait on his spinner. When he got to his place above me he cast this out and let it down, and held his rod stationary. I could see his line and it was not three feet from where I stood.

Now what would happen? I looked for Lone Angler and R. C. Both of them waved at me, and not at all sympathetically. In a few moments that native angler hooked another steelhead right by my feet. And he went ashore, and downstream with it, landing a seven-pounder in less than seven minutes. He came back, and soon he had another on. This was too much. It filled me with despair. I changed my fly for a spinner and began to cast that.

It seemed to me that I might just as well have had an onion on for bait. Presently the native picked up another steelhead, right off my boots, and this one turned out to be a big one. It made a leap on the first run, a splendid diving leap, came out again fifty feet farther down, and churned the water white again. The fisherman was not able to get ashore quickly enough, so that he could run and follow this fish, and it took out all his line and broke off.

"Thet there was a twelve-pounder," he told me as he came back. "Ketched two like him yestiddy down below. Ain't you hevin' any luck?"

I acquainted him with the direful state of my angling fortunes, whereupon he gave me a small crawfish and told me to put that on. Gratefully I did so. I fished alongside of him with great expectancy, but nothing happened to either of us. The steelhead had quit biting.

Sunset had passed, and the dusky violet and purple lights fell over mountains and river. R. C. reported a fish hooked and lost, and Lone Angler said he had not caught anything but scenery.

The next day found us faithfully on the job, but the morning yielded nothing. In the afternoon we went again to the dam to see the steelhead and salmon. Again we were delighted and dejected by sight of wonderful schools of fish. We idled there for two hours, and then we returned to Pierce Riffle.

The sun was westering low and showed a dull magenta through the pall of smoky haze. The river seemed a moving medium of rose and lilac, incredible to the eye. Hot and oppressive, the dry air was full of odorous penetrating fragrance. Not a single fisherman marred the beautiful landscape for us. The loneliness, the charm of the place, the mellow changing roar of the rapids, and the leaping of steelhead everywhere inspired us once more to hope and action.

R. C. got there first, and on his initial cast he raised something big. I saw his spoon hit the water, and then something strike it. A wide breaking swirl attested to the power of the fish. How incredibly fast he shot downstream! R. C. had no time to move out of his tracks before the fish was gone.

I was the last to get ready, and before I stepped into the water R. C. had another strike—missed—and Lone Angler had a steelhead on. It took him the whole length of the swift water, and farther still, not a leaping fish, but a good one of five pounds. This sudden windfall of luck changed the aspect of things. With thrilling zest we went at it, and I held to my desire to catch a steelhead on a fly. The difficulties I had discovered at first hand, and the fact that few steelhead, comparatively, were taken on a fly, spurred me on to an accomplishment of that worthy feat.

R. C. soon struck another snag in the shape of a salmon. One of the heavy Chinook appropriated his spoon and started away from that place. Valiantly and wondrously my brother performed and pursued, but that salmon had a jaw of iron and an unconquerable spirit. He could not be held.

"Looks as if I were going to get mine today," said R. C. to me. "Thought I could lick anything with this tackle."

He had rigged up one of my green Leonard bait-rods, nine and one half feet, ten ounces, that I had had built for bonefish, with a good-sized reel full of silk line. He waded in above me, made a wonderful cast clear across the river into the shade of the willows, and a big steelhead leaped out with the spoon in his mouth. Sharp and hard R. C. came up on him, and out he sprang again, a curved quivering opal shape, flashing the ruddy diamond drops of water. I let out a whoop and R. C. yelled, "Run, you son-of-a-gun—run!"

R. C. never moved from his tracks. He held his rod well up, and apparently lightly thumbed the reel. I could hear it screech—screech—screech. Below us stretched the hundred yards of swift water, white and choppy close at hand, and gradually quieting down into the broad deep pool. That steelhead tumbled over the white waves in the most bewildering exhibition I had ever seen. He did not seem to go under at all. He danced like a will-o'-the-wisp, like a twisting light, over and over, with a speed unbelievable. He surely ran that hundred yards in less than ten seconds. He ended this run with a big high leap. Then he sounded.

R. C. came wading down to me. His face was beaming in spite of its tensity. His eyes were alight.

"Say, did you ever see the beat of that? Sure, this steelhead game has got me," he said. "Run, you Indian! That's what all this line is for."

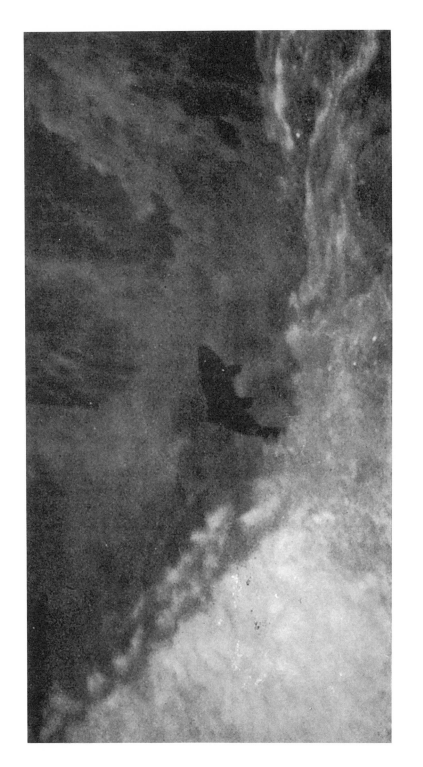

A Leaping Chinook Salmon

plate xxxviii

The River Beautiful

PLATE XXXIX

Before the steelhead slowed down he ran off another hundred yards of line. Then R. C. waded out and went with him downstream. Lone Angler accompanied him, and then I, unable to withstand the temptation, waded out, laid down my tackle, and joined them. R. C. gave an admirable performance with that steelhead, handling him perfectly, and eventually beaching him far around the curve of the big pool. Seven and one half pounds!

We went back to the rapid, and in a very few moments R. C. had hooked another, a different kind of fighter. He did not leap and he wanted to go upstream. What with bucking that swift current and R. C.'s strain on the line he soon tired, and gradually dropped down to the still water. There he was dragged over the shoal and landed. Six and one half pounds.

My ethical ambition expired for the time being and I put on a spinner. I made, more or less, nine hundred casts without avail. Then as I was letting my line drift, looking back at Lone Angler, totally unprepared for anything, I had a most tremendous strike. Thirty yards of fly-casting line went by the board in a flash and the green linen line followed. I burned my fingers and thumbs. All the hundred yards of linen line whizzed off the reel. Then this thunderbolt of a fish slowed up. Seizing the opportunity, I nearly drowned myself wading ashore below where I should have gone. Then I ran along the river, downstream. Soon I found that my fish had snagged the line on the bottom. How sickening was that realization! I worked for a long time to save the line, and finally did so, but the steelhead was gone. Never will I forget that strike.

The run of a bonefish, after he is hooked, is certainly great, but this strike of a steelhead is all run. You have no choice but to run yourself. That day indeed was a red-letter day along the Rogue.

Next day Burnham took us up the river, five miles beyond the dam, to a place he called the Suspension Bridge. A couple of wire cables sagged across the water between high banks, and to these were attached loops of chicken-fence wire, which in turn supported some rotten loose boards. The contrivance must have been as old as the oldest Oregon pioneer; it swayed at every step, and was certainly alarming to one unused to it. Burnham had a lot of fun leading us across this bridge, and I was sure he started it swaying by his own movements.

The stretch of Rogue River here was Burnham's favorite place. No wonder! It surpassed any stretch of fishing water I ever encountered. The bank from which we had crossed was high, a rocky rugged cliff, green with moss and vines, and covered on top with heavy timber, consisting in part of giant pines. The bank we approached was high, too, but sloping, and we descended it through thickets to the shallow rocky-floored stream. A narrow riffle roared at the head of this stretch, and sent its swift current along the far shore under the cliff, and through deep channels cut in the flat rock of the stream bed.

R. C. and Wiborn waded out to the riffle. I saw the former hook and lose a steelhead in the white water. Then I essayed to follow Burnham. I had a task. He stood over six feet tall and wore seven-league wading-boots, and deep or shallow was all the same to him. He worked downstream.

Nevertheless, here was a place where I could wade out as far as I liked and reach all but the farthermost spots. For a hundred yards out the water ran scarcely a foot deep over level rock, and led to where the deep ruts and channels and lanes could be reached. These deeper aisles in the rocky formation of the river bed were wonderful places to fish. The water ran dark and eddying through them. The river here was very wide, bank full, so that no bars or gravel beds or ragged rocks showed from one green shore to the other. The farther down we progressed the more beautiful grew the forest-topped cliff. Meadow larks and orioles sang melodiously in the trees, accompanied by the low murmur of the swift water. White ships of clouds sailed in the blue sky, and the sunlight shone golden on the foliage.

The steelhead were not there or would not rise. Burnham said this stretch seldom failed and we should keep on. What a wonderful sight to see him cast a fly! It fascinated me. It seemed so easy. His fly gleamed like a spark of gold in the sun. It shot out and back, forward and back, and his line seemed to wave, to undulate, to sweep up in a great curve, and at last stretch out low over the water, to drop the deceiving wisp of feathers like thistledown. He always cast quartering a little across the channel so that the bag in his line would drag the fly faster than the current. He said a steelhead rose to a fly and followed it downstream, and struck it so hard that it hooked itself. Twice he raised fish, and both times he let out a lusty yell. But he missed them, to my great disappointment.

Toward the lower end of that magnificent stretch of river the water deepened somewhat and the channels appeared harder for me to reach with a fly. I could not cast over into the shady ruts under the cliff, and it was here that Burnham was raising fish. I would make half a dozen attempts, and that meant at least six sweeps of my rod for each cast, and then I would rest my tired arm and watch Burnham.

I came to a place Burnham had left for me, a joining of two dark channels above a flat rock, behind which swirled and eddied the most haunting and beautiful little pool imaginable. It was fully sixty feet away, a prodigious cast for me. But I essayed it, more in the persistence and pride of practice than in a hope of raising a fish. Straining nerve and muscle, I swept my rod forward and back, forward and back, watching my fly, letting out more line, until I reached the limit. The fly dropped perfectly. I saw it sink and float under the surface, and then as the current caught the bag of line it dragged my fly a little more swiftly. The sight pleased me.

Then out of the dark eddying depths of that pool loomed a shape, dim at first, gathering color and life, until it became the reality of a steelhead, huge and broad as he swerved half over to follow the fly, shining pink and silver through the water. My heart leaped to my throat. Just as he reached the fly I jerked—and pulled it away from him. The action was involuntary. Then one instant I thrilled and shook, and the next my heart turned to lead and I groaned at my stupidity. Many and many a time I cast again over that pool, but all to no avail.

Suddenly my attention was attracted by Burnham's yell, and then shouts of onlookers up on the cliff opposite his position. He had hooked a steelhead. I saw it leaping. He called for me to hurry down and take the rod. I yelled back no. But he insisted. By the time I covered the goodly stretch of distance between us the fish had stopped leaping. But he had out nearly all of Burnham's line. So I took his rod, much to the amusement and interest of the audience on the cliff, and I waded after that steelhead. It took me fully a quarter of an hour to get back that line, and longer to lead the steelhead ashore. My left arm felt dead. The fish was not large, but on Burnham's light rod he was indeed heavy.

After that we fished down to the end of the stretch of good water, with no success. Then we waded to the narrow shore and headed back toward the bridge.

Next day the three of us tried Pierce Riffle again, and struck another off day. The following morning we left at daylight to motor twenty-five miles down the river to meet Burnham at the end of the road.

Our drive over the rugged bluffs above the Rogue, and the accidents we had, and the times we lost the way, would make a story. All I have space for is mention of the picturesque beauty of the Rogue River below Grants Pass. The farther we went and the higher we climbed the more beautiful grew the vistas of river, seen through the iron-walled gorges, or winding white-wreathed between dark and lofty timbered mountains, or meandering through a wide fertile valley of golden cornfields and fertile orchards.

Eventually we found the end of the road and the ranch where Burnham was staying. Late that afternoon he took us to a place called Chair Riffle, where the night before he and a Mr. Carlon had taken a dozen steelhead.

Naturally we were both excited and elated. Chair Riffle owed its name to a chair-shaped stone, on which an angler could sit and fish to his heart's content. This stretch of the Rogue revealed a long wide sweep of water, running four feet deep over gravel beds, where the steelhead lay in certain currents. They loved swift water. Burnham said it was necessary to learn where they lay. This evening, however, they did not lie anywhere in that riffle. They had moved on. We were too late. But I enjoyed sitting in the stone chair, watching, and listening to the river. This was wild country. I saw cougar and bear tracks along the shore, and deer were numerous. The mountains were high, cone-shaped, heavily timbered on some slopes. From this point on through the Coast Range to the Pacific there was unsettled rugged country, full of game and fish.

Next day Burnham and Mr. Carlon extended themselves in efforts to see that I hooked a steelhead on a fly. I enjoyed these kindly sportsman-like offices, but in my secret heart I did not believe the fish god himself could connect me with a steelhead. But you never can tell!

Toward sunset we motored several miles back upstream from the ranch, to Mr. Carlon's favorite fishing water. It was at the foot of a rapid that foamed in many white channels around and between many little islands, all of which were covered by a long heavy green grass. Burnham took Lone Angler and R. C. up above this rapid, while Mr. Carlon rowed a skiff through tortuous swift channels and in all kinds of difficult places in order to get me just where he wanted me. In half a dozen spots he held the boat and instructed me to cast here and there. What swirling eddies, and holes under shelving rocks, and little deep pools overhung by willows! Always behind us on the other side of the ledges of rock was the main roaring white channel.

At last this genial and indefatigable gentleman hauled the boat up on the edge of a rocky island, right in the middle of the lower fall of the rapid. Below us a long irregular sunken ledge of rock divided the deep heavy water from the eddies and pools on the other side.

"Never have I failed to catch a steelhead here," he said. "You must cast farther. Watch me."

Then he swept his line out over the water without letting it touch, farther and farther, with a wonderful grace and skill. It undulated as had Burnham's, only in longer higher waves, and it seemed instinct with life. Reeling in, he took a position directly behind me, and grasping my rod hand he gave my wrist quick powerful jerks, getting my line out with the sweep that had characterized his. In a few moments he had taught me the swing of it.

"Now try it," he said, finally, turning toward the channel of swift deep water. "Cast across and down. Don't drop your fly until it is as far out as you can cast. Then let it float down along that ledge."

I complied to the best of my new-found ability, succeeding fairly well in reaching the spot designated. But I did not see my fly float under the ledge. The ruddy glow of sun on the water dazzled my eyes.

"There! You raised one!" shouted Carlon.

Then my rod sprang down, straightened by a violent tug, so energetic and electrifying that I was astounded. The scream of my reel told me what had happened. I swept up the rod to feel the strong pull of a steelhead taking line. Carlon called something that I could not distinguish above the roar of the water. But I thought he said the fish was leaping. Facing directly in the sun, I was dazzled and could not see downstream. My fish took a hundred yards of line, out into that swift channel, and there he hung. As good luck would have it, R. C. and Lone Angler with Burnham came along down the rocky shore and provided me with an inspiring audience.

If moments could be wholly all-satisfying with thrills and starts, and dreads and hopes, and vague, deep, full sense of the wild beauty of environment, and the vain boyish joy in showing my comrades my luck and my skill—if any moments of life could utterly satisfy, I experienced them then. It took what seemed a very long time to tire and lead that steelhead, but at last I accomplished it. When he bored under the ledge of rock he alarmed me considerably, and evidently worried Carlon, who wanted to take me in the boat and row around the ledge. This I feared might be needful, and was about to comply when the steelhead came out where I could lead him over the ledge. For five minutes he swam in the shallows below me, showing plainly, dark-backed, rosy-sided, gradually slowing in action until he turned on his side, his broad tail curling, his fins waving. That was the moment to have released him. I had the motive, but not the unselfish appreciation of him and his beautiful Rogue—not that time. He had been too hard to catch and there across the river stood those comrades of mine. Instead I lifted him up in the sunlight for them to see.

ROCKY RIFFLE

THAT old adage "the third time is the charm" worked truth-fully for me on my 1924 trip to Oregon. It was a wonderful fishing experience, beginning disastrously for me, wearing on through the most miserable and inexplicable bad luck, and wind-ing up gloriously.

It had been the driest of seven successive dry seasons. Mt. Shasta was bare of snow, a remarkable evidence of a lack of pre-cipitation in that region, and the Oregon peaks shone naked in the sunlight. The forests were as crisp as tinder. At Medford we learned the Rogue was nearly two feet lower than for many years. R. C. and I hailed this information with satisfaction, as we had not forgotten that formidable river of swift currents, treacherous rocks, and deep icy waters. Also, and what was even more gratify-ing, we learned that an unprecedented run of steelhead trout was on. Fine catches fell to anglers all the way from Medford to Grants Pass. Most of these fish were being taken on spinners, which lures R. C. and I were averse to, unless as a last resource.

At Grants Pass, however, Mr. Wharton, the genial sporting-goods man of that town, and also an expert angler, informed us the fly-fishing for steelhead was the best he had experienced in all his years there. He could not account for this remarkable fact, especially as a low river was not supposed to yield good fishing. Steelhead come up from the sea in two runs, usually in July and September, the latter being considered the best.

We purchased about all the waders, flies, lines Mr. Wharton had in stock, besides a goodly supply of other tackle, and with a truck full of camping essentials and food we made haste to the place I called Rocky Riffle. No doubt it had other names, but I never heard them.

It was on September 23rd that we pitched our tents on a high open bank above the Rogue. We calculated on getting the morning sun and afternoon shade, always a desirable arrangement for a camping trip. The day was hot and work pleasant. A smoky haze of Indian summer filled the winding valley. High mountains, densely wooded, sloped up from the green-and-white river. In fact, the river valley was V-shaped, with high banks and benches at the base of the mountains. Behind our camp rose the dark green wall of the forest. Great fir trees lorded it over the pines, oaks, and maples. The gold and red and purple of autumn contrasted beautifully with the rich green. In several places we could look up through a notch between high slopes to see wild black-fringed peaks, sharp against the blue sky. Just below us the river made a wide bend full of rapids from which an incessant and murmurous melody came.

This delightful camp site had one bad drawback, and that was the river road which skirted the base of the mountains. Fortunately we could not see it and were aware of it only when the hum of a motor car sounded above the roar of the river. If there is anything I abominate on a hunting or fishing trip it is sight or sound of an automobile. In a case like this, however, there did not seem to be an alternative, and I had to swallow my resentment.

On this trip, R. C. and Takahashi, long uncomplaining subjects for my writing proclivities, had been reinforced by new comrades, Ed and Ken, who drove up the cars for me, and Chester, one of Mr. Lasky's camera boys. Altogether they bade fair to fulfill my exacting expectations for sport and fun. Chester cared only to fish with a camera, but Ken and Ed, having had some little trout fishing, were keen as whips to see something of the wonderful steelhead. R. C., remembering his failure to achieve success on our two former trips, was eager and determined. And lastly, Takahashi, the great little Japanese man who had helped make so many adventures profitable for me, seemed to present the best possibilities for an inquiring story-teller. George had fished in the ocean at Avalon and he had shown signs of obsession. But the kind of fishing we expected to do on the Rogue was Greek to him. I had provided him with some good tackle and was ready to give him instructions. Now George never took kindly to instruction. Sometimes he would ask for information or advice, though not often. I knew how to inspire him, and at once began dropping judicious remarks to that end. He was remarkably intelligent, could lay his hand to anything, and was exceedingly skillful. George had more patience, persistence, and ambition than any man I had ever encountered. Physically he was a marvel, but his small stature would handicap him tremendously in the wading necessary to fish the Rogue River. George was not much over four feet high. He would be lost in a man's-size set of waders. So what with the delicacy of manipulation in casting a fly, and George's inordinate assurance, and the tremendous handicap under which he must labor, I anticipated immense fun out of him. In fact, my calculations regarding all my comrades seemed tinglingly full of thrill.

By four o'clock we had our tasks of making camp complete and George was getting early supper. Owing to the high mountains in the west the sunset fell quickly, and with the shade and shadows came cool air that gave our camp fire an added charm. George was burning dead oak, a hard wood that makes a wonderful fire. The smoke was not so bad for the eyes as that from pine or cottonwood or cedar. "Oak wood fine for burn," said George, "but aspen wood more better."

How pleasant and restful the camp! It afforded me an immense relief. For three months I had endured the glare of the sea, the blaze of the sun, the strange enmity of the vast water wastes. Two months at Avalon angling for swordfish, and one in Nova Scotia for tuna, and then the travel, had tired me out more than I had realized. How good to be here, in the green, dark, cool mountains, near a ruddy camp fire, with loneliness and beauty of nature at hand, and in my ears the music of a murmuring stream!

After a bounteous supper, which included apple sauce made from Oregon apples—than which no more luscious dessert could be concocted for me—I undertook the pleasant task of talking to the boys.

"This Rogue is a dangerous river. The rocks are slippery and deceiving," I held forth. "The current is strong and swift, and the water cold as ice. You simply must not lose your balance and slip at a bad place. If you do it is all day with you. Hobnailed boots are necessary, and waders, too. That is why it is so dangerous to fall in. I, for one, couldn't swim weighted down. But I can't stand this ice-water without waders. It's a good idea for two fellows to fish close together, so in case of accident one can help the other. . . . Now as to fishing for these steelhead, try fly-casting. Practice casting until you can place a fly forty or fifty feet. If you can't catch them on a fly, try a spinner. But if you ever do catch a steelhead on a fly you will not care for any other method. You must learn where to look for steelhead. They favor swift water at the head of rapids or at the foot. They like eddies behind rocks, and deep places under ledges, and clean gravelly bars. The matter of finding them is something you will have to learn."

Although I talked with assurance, I knew perfectly well that I had a great deal to learn, myself. I had fished with Wharton and Adair, the Grants Pass anglers; and most of my instruction had come personally from Fred Burnham and Mr. Carlon, both wonderful exponents of the highest class of fly-fishing. I knew enough to realize that the Rogue River steelhead had no equal in fresh water for speed, strength, cunning, and endurance. Why these trout are peculiarly savage and game, infinitely more so than other species, even than steelhead in other rivers, I cannot say. Theories have been advanced for this remarkable fact, but they are scarcely convincing to me. The one thing that I lean to as an explanation is the ice-cold water. The Rogue, no doubt, has its source under the cold depths of Crater Lake.

The boys were enthusiastic and got out their tackle, and began to cast in the open glade before our camp. They were all amusing, but George Takahashi was the funniest. If he had not been so deadly serious I would have laughed as he tried to follow my casting instructions. Ed and Ken were born rivals, just as R. C. and I had been as boys, and were still.

It occurred to me that it might be well for me to rig up my own tackle and make a few casts before dark. While at home in Altadena I had practiced faithfully, and I could do fairly well, as casting goes. Of course I had fished for years in the East, using a fly for both trout and bass. But I measured my abilities by the marvelous casting of Burnham and Carlon, and had no illusions about myself. Still I could attain sixty feet, sometimes at rare intervals better than that. Such distance, however, in my opinion, was far from enough in the Rogue River. I had pinned my faith on an eight-ounce Kosmic fly-rod, one of the marvelous old rods not made any more. It was heavy, and tired me when I practiced, but I imagined I could use it. On the occasion of my fishing trip to the Rogue the year before, Burnham had used a seven-and-three-quarter-ounce rod, and Carlon one almost the same. So I thought I was on the right track. I had given the boys seven-and-one-half-ounce rods, and R. C.'s was seven. The idea of trying to whip these desperately fighting steelhead on a light rod had not yet occurred to me as possible. And, it seemed, on this evening my preliminary casting left nothing to be desired.

Twilight had begun to steal down the valley. I went through the trees to the bank of the river, to have a look at the rapids and to be alone a little before night set in.

The bank was high, and densely wooded, and thick with deep grass and vines. I found a huge fallen fir tree, fully two hundred feet long, that projected out over the bank, beyond the foliage, and almost to the water. It slanted at a rather precarious angle, but I walked down the trunk until I reached the branches, and from there found safe going until I got out over the water. Here I took a comfortable seat.

The Rogue made a big bend at this point, and all that bend was rapid water, some of it white. On my side the bank sheered down straight, dark and green with timber. Across the river a wide gravel bar led to a bold red bluff, spotted with pines and oaks, and this in turn led the eye to the black towering mountain beyond. On the moment an eagle sailed across the purpling sky.

The air seemed filled with rush and roar of water. No other sound was distinguishable. I could see where the wide stream, gliding from round the bend above, grew swifter with a glancing smooth current, and divided its hurrying volume over a gravel bar on the far side and dark deep channels between brown ledges on my side. Below these, the water broke into a most alluring ripple, and then went on into swift massed volume, to pour white and roaring over a ledge into a rough pool, and from that over another and lesser fall into a narrow curved channel which soon glided, spotted with foam, round another bend.

The beauty and melody of this river bend quite hindered for some moments the thought of fishing there. Finally, when that did occur to me it gave me a thrill, and at the same instant a sensation of dismay. For if any of us did succeed in hooking one of these fighting trout at the head of that rapid, how in the world would we ever catch him? No doubt about the fish rushing down the glancing incline, into the heavy current, over the roaring fall, and on through—assuredly to freedom! Nevertheless, the idea of such adventure was alluring. And I soliloquized, "A fellow might get out on the bank and chase the steelhead downstream."

After that calculation I spent a quiet half-hour there above the murmuring stream, into which reverie dreams of fish did not enter.

The place was lonely, beautiful, wild; melancholy, too, with the autumn colors and the imminence of night. I was surprised to find the air only pleasantly cool, despite the lateness of the season. It seemed like a summer evening in the mountains. In fact, the atmosphere felt a little as if it presaged rain. Finally, the darkening shadows warned me to make an ascent of the fallen tree before it was too late to see. This I did, and soon espied a bright red camp fire through the foliage.

Like the Indians, I had pitched my tepee with the door facing the east, so that I would be awakened by the sun. But this morning it was a rustling patter of rain that roused me from peaceful slumber.

The valley was full of gray cloud; only the lower part of the timbered slopes could be seen; and a warm showery rain was falling. Rain to a camper is not usually welcome, but in this case we were all thankful for it. Oregon was as dry as tinder. There were some forest fires, and all the remote wooded districts were threatened. "Let it rain!" quoth R. C., surprisingly facetious for him, considering the early hour and his antipathy for any weather except California sunshine.

After breakfast R. C. and I donned waders and rubber coats, and sallied forth valorously to meet certain defeat. We had been there before. And the boys, equipped to suit their particular fancies, started off with the air of conquerors.

R. C. and I had been told to cross the river below the fall, and fish the ripples beyond the bend. Whereupon we took a trail leading down through the woods and eventually found an old flat-bottom skiff, half full of water. Sight of it recalled our many years of bass fishing on the Delaware. What R. C. and I did not know about flat-bottom skiffs and rocky rifts was hardly worth learning. And in fact the Rogue resembled the Delaware, only it was deeper, narrower, swifter, and marked more by rapids and high mountains and lonely wild stretches. We bailed out the boat with tin cans, and in place of oars we used a couple of boards as paddles. I did not quite like the idea of trusting this old scow in the deep swift current we had to cross, especially as it led into rapids a hundred yards below. But fishermen incur risks, and perhaps Providence has more a care of them than of hunters. By paddling strenuously we crossed safely.

Then we went downstream round the bend, where we saw a goodly stretch of fast water leading into a widening riffle. The day was dark, with lowering clouds and drizzling rain, quite an ideal day for steelhead, though I did not fully appreciate it then.

At the head of this rapid big rocks split the current, and little grassy islands helped to make the spot an attractive and difficult place to fish.

R. C. and I separated, and waded in up to our hips, and began casting. Alas for thrilling expectations and vain assurances! I could not reach the places where I was sure the steelhead lay. The rocks and grass behind me, and willows on the bank, at once interfered with my back cast. Half the time I was snagged and the other half was devoted to freeing myself. I moved slowly downstream, and came at length to a part of the shallow water and bank clear of high obstructions. Once or twice on the back cast my fly ticked something. I got it out fairly well and tinglingly watched it float down to disappear. But nothing happened in the way of a strike. Often I glanced downstream to see what R. C. was doing. He was casting laboriously and having his troubles wading over the slippery rocks.

The exercise was little short of strenuous. Encumbered with the heavy rubber coat, I became uncomfortably warm. I took it off. The rain had a habit of showering profusely and then letting up for a while. Besides, it was not a cold rain. In fact it appeared pleasant, wetting face and hands. After casting for a long time I happened to look at my fly. The point of the hook had been broken off. Whereupon I sat down to meditate. I had been fishing all the time with a barbless hook. Slowly the old associations awakened in my memory. This kind of accident had been the bane of my fly-fishing on former trips. As I changed my fly I had a queer mental reaction. "Well," I ejaculated, soberly, "I bet I have a time getting on to this steelhead game!"

Somehow I just felt that way. Both former trips to the Rogue had only acquainted me with the fascination and difficulty of catching these steelhead on a fly. I would be extremely fortunate if I succeeded in taking even some small ones. So that incident struck a rather discordant note, which I could not dispel. Perhaps a fisherman is superstitious. Assuredly he is moved by many illogical fancies. "I've a hunch it's a bad start," I concluded, standing up and wading out.

Yet even on the moment I realized how perfectly foolish that was. I wondered how many anglers would ridicule this attitude and how many would understand. Thousands of fishing excursions had started badly for me. It seemed, on retrospection, that they had all started so. It was a fatality. I was beset by a bad-luck complex. There was nothing to do then but fling defiance to the gods of the fishes and, whatever befell, make this present fishing trip turn out well.

I spent hours wading, casting, then resting a moment, and going on. I never had a strike or saw a fish. Rain fell intermittently. The clouds lightened and darkened. The Rogue rolled on melodiously, with its babble and gurgle and roar. Wild fowl winged swift flight up and down the river. Time passed, and at length R. C.'s voice hailed me from the bank. I waded out to where he sat on a rock.

"Raise any steelhead?" he inquired.

"I don't believe there's a fish of any kind in this river," I replied, wearily.

"I had two strikes and saw one trout," he said, reflectively. "I couldn't get my fly where I wanted it. . . . I'm tired. It sure is hard work. Let's mosey back to camp."

To my amaze, it was nearly three o'clock when we got there.

The boys were all back and I observed they appeared partial to the camp fire. Light misty rain was falling. Ken and Ed reported that they had tried fishing from the bank at various places. The hip boots I had given them were worse than none at all, they said. They slipped at every step.

"Awful river!" concluded Ed. "I'm going to wade without boots, so when I fall in I won't drown. We saw fish jump. I'll bet there's lots of them. George Takahashi broke his tackle on one."

My eager interrogation of George elicited a smiling reply from him.

"Sure had big one on," he said. "I fish while with fly. No good. Then I use spoon. Right down by camp where water all swift. I throw spoon long time. Then I have bite. He pull awful hard. Run far! My! he run all line off reel. I try go along bank. But he swim fast an' break my leader."

"Well!" I exclaimed, with a thrill. "Did you see the fish?"

"Sure. He jump first thing. Great big white fish all pink. He jump lots. An' shake himself like dog."

"Steelhead," said R. C. "Too bad, George. You must run downstream after these fish."

"I run fast. But no good. Awful bad place. Fish take line all off. I fall down. He give hard jerk. Bust!"

"George," I replied, with a laugh. "You have given an eloquent and exact prophecy of what is going to happen to me."

Next day was cloudy and rainy also, though it showed indications of clearing weather. But as it had rained hard in the early morning we had chosen to let the fishing go and attend to gathering firewood and other necessary camp tasks.

About noon we had visitors in shape of Wiborn, of Lone Angler fame, and Fred Burnham, who had motored down to stay at a farmhouse along the road and have a try for steelhead on Rocky Riffle.

"You ought to be out fishing," said Burnham. "The river is full of steelhead. Never saw the like before! It's been that way for a month. They're taking dark flies best. March Brown is good. Golden Pheasant better. It's a grand run of big savage steelhead. And this is the kind of a day I've been wishing for. It's been too dry. Jump into your waders and come on."

"Well, you're most encouraging," I replied. "Last night I was convinced there were no fish in the river. I'll try awhile along toward evening."

Scarcely more than two hours later, while we were having dinner, we heard Burnham coming back up the road in his car. He stopped at a point opposite our camp. Presently he emerged from the green, wagging along with two enormous steelhead, one in each hand. He strode into camp and laid them down on the grass. To say that I had a thrill would be putting it mildly. I had never seen such steelhead.

"Ten and a half pounds and nine and three-quarters," announced the Angler. "You don't often see a brace to beat this. . . . I caught five in one hole. First fish I hooked cleaned me out. He didn't jump, so I don't know how big he was. But twelve pounds easy. . . . They're taking dark flies here, same as up Medford way. You want a Number Four, dark, with a bit of yellow."

Burnham's talk had a singular effect upon me. Not only was it thrilling and inspiring, but likewise dismaying. I felt helpless and yearning before those two wonderful steelhead. They were long, broad, wide, thick, all muscle, with a great spread of tail and the small snub-nosed head of the gamy trout. They resembled salmon to me.

"How long did it take you to land the bigger one?" I queried.

"Not very long. But I was a half-hour on the other one. He was sure a fighter. I had to follow him."

"Do you often hook fish like these?" I went on, curiously.

"Every day. And often I hook bigger ones," he returned. "Last week I raised a whale of a steelhead. He would float up and look at my fly, and refuse it. I changed flies I don't know how many times. Finally he took one—same as I used today— and I nailed him. That steelhead beat any fish I ever hooked. Fast! Why, he was like a flash. And strong! I couldn't do a thing with him. He took me through the rapids. I had to swim the river twice. And after fighting him over an hour I lost him a mile below where I hooked him."

"Good night!" ejaculated R. C., in wonder.

"My goodnish!" exclaimed Takahashi, who was an attentive listener. The other boys exclaimed, "What do you know about that!" But my feelings were not provocative of expression. Fortunately Burnham asked me about my tuna of 758 pounds, which I had caught in Nova Scotia some weeks before, and that liberated my speech. I told him about the hooking of the great bluefin and the battle. It afforded me some little satisfaction to see that my narrative stirred Burnham in some degree as his had me. Fishermen are all alike. Lastly I got out some pictures of the tuna. Burnham gazed at them spellbound. His tanned face expressed delight, awe, incredulity.

"Good Heavens, what a fish!" he exclaimed. "There isn't such an animal! . . . Say, boy, but wouldn't I like to hook one like this!"

"No more than I would the steelhead you had such a battle with," I replied. "Fishermen are never satisfied. There's always an unattainable fish. I don't believe I'll ever catch a big steelhead, though I swear I shall. This is my third trip to the Rogue. And yesterday I cast a whole hour with a broken hook."

"It's nothing to do that," he said, with a smile. "I break hooks often. The thing to do is watch your back cast and if you tick anything, reel in and look at your fly. These big hooks catch on the rocks and break. Sometimes you can scarcely hear the snap. Wade out far, and in bad places make a false cast in the clear, then cast again where you want your fly to light. Practice. You'll hook some steelhead, and catch some, too. That'll not be hard. But to me it's a grand game because there are always steelhead too big and fast and strong to catch."

"That applies to all fishes in all waters," I rejoined, "though I can appreciate how it holds true with steelhead to a far greater extent."

Late that afternoon R. C. and I went down to try our luck again. We crossed the river at the same place. I fancied the water was not quite so clear as it had been the day before. But as the sky was overcast and light not strong I could not be certain.

This time we went upstream to the head of the rapids. The usual difficulty presented itself. We could not reach the likely runs and channels and eddies, and as the current ran like a mill race we dared not wade in deeper than halfway to our hips. Nevertheless, we cast persistently and with boundless hope all the way down that rapid. It seemed a fishless river. I found that to wield my eight-ounce rod for half an hour was extremely fatiguing. I had to rest my arm. We went on down to the lower riffle and tried again. I decorated the willow bushes with three perfectly good flies, and noted to my secret delight that my brother did almost as well. Along about twilight I gave up for the day and strolled along the shore watching R. C. Presently he abandoned his fly-rod for a bait-casting rod he had brought with him. Putting a good-sized spinner and a small sinker on his leader, he waded back with the grim remark, "I'll bet I can reach where I want to with this."

R. C. and I had never used the casting plugs so much in vogue with modern anglers, but we had spent years casting black-bass and bonefish baits. R. C. had a long, sweeping, graceful left-handed cast. The very first time he placed the spinner far across the river, close to a dark ledge of rock, where the water ran deep. Smash! The water burst and foamed.

"Wow!" yelled R. C. with swift sharp upsweep of rod. His reel gave forth a screech and the rod bent double. He had hooked a steelhead. It ran downstream fifty yards without a break on the surface. R. C. waded out and strode down the shore. I followed. Then the fish scurried and threshed half out of the water, then he ran upstream against the swift current, and hung there for a long time, doggedly plugging to free himself. Eventually he turned back and worked down the river, with shortening runs, until finally he gave up. R. C. beached his first fish of the trip, a five-pounder that shone even in the dusk with a beautiful effulgence.

"Look how I had him hooked," said R. C. "These gang hooks on spoons are not fair. No chance at all! Yet he sure fooled me. I believe these steelhead are extraordinary fish. We've got something coming."

R. C. made a few more casts without a rise; and then, as darkness was settling down, we turned campward. Arriving there we found a warm supper, bright fire, and several very disgruntled fishermen. Their usual cheerful responsiveness was entirely wanting. Takahashi winked at me, which had the effect of silencing my good-natured queries. R. C. gave me an amused and knowing glance. When I had gotten out of my waders and into warm clothes, Takahashi accosted me in a stage whisper.

"Ed an' Ken must have hell of time. Come back camp all wet an' mad. I say nothin' but I watch sharp. I see busted leaders all same like mine. No feesh!"

Manifestly the boys had taken ill luck to heart. They were novices in the art of angling and this was the hardest kind of a game. They reminded me of my boy Romer, whose enthusiasm for fishing often ended in grief. A hot supper, such as Takahashi excels in getting, a little time round the genial glow of the camp fire, gradually worked on Ed and Ken. Then a sympathetic query or two brought forth a bewildering and remarkable narrative of angling misfortune. It was with extreme difficulty that I arrived at several facts. They had lost all the leaders, flies, spinners which I had given them. How these were lost did not appear clear, but I gathered an impression that a school of steelhead had attacked the boys. Ed managed several times to repeat a rational statement.

"I'd cast out anything. Bingo! Up comes a steelhead!"

What happened after these occurrences he did not seem able to explain. Ed tried to tell what had happened to Ken, and Ken just as excitedly endeavored to give us some inkling of the marvelous things that had befallen to Ed.

"Ken cast out a spinner," quoth Ed. "Bingo! Up comes a big steelhead. He jumped way out. Then he ran, and, bingo! up he jumps again, right into the middle of that little grass island. Ken, the darn fool, went trying to wade across that deep swift channel where he'd hooked the fish. He'd drowned sure. I pulled him back. An' he was goin' to punch me because he lost the steelhead."

"Aw, Ed's out of his head," declared Ken, with most earnest disdain. "It didn't happen that way at all. . . . I wasn't casting in the swift place. I was wading down, letting my fly float. Sure a steelhead grabbed it. He jumped a mile high. Say, you should have seen him. Then he ran. Then he jumped clear over the little grass island. My line caught in the grass. I was going to wade in far enough to free it when Ed stopped me. We were tussling there when the fish got away."

"I saved your life," declared Ed, vociferously. "Next time you can drown. . . . And your steelhead is layin' right now on that grass island."

"Well, boys, don't quarrel," I replied. "Looks as if we're all in for some excitement."

Further inquiry elicited the opinion that it was impossible to wade the Rogue safely in rubber boots. I certainly sustained this, and I emptied my duffle-bag to see what might be left in the way of waders to give the boys. I found one long pair of waders that reached well up around the waist, and one short pair. These I donated to Ken and George, respectively, as suitable for their height. To Ed I gave all that was left—a pair of heavy rubber waders with rubber boots attached. These were abominable and had nearly drowned me more than once, and I warned him. Ed, however, took them eagerly, and proceeded to pound hobnails in the soles. George and Ken, likewise, hobnailed their heavy shoes, which were to be worn over the waders. Altogether we were that night a serious and speculative group of anglers.

Before I went to my tent I saw the clouds breaking away and stars white in the blue sky. The air was cooler. Next morning when I got up a thick fog obscured the upper half of the mountains. It was not cloud, for it had that deep-blue tinge which characterizes the morning mist in the mountains. It presaged a fine day.

Presently a silver blaze lightened the fog. That was the sun rising over the mountains. It soon dispelled the mist. We were not long in getting ready for fishing. R. C. and I found the river a foot higher and somewhat discolored. We attributed this to the rain. We tried fishing with spinners for a while, to no avail. Then we returned to camp. Warm sunshine had dried grass and trees and tents. I observed that the rain had heightened the autumn colors. Gold and red and purple contrasted vividly with the massed green. The air was fragrant with the tang of the mountains and the odor of wood smoke. Birds were singing in the trees. Camp was indeed a beautiful and delightful place.

Chester had gone deer hunting. The other boys one by one

came back from the river, minus fish. We idled away the day, except for those inspired intervals when I could get everybody to practice casting. Takahashi was the most industrious, but he could not get the knack of it.

We learned that the rise in the river was not all due to the rain, but to the opening of the dam above Grants Pass. Naturally we expected the high and roily water to subside quickly; and at different times we all took stock of the river. Toward evening R. C. reported the water falling and clearing. Burnham and Wiborn called on us and added to a pleasant hour round the camp fire.

"River ought to be clear and low again tomorrow," announced Burnham, in reply to eager query. "Queer river this year. Have you noticed that the steelhead and salmon are not jumping, playing on the surface, as usual during their run? Perhaps that's on account of low water. Early morning is not good. At this time of year steelhead do not rise until the sun burns away the mist rising from the water. From nine till four is best. Wade downstream, and cast quarteringly across. Try to make your fly light first on the water. Let it float till your line straightens out below you. Then cast again. Make a few casts over one spot, then wade down a few yards. When you get as far down the river as you want, go back and fish the water over again. Sometimes I raise steelhead on the third or fourth trip."

Like all really great anglers, Burnham was generous and kindly, taking keen interest in our tackle, equipment, and fishing. He seemed particularly anxious to have me appreciate what a wonderful river the Rogue was and how incomparable the steelhead fishing.

"Well, as to that, I think I'm already convinced," I told him. "Anyone can see that the Rogue is in a class by itself. And what you have told me about steelhead is certainly enough for me to place them equal to the Atlantic salmon, pound for pound. But I'm afraid if I write anything about my own fishing it will be only a record of awkwardness and bad luck."

Chester returned at dark, tired out and hungry. He had tramped thirty miles. He had seen several deer and heard many breaking through the brush. The nature of the country, densely wooded

canyons and sharp mountain ridges, made stalking deer exceed•
ingly difficult. He had also seen quail and grouse and some fresh
bear sign.

That night the moon cast fantastic shadows on my tent; the
pine needles rustled down, pattering like light rain; the crickets
chirped their lonely night refrain; a fox barked raucously from
the bluff opposite; and always the stream made melody, murmurous
and melancholy, pervading even my dreams.

At six o'clock next morning I was up in the silver gray of
dawn, ringing the ax on an oak log. This was my way—some•
times—of awakening my comrades. I heard Takahashi say to
R. C., whose tent he shared: "My goodnish! Chief up choppin'
wood. He early bird!"

I made note of the fact that my chopping called forth only
George and Chester. Whereupon I visited the tents. R. C. said
he was sick or something; Ed answered sleepily and Ken roared
like a mad bull. Later Ed confided to me, with great gravity,
the fact that Ken hated to wake up in the morning. "You mustn't
wake him," avowed Ed. "He might kill some of us."

Despite all this we had an early breakfast and reached the lower
rapid, which I called Rocky Riffle, before the sun had dissolved
the mist. It was indeed a glorious morning. The silver veils of
mist lifted from the purple canyons; the blue sky appeared; the
sun blazed white over the fringed mountain tops; and the river
was a thing of swiftly-moving joy and beauty.

Along that mile stretch we separated, R. C. leaving us first.
The river had returned to its former stage. I took casual note of
the wide shallow place where R. C. waded in. Narrow deep
channels showed far on the other side. That particular part of
the river did not strike me as especially auspicious. Ken started
in several hundred yards below and I did not look twice at the
section of river he chose. George disappeared somewhere, but as
he was so diminutive in stature I did not think anything of that.
Ed with rod and Chester with camera trudged on ahead of me.

Presently I arrived at a swift break in this riffle, where shallow
water ran into deep, and the river narrowed, with gravelly bar
on my side and rocky shelf on the other. As I rigged up my rod
I had a vague sensation of the sweetness, peace, and beauty of time

and place. Something haunting and far away attended my mental
state. I waded in and began to cast, as best I could. It was not
that I was conscientious or determined. Mind and eye and muscle
merely answered to a dreamy instinct. I was fishing. All was
well with the world and forgotten. I did not expect to catch a
fish and did not care whether I did or not. I waded down my
quarter-mile stretch, cast my fly a thousand times, more or less,
went back to repeat the performance, and then again. The sun
rose high and warm; the river murmured and flowed on; the
enchantment of day and place strengthened rather than lost its
hold on me. For all I knew there might not have been a fish
in that part of Oregon. But I did find that my arm gave out.
Wielding the heavy eight-ounce rod for hours was harder, at least
on that arm, than pulling at a swordfish. So I sat down to rest.

Naturally then I remembered my comrades. Far below me Ed
appeared to be imitating the evolutions of a tight-wire performer.
His rod was a balancing pole. Midway between him and me
perched Chester, high on a rock, camera in hand, waiting for us
to give him some action to photograph. In the other direction I
espied Ken standing knee-deep in swift water close to the opposite
shore. He appeared to be precisely where he had started for,
upon leaving us. I watched him cast, and then leave his fly in the
water a long time as if it were a bait. He had been there so long,
and he had such an air of patience and expectation, that I wondered what had happened to him. Presently R. C. emerged from
the willows close by. He carried a steelhead dangling from a
string—a shiny fish between five and six pounds in weight.

When he reached my side I made note of his beaming face and
bright eyes, and the unmistakable pride that emanated from him.

"Any strikes?" he queried, cheerfully.

"Nary one. Reckon this particular stretch of river is devoid
of steelhead," I replied, nonchalantly. "Don't tell me you caught
yours on a fly, for I'll not believe you."

"But I did, by jingo! My first steelhead on a fly! . . . And
I'm telling you, brother, that it was some sport. I waded out on
the gravel bar up there to where it drops off into deep water with
submerged rocks making riffles and eddies. I had no more than
forty feet to cast. And I'm a son-of-a-gun if I didn't raise a steel-

head the very first cast. Saw him! But he missed the fly. I cast
again and again. I let my fly float down and was just about
to whip it back, when, 'bingo!' as Ed says, I had a hard jerk.
It sure made me tingle. But I wasn't ready. After that I settled
down to mind my business. And a little below that place I hooked
this bird. He shot up five feet out of that swift water. Leap!
Say, these steelhead are wonders. This one came out five times
while running downstream a hundred yards or more. He made
the best fight any small fish ever gave me."

"Well, that's fine. I'll take back what I said and believe you,"
I replied.

"Did you hear Ken yell? I looked and saw his rod bent double,
and a smash on the water. He had a big one on. But the darn
fool pointed his rod right at it and pulled even when the fish
was running. He forgot to run downstream. But that's a bad
place where he is. Maybe he couldn't. He had the fish on only
ten seconds. When it broke off Ken nearly lost his balance. And
he's been there ever since."

"Looks as if Ken and Ed, and George Takahashi, too, were going
to get dippy over this Rogue River fishing," I said, with amusement.

"Who wouldn't?" declared my erstwhile practical and unemo-
tional brother. "I've fallen for it with a dull thud. It's just
getting under my skin. I begin to understand Burnham's coming
here for so many years. And I know well as I'm alive that you will
pronounce fly-fishing for steelhead on the Rogue just what Burnham thinks it is. You see, the fly makes the difference. I can't
explain what that is. Hard as steelhead fight on a bait-rod and
spinner, it is nothing to what they do when hooked on a fly. It's
simply great. Just you wait!"

While we relished our sandwiches and argued about the unknown
and alluring qualities of this species of trout, the other boys made
their way back to us.

"By golly! I had a big one!" announced Ken, and then for
a space he raved about the fish, giving a remarkably different angle
from that reported by R. C.

Ed was not wanting in weird narrative as to his piscatorial
adventures during the morning. From it all I gathered that he had

WHERE ROLLS THE ROGUE (Plates xl to xliv)

PLATE XL

PLATE XLI

PLATE XLII

PLATE XLIII

PLATE XLIV

WHAT FLY TO USE!

PLATE XLV

several strikes and had left a fly sticking in the jaw of a fish or on the willows, he was not certain which.

George Takahashi was the last to arrive, and he had a broad grin and noncommittal air. "I show you some day," he said.

While we were talking a Ford car hummed out of the willows behind us and bumped down the rocky slope to the gravel bar. Several immensely long bamboo fishing poles waved and wagged from the side of the car. Three native fishermen piled out, to grasp the poles and come striding down toward the river.

In my interest I quite missed the loquacious remarks of my comrades. If ever I saw assurance, certainty, in the demeanor of fishermen I saw it in them. They advanced as if they meant to stride straight across the river. But they halted at the edge. Not one of them was clad for wading. They shouted gay badinage from one to the other, anent the immediate catching of fish.

These bamboo fishing-poles fascinated me. They recalled boyhood days. I had learned to fish with one, though indeed not one so enormously long. That of the tallest native was fully twenty feet in length and quite limber. It had a small reel some two feet from the butt, and guides for the line. What a formidable tackle! When that lanky native fisherman clambered upon the highest rock along the bank, and waved that huge pole, I was stunned with the certainty that he would do terrible execution with it.

He grasped the end of the butt in the hollow of his left hand and with his right held the pole above the reel. His lure was a small brass spinner, not the smallest made, but about the second in size. It bore a fairly large gang of three hooks. I noted that he used a six-foot leader, but whether it was wire or gut I could not tell.

Then he began to wave the long pole. The line hissed out; the spinner whistled. He cast to get out line, not letting his spinner down to the water. His action appeared to be a powerful jerk with right arm, both forward and back. His left hand furnished only a fulcrum. The pole was limber, as I said, and it bent almost double. In a surprisingly few waves of it he had that spinner shooting out over the river, back over the bar, out again, farther and farther. until I calculated over a hundred feet of line was out. It was an amazing performance. Then he dropped the spinner precisely alongside a dark ledge of rock, a place that I had so slaved to reach with fly and failed, and he let it float down with the current. When the line straightened out he jerked back with powerful sweep and made another cast. This time there was a swirl on the water. Then we all exclaimed simultaneously as he hooked a fish.

It swung downstream, pulling hard, but did not leap. The fisherman drew back upon the bent rod while his comrades yelled at him. Then stepping down from his perch he walked backward and downstream a little, drawing the fish toward shore. It swept up and down, lunged and threshed on the surface, fighting desperately hard. But it could not break the tackle or get away. Without winding in the line the fisherman walked backward on the bar and dragged the fish out on the sand. It flopped with tremendous energy until all its silver and rose sheen was covered with dirty sand. Then the fisherman hit it on the head with a rock.

Naturally we all had something to say among ourselves, and most of it was unprintable. Then a lusty shout from another of the native anglers wheeled us to see that he had hooked a fish. He stood some fifty feet above our position, in quite swift water. Did he walk downstream and let the steelhead have some line? He did not. He yelled as if at the fish, holding hard on the pole. The steelhead made a magnificent leap and threw the spinner. Then it was our turn to yell. We were far from kindly about it, but the fellow took it good-naturedly.

"Aw, I'll snag another in a minnit," he called, cheerfully.

My attention reverted to the tallest native, whom I instinctively recognized as a master of this kind of fishing. Precisely upon his third cast he raised and hooked another fish. It made a deep stubborn fight for about two minutes, and when dragged forth from its element proved to be a jack-salmon, a bronze-colored, black-spotted fish of about nine pounds.

Next the third native, fishing below, caught a small steelhead which he unceremoniously hauled out. We sat there then, spellbound, and saw these natives catch eight more steelhead, five of which were taken by the tall fellow. He certainly was a machine for extracting steelhead from under the dark submerged rocks. He could pick them out of the farthest edge of the channel, a hundred and twenty-five feet across the river. He could hit any spot he aimed at. He never missed a strike. A steelhead, no matter how big, had no chance with him. The largest he took, which I estimated to weigh between eight and nine pounds, was literally jerked out before it had gotten its head.

Then the steelhead ceased rising. The native fishermen, laughing and joking, threw their catch into the Ford, tied on their wagging rods, and with loud and raucous guffaw, probably meant for us city fishermen, they rode away. They had been with us about one half-hour.

For me the incident was tragic. It hurt me deeply to see these magnificent trout treated like German carp.

"I be damn'! Just like Jap fishermenz," said George Takahashi. "No monkey! Pull 'em out quick."

"Bingo! What do you know about that?" exclaimed Ed, with fire in his eye.

"Seems all right to me," added the practical Ken. "It's their river. They catch fish to eat and salt for winter. It's none of our business. And we needn't be sore because they showed us how to catch steelhead."

"Ken, you've got the wrong idea, common to most Americans," spoke up R. C. "If you ever have a son he will never know the thrill of catching a steelhead, let alone having one to eat. . . . Because the steelhead will be gone! You've just seen one of the reasons."

I had little to say, but I was thinking hard. I wondered what was Burnham's opinion of this sort of thing. For the time being, that slaughter absolutely sickened me. It was almost as bad as seeing four five-hundred-pound tuna murdered with mattocks in a net in Nova Scotia. It brought to mind the bugbear of all thoughtful anglers, compelling them to dwell on queries and facts that were disagreeable and disheartening. Our wild life, our forests and fish, were vanishing. What was a broad point of view and what a narrow? It seemed to me that in this particular case if the fish were eaten there was no room for argument. But I had traveled to many places, remote and otherwise, and had collected a vast fund of information relative to this Vanishing America, and I was skeptical about the legitimate cutting of forests and their adequate protection from fire, and the regard for fish and game laws, and the interest of the great public in preserving anything.

That time, however, did not appear to be the right one for me to dwell on conservation; so forthwith I set off whistling to whip my stretch of water again. R. C. called after me, as in the old baseball days.

"Hey, you've got a game leg and a bum arm. Let's go back to camp and rest."

But I was bound to have my last fling, which really was a defiance of the native fishermen and my morbid reflections. So I began to cast, while the boys looked on and waited. Remarkable to see, even with the kind of arm R. C. said I had, I could cast farther and better. I had learned while I rested. It encouraged me. Turning a deaf ear to my lazy and facetious comrades, I waded in deeper and essayed to make more of those casts that had astonished and pleased me. They improved even though my arm gave aching premonitions of weakening. But I waded and cast on. It was practice and perseverance. Steelhead I had forgotten! I wanted to see how far out I could cast that Golden Pheasant and how deftly I could make it alight. So I gradually drew away from the others, on down toward the middle and best part of that riffle.

At length I made such a splendid cast, for me, that I uttered an admiring exclamation. "Oh, pretty poor, I don't think! Eh what?"

Then something remarkable happened. A curling wave appeared behind my floating fly. A sharp splash followed. The slack line I was holding in my left hand flipped quick as a flash out of my grasp. It twanged tight on the rod. Then a powerful violent jerk all but took the rod away from me.

Too late I realized and pulled. But the steelhead had let go and gone. "Oh! what a strike!" I cried, tingling all over. Next disappointment assailed me, then fury at my absent-mindedness, and lastly dismay at what seemed more bad luck. Still I went on casting until I was so tired I could not cast any longer. Thereupon I wearily waded out and trudged back over the boulders to where the others waited.

"Say, didn't you get a strike?" queried the keen-eyed R. C.

"Me? Oh, that! Guess maybe it was," I replied, casually.

"Humph! Thought I saw a wave and a smash. You acted funny, too," he replied, dubiously.

"Well, brother," I replied, resignedly, "if you keep strict tab on me you're liable to see lots that's funny."

Tramping back to camp over boulders and through dragging sand and up brushy trails, burdened by wet waders and heavy brogans, was tedious and wearisome toil. The sun shone hot. There was a drowsy hum of insects. This afternoon I appeared to be pretty much all in when I reached camp. Yet as soon as I changed to dry comfortable clothes and had stretched out in the shade, the sense of rest and ease was so delightful that I rejoiced in the pangs which had made possible the contrast.

A low soft sigh of wind stirred the lofty firs and pines; colored leaves floated down from the oaks and maples; the black slopes of the mountains heaved toward the sky; white columnar clouds sailed across the blue; and always the river murmured and babbled and roared down its stony bed.

After supper the hour was still early, with the sun still topping the high mountain. R. C. amazed me by appearing in waders and with a very determined expression. He went upriver, to disappear in the thick brush along the bank. The other boys likewise went off fishing.

For a while I deliberated as to whether I should follow suit or not, and came to the conclusion that not always to be doing my darndest—of which I had been accused—might be a welcome change. It even might change my bad luck. My arm was almost as sore as it used to get after pitching a hard game of baseball. I rubbed it with liniment.

That done, I went down through the trees to the bank where the great fallen fir overhung the river. Climbing to the trunk, I found my way carefully down to the thick foliage of vines that enveloped its branches, and there I sat hidden. My intention was to spy upon the innocent fishing evolutions of the boys. But no one was in sight.

My position appeared to be about twenty feet above the river, at a point where the water ran a few inches deep over flat dark rock. Suddenly as luck would have it a bird came flitting down the shaded shore under the foliage and alighted right under me.

It was a water ousel, one of the few of that species I had ever seen, and this was very close to me. To me birds had always been beautiful, mystical, exquisite creatures to be loved. A water ousel is the rarest and wildest of birds, exceedingly shy, and almost impossible to approach. It haunts the lonely swift mountain streams, and is very seldom seen.

This water ousel was unaware of me. Yet its every motion was indicative of its wild nature. It was about the size and color of a catbird except that it might have been a little heavier and shorter, and also minus the long tail. The color was a dark slate, unrelieved by lighter touch. It had a sleek, small, fine head with small dark eyes and bill. Its legs and feet were dark, too, and though I could see the toes I was unable to make sure whether or not they were webbed. I thought not.

Now this water ousel had the strangest actions of any bird I ever watched. In the first place he was most vitally and keenly alert. Every second he looked here, there, up and down, everywhere. I could see him turn his head and peer up into the foliage as if he suspected an enemy hidden there. All the time he bobbed up and down. It was a singular springy action, and seemed to be a constant precursor of flight. In fact, he teetered on his tiny feet, quick, nervous, intense. At the same time he waded the shallow places, searching for food. Often when he pecked at something his head went underwater. At others when he got in a little deep he breasted the current like a duck. Then, most strange to see, he went wholly under. He dipped rather than dove. I could not be sure, but I thought he walked underwater. He did not swim.

While craning my neck the better to follow the movements of the bird, I rustled the foliage. This alarmed him. He stood in one place and bobbed up and down, uttering the sweetest, wildest bird notes it had ever been my fortune to hear. On the moment I thought of Hudson, the English naturalist, and how beautifully he could describe the music made by birds. How impossible for me to give an adequate sense of the actual sounds I caught! I heard the bird utter his sweet, sharp, delicate note many times, and thought I would never forget it. Suddenly the bird flitted away as swiftly as he had come. And I found that he had left me with a vague haunting echo of his bird-cry, something too soft, too wild and strange, to be imitated in words. It was indeed the very essence of the lonely nature of this water ousel.

It would be wonderful to know all about such a bird. Haunter of rushing clear mountain torrents, mossy-bouldered, fir-shaded, he represented the very soul of all that was alien and aloof to civilization. He was the unattainable in nature. Naturalists tell us that all birds evolved from reptiles; that during long dry eons of the past feathers had to be developed to cover distances in search of water and food. No doubt this is true. Many scientific facts are stunning and incredible, not to say ugly. But if this water ousel did not have a soul, then the illusive and elevating thing I felt was in me. Still that bird-creature would have expressed the same, absolutely alone in his primeval haunts.

How and when did he court his mate? Where did they build their nest? What were the eggs like, and the baby birds? Whence came that wild fugitive alertness, that eternal vigilance? Did it emanate from knowledge of man? How infinite the knowledge of the nature lover who could learn the past and present life history of a water ousel!

Next morning I stole a march on the boys, and before they had finished breakfast I was on my way down to the river.

Though the hour was early and the sun not yet silvering the fog mantle over the eastern mountain range, the air was pleasant, almost balmy. This Oregon climate was new to me. Oregonians have a slogan, "It is the climate," and I am bound to admit there is reason. Wherever else I had hunted and fished, the early hours of late October had been characterized by frost. Here was developing that enchanted time called Indian summer.

As I strode along I was aware of my hurry and that I did not attend to sights and sounds and smells as faithfully as was usually my wont. I saw a flock of gray birds, larger than doves, and concluded they were pigeons. And once my eye caught a blue-gray flash of a deer in an opening of the woods across the river. But for the most part I saw only the river, searching for widening rippling circles on smooth eddies, and the flip of a silver fish out of the riffles. Burnham had said the salmon and steelhead were showing very infrequently this season, a fact for which he could not account, unless it was because of the unusually low water.

It disappointed me keenly, for there is nothing I like more than to see any kind of game fish show on the surface. Still, I had not wholly missed this pleasure of the watchful angler.

The early bird catches the worm—in fishing as in less charming walks of life. R. C. had cast a suspicious and knowing glance upon me. And Ken had yelled after me, "Keep away from my fishin' hole." Takahashi, who took profound interest in my fishing fortunes, also called out, "More better luck today mebbe!"

My chivalry in passing by R. C.'s place and Ken's hole was little to my credit, because I had quite a fight to attain it. Those respective lurking-places for steelhead looked singularly alluring, and somehow I knew positively I could have gotten a strike out of both. But I went on, absorbed in thoughtfulness and vaguely happy.

It afforded me considerable satisfaction to fish that half-mile stretch of riffle, the best water on the river, before any other anglers hove in sight. I was turning back for my second lap when I espied the boys wading in above. A second faithful whipping of the same water did not earn me a strike. Upon my return to the head of the riffle, where it was deep and swift, I laid aside my fly-rod, and tried my bait-rod with spinner for a while. No luck!

Then I resorted to desperate ends in my craving to break my ill fortune. I began to hunt in the shallow water for crawfish. The river was evidently full of them, many big red ones showing on the rocks. Small soft-shelled crawfish were not numerous, and hard to find. This pursuit had an unlooked-for pleasure—that of reminding me of catching crawfish and hellgramites in boyhood days. But, alas! I was to find that I could not catch them as deftly as I used to. Finally I discovered several which might do, one of which especially appeared a most attractive bait for a steelhead.

Putting on a larger spoon, I fastened this bait on the hook and cast out over the swift water, and let it go with the current. Then

R. C. with Fine Steelhead

PLATE XLVI

Under the Dark, Cool Shade of the Mountain

PLATE XLVII

I wound in and tried again. I could cast clear across the river to the identical spot where the native fishermen had raised their fish. And I had a feeling that I would get a strike. Meanwhile R. C. had come along, carrying a four-pound steelhead, and he leisurely sat down to watch me.

On my fourth cast I had a smashing strike. Despite my expectations I was startled. The fish took a short vicious run. Then he split the water with a crack and tumbled aloft, an enormous steelhead. I heard him shake himself, and the spoon jingled high in the air. He had thrown it.

"Wow!" yelled R. C., leaping up. "Oh, he tore out! . . . Wasn't that a lunker? By golly! I believe a spoon's the thing to raise the biggest ones."

"I had a crawfish on this spoon," I told R. C., as I slowly wound in, manfully repressing my desire to swear to the high heavens.

Another crawfish, cast for half an hour over all that swift deep place, failed to raise any more fish. Then R. C. tried it. While we were laboring thus Ed had caught his first steelhead, which he brought proudly to exhibit. "Bingo! he grabbed my fly!" exclaimed Ed, with eyes alight. "Not very big, but he was the fightenist cuss I ever hooked. I've sure fallen for this steelhead stuff. An' say, look at Ken up there. He's whipped that hole all mornin'. Worse'n me!"

At this juncture Burnham and Wiborn appeared below, making their way down the boulder-strewn slope toward the river. R. C. and I went to meet them. They had been two miles below, at another good riffle, where they had caught several steelhead, all small.

"Anything doing on Rocky Riffle today?" inquired Burnham. And upon being informed that we thought it was no good he laughed and said he would show us how to catch one.

Burnham was a stalwart figure, looking like a guard on a Yale football team. He was over six feet tall and would weigh around two hundred. He wore wading boots with very heavy soles thickly studded with nails. When he ploughed into the water R. C. remarked that it was not any wonder he could wade the Rogue. Some of us would have drowned where Burnham comfortably lighted cigarettes. His weight and height, of course, helped him to be such a wonderful wader; and wading was half the secret of Rogue River fishing.

Burnham's casting was a thing of beauty. Two sharp motions of his wrist! It seemed so easy. He now used a short rather stiff five-and-one-half-ounce Leonard rod. On his forward cast the line shot out gracefully in high rolling waves. The last half-circle of the line would straighten out, sweeping the long leader ahead, and letting the fly light first. Like a feather it dropped. Burnham allowed it to float until it reached its limit below him, then he cast again. He could place his fly in all the dark holes and channels, behind the submerged rocks, along the sunken ledges. If it was fascinating to watch him, how much more so would it have been to be able to fish that way! He covered the whole stretch of water before us, however, without raising a fish. R. C. and I followed along, learning more from watching him work than we could out of any amount of practice.

At the bottom of this riffle the river broke, the main body of water going through a swift channel near the left shore, and on the right a wide space of shallow water glided over flat corrugated rock, hurrying faster and faster, at last to rush in rippling channels down into what appeared a wonderful dark pool.

"That's my favorite place on this river," said Burnham, pointing across. "I can always get a rise there."

He waded the deep swift channel, which had appeared more formidable than it really was. It was too far for me to see clearly the kind of water, but it looked as if on his very first cast he hooked one right at his feet. The steelhead began to run and jump, and got out in the pool, and finally reached the heavy current. Then Burnham had to move out of there. Holding his rod up high, he piled off the ledge into deep swift water, and I was sure if the current had not been behind him he would have lost his balance. He went downstream while he crossed, and eventually reached the gravel bar and was able to recover line. It amazed me to see how hard he pulled on that steelhead. Still, he took what seemed a long time. When the fish was whipped Burnham walked backward up the bar and carefully drew it out on the sand. It was a beautiful specimen, a male fish, he said, weighing close to seven pounds.

"I'm going to take you over there," he announced. And forthwith he dragged me into the river and held on to me while he waded. In the middle of that channel the water reached up to my waist. I could see the bottom plainly, and made a mental picture of the course. I noted he waded diagonally downstream. The hardest part was getting out on the flat ledge. The action of the current had worn the rock into ruts, sharp, curved, and as slippery as ice. Once beyond that zone the wading was comparatively easy. Burnham halted me within fifty feet of the most beautiful place to fish that I had ever seen in my life. It beggared description. I devoured it with my eyes.

We stood up to our knees in fairly swift water. In front it poured off a slanting yellow ledge into a riffle that smoothed out in a deep dark pool. To the right a glancing incline of water came gliding from under the high wooded bank and swept with low roar into the pool. Between riffle and channel some golden rocks just showed under the surface. Green and amber depths, white water and eddying foam, shelving ruts reaching under the ledge, and beyond them the black pool whirling round, mirroring the great mountain slope—these certainly called to all that was thrilling for a fisherman.

Burnham showed me where to cast. It was not beyond my reach, and my fly alighted very creditably for me, floated down, disappeared. I felt a slow draw that I fancied was the current.

"Hook him!" shouted Burnham.

But I was a fraction of a second too late. I just felt the fish as he ejected the fly.

"Didn't you see that fish rise?" queried Burnham. "He was a big lazy duffer. He just sucked the fly in. Sometimes steelhead will do that. Then if you don't see them you're out of luck. Try again. There's a bunch of fish at the foot of that current."

The moment was a little too exciting for me to maintain perfect calm. I cast well enough, but I was certainly shaky. On my third cast I had the sharpest kind of a strike, quick as lightning. The steelhead was gone before I knew what had happened.

"Always raise your tip after casting, and hold your line tight in your left hand," advised Burnham.

Further casting on my part failed to raise another steelhead. Then Burnham tried his hand without success. Whereupon we waded back to the other shore and found comfortable seats where we rested and discoursed about fish in general and steelhead in particular.

There is only one thing wrong with a fishing day—its staggering brevity. If a man spent all his days fishing, life would seem to be a swift dream.

We arrived at length at the subject of angling books. Marvelous to realize, I actually have more fishing-books than fishing-rods. I was asked why I so obviously thought the English fishing-books superior to the American.

"I suppose because the English anglers write better," was my reply. "Then they have infinitely more background and tradition. If they had such a river as this Rogue, such wonderful fish as steelhead, what wouldn't they write!"

"Izaak Walton is of course your favorite?" was another query.

"My choice of all fishing-books is *Fishing from the Earliest Times*, by William Radcliffe, an English author and Oxford man. This is so great a book that I have never felt equal to writing the review of it I promised for American publication. The best of angling authors fill their books with the beauty, the thrill, the recreation, the peace and joy of fishing. And the myriad of ordinary writers on fishing are well worth reading because they deal with actual experience. They tell simply of adventure on the water. It remained for William Radcliffe to spend twenty years of his life translating Greek, Roman, Hebrew, Chinese, all the ancient languages where there was any word of fishing. And he traveled as industriously as he read. All to get at the antiquity, the source of fishing!

"*Fishing from the Earliest Times* is a monumental work. It is scientific, scholarly, narrative, poetic, philosophic. It is a treasure-mine of truth about the oldest sport and one of the earliest trades known to men. Fishing has history little suspected by the mass of men who love to follow it. My father used to punish me for running off to fish when I should have mowed the lawn or swept out his office. He declared the only good fishermen who had ever lived were Christ's four fishermen disciples. My father was sure I would come to some bad end because I loved to fish. But he was wrong. And all fathers of youthful Izaak Waltons or angling Rip Van Winkles should read this wonderful book and learn how fortunate they are in having such inspired sons. For fishing has a dignity, a simplicity, a ruggedness and honesty little dreamed of in this materialistic world. Its history is profoundly revealing and tremendously interesting to the angler, whether he be naturalist or not. But every fisherman, unconsciously or otherwise, is something of a naturalist.

"Why men love to fish is much more easily understood than how they came to learn it. For all fishing skill and implements are but evolutions of the past. Where did fishing originate? Who were the first men to practice it? What kind of tackle did they use? How far back into the dim and mystic past can fishing be traced?

"It seems to me that every earnest student of angling should read Radcliffe's incomparable book. Even the humble market fisherman or the loafer fisherman could not help but be enthralled. For the facts about a man's calling, his toil, or his unbreakable habits are bound to be interesting. When rightly presented they take hold of his bosom. I have tried this out in many ways, on boatmen, on fishermen by trade, on the worthless idlers who lived only to hunt and fish. I never found it hard to get their attention. I would tell them that one of the first fish-hooks used by prehistoric man came from the hind leg of an insect that had a long stout recurved spur. Or about how early Aristotle claimed that fishes really did hear. Or why the dolphin and tuna were mentioned by so many ancient writers. Or about how fish in early Roman days became luxuries for which fabulous sums of money were paid. Or about the earliest drawing or representation of fishing in 2000 B.C. Or that early fishing lines were sometimes made from the hair of dead human beings. Or the mention of fishes in the Bible and in the various interpretations of the Deluge. Or any other of the innumerable quotations, anecdotes, and scientific deductions with which this book is packed.

"Best of all, *Fishing from the Earliest Times* gave me infinite respect for this form of outdoor life which means most to me. The joy of fishing, the thrill of it, the fascination, and the wholesome strength-renewing virtues that attend its practice were things I never needed to learn from a book. Then quite by myself I felt that I had discovered some secret mind-saving soul-healing property concealed in this gentle art. But it remained for *Fishing from the Earliest Times* to invest my favorite outdoor pursuit with the dignity of education, of culture, of an affinity with great minds of the past, with an important place in the history and progress of the world."

Ten days passed. Idyllic days they were, verily the dream days of an angler. October brought out the intense golds and reds of the forest; cool, clear, silent nights with myriads of white stars; crisp dawns with the purple mist veils changing to silver; and warm drowsy days in which it seemed always afternoon.

Many things happened during that period of ten days. A fresh run of steelhead reached Rocky Riffle and lingered there, as if loath to pass the long channel with its level gravel bars and its shelving ledges, and the deep bend in the river where the white water roared down under the shade of the dark forest.

I saw the native long-pole fishermen drag many and many a steelhead out on the rocks. I even talked with them, and found that they fished for fun, and not, as I had supposed, for the meat. They fished all the riffles along the river, driving from one to another, seldom spending more than an hour at any one place. One fellow informed me he caught a steelhead forty-two inches in length and a foot wide, and never weighed it. Then the crack fisherman of that group told me he had come to Rocky Riffle one evening just at dusk. He said the steelhead were thick. One at each cast! They hung close inshore and he could see their bright sides gleaming in the shallow water. He caught one that weighed close to fourteen pounds. I summoned temerity enough to ask if that fish had fought hard. "Reckon he did," was the reply. "Nearly busted my pole an' yanked me clear down round the bend." Somehow that succinct reply afforded balm to my wounded spirit.

All my life I have envied country boys, backwoodsmen, native fishermen, and the hardy men who eke out a living from the deep.

For they see most of nature's wonders. They are always there, daybreak and sunset, and they catch the most and biggest fish. I often wonder if I do not care too much about fish and fishing. Such a mental attitude does not enhance skill, and it certainly seems to be a loadstone for ill luck.

Up to this time R. C. had wonderful good fortune. Fourteen steelhead to his rod, all caught on a fly! The largest weighed seven pounds. I saw the fish leap eleven times. Only one bad day fell to R. C.'s lot, and that was early in the ten days. He had become obsessed with the idea of catching a large steelhead on a spoon, and to this end he devoted one whole day. He hooked three great steelhead, all between twelve and fifteen pounds, and was not able to land one of them. The first and largest gave a wonderful exhibition in swift water, at last twisting out the hold of the hook. So many of the larger steelhead do that. After this day R. C. devoted himself solely to fly-fishing. He became charmed, intoxicated with the sport. He gave it precedence over all other kinds of angling. He would babble as long as anyone would listen—which conduct was remarkable for R. C. Contrary to my usual self, I was a poor listener. I went to bed early these days. The remarks of my well-meaning but misguided comrades were insupportable. They had all surpassed me. Ken had caught eleven steelhead on a fly. Ed had seven to his credit. Takahashi two! And I had none. These miserable lucky fishermen undertook to teach me how to catch steelhead!

"Well, I'll tell you," R. C. would begin. "You've got to be a real guy to catch these birds. You've got to be on the job when they strike—or before. No dreaming stories or watching the sunrise on yon bank!"

"You want to find a good hole and stick there," advised Ken, knowingly. "Cast till one sails up and soak the hook in his jaw. Then run."

"You've changed tackle too much," added Ed, with the air of an old expert. "And you want to wade in deep and cast far, and when you see a swirl—bingo! nail him!"

Then when my quondam ally George Takahashi would join the ranks of these vastly experienced anglers and say, "You awful rotten fishermanz this trip," it was time for me to steal away like an Arab to my tent.

I saved Ken's life one morning. After his usual two hours of casting in the same identical spot he hooked a husky and lively steelhead. It ran off all the line. Ken followed fast as he could, encumbered with heavy waders and boots, forgetting absolutely the deep channel below. He was bent on keeping that steelhead from breaking off. Ploughing and splashing, he hurried downstream the whole of that five-hundred-yard stretch. And he got into water up to his waist and too swift for him to stand still. But though I yelled and yelled, he did not appear to realize that fifty yards more, in a direct line, would take him into water from which he never would be able to get out. I ran up the shore and plunged into the river, and by dint of stentorian profanity I got him to realize where he was heading. Then he had a hard time to work across the channel, when the current was forcing him down. He just made it—a close shave. And all the son-of-a-gun thought of was the steelhead which was still on his line. Eventually he captured it, a six-and-a-half-pounder, his largest. Sight of his imperturbability and also the beautiful steelhead prompted me to a remark that really was worthy of R. C.

"Say, Ken," I said, "what do you want to take risks like that for? You might drown, and then who would drive the truck home?"

Another morning Ed took chances as perilous; however, inspired to capture his largest fish, almost equal to Ken's, he took them deliberately. He crossed the river at the place where Burnham had assisted me. How he ever accomplished it I had no idea. For a little space of time all we could see was his hat and his rod. But he got over to Burnham's favorite pool, and quicker than it takes to tell it he had hooked a steelhead.

Ken was below R. C. and me. As the fish began to run away across that pool, toward the heavy swift channel, and at length got into it, Ken threw down his rod and ran along the bank to a point even with Ed.

"He oughtn't try to wade across there," said R. C., gravely. "Why, it was all Burnham could do!"

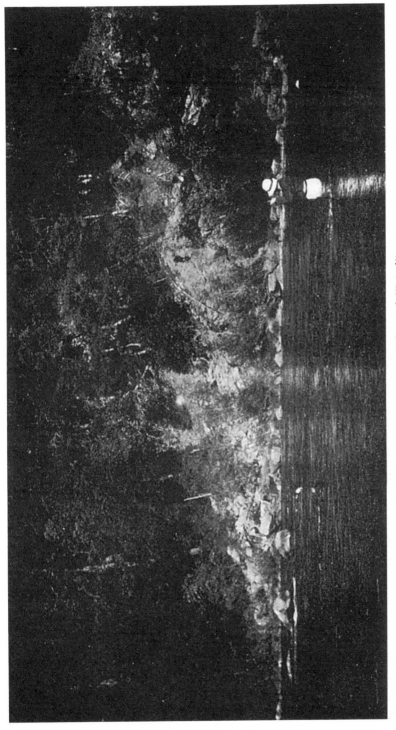

LEAPING STEELHEAD (Plates xlviii to li)

PLATE XLVIII

PLATE XLIX

PLATE L

PLATE LI

"Let's hurry," I replied. So we ran down the river shore, watching as we went.

Ed was having trouble with the steelhead, but more with the wading. The fish leaped again, showing he was broad and heavy. He got in the strong current and took all Ed's line, as I could tell by the forward jerking of his rod. Plain to all then was Ed's intention. He did not care anything about the swift channel. He hardly looked before he leaped off the ledge.

"You darn fool!" screamed Ken, beside himself with fear and anger. "Don't try to cross there. . . . Hell with the fish!"

But in four or five steps Ed went in deep, and then clear under. Only his right hand and the bent rod showed above the water. It was indeed a strange sight. Suddenly he reappeared some yards below. His head and shoulders came up, and be blew like a porpoise. That reassured us. But Ken kept on wading and yelling. To my dismay, Ed suddenly disappeared again.

"Boys, let's run below. Out on the bar!" I yelled.

Ed bobbed up again, still farther down. Neck deep, he then waded diagonally across the very end of that channel, just above where it poured over into the deep rapids. When he got out it was to discover that the steelhead had torn loose from the hook. Despite his icy bath, Ed was beaming. He had rosy cheeks and his eyes shone bright.

"See me walking underwater?" he ejaculated. "Burnham has nothin' on me. . . . Oh, boy, that was a steelhead! He had every darn inch of my line out."

Now Ken, though not a great deal older than Ed, had always exercised a brotherly, even a paternal, guardianship over the lad. He had been terribly frightened, which was no great wonder, for I had been so, myself.

"You—you darn fool!" he fumed, red in the face. "Haven't you sense enough not to cross a place like this?"

"What's eatin' you?" demanded Ed, firing up. "I had sense enough to hook a big steelhead, didn't I?"

"What's a steelhead, even if he's a whale? You poor fish! . . . You damned near drowned and scared me to death."

"Say, I'll drown if I want to," yelled Ed, also red in the face. "I'm going right back across there."

"Ed Bowen, if you try it I'll punch your thick head!"

I strongly objected to this, myself, and told Ed so, though in a kindly and conciliatory manner; then R. C. and I turned away, trying to hide our mirth, though we left the boys on the point of blows.

Another morning, after hours of patient fishing I was resting alone in the shade of some willows near the water. Presently I espied Takahashi on the opposite side of the river. He was sitting on a point of rock, evidently fishing, for I saw the glint of his rod.

The Jap was always worth watching, and in a case like this, when I had nothing particular to do, observing him would certainly pass the time pleasurably for me. I was convinced that a true screen chronicle of George's fishing activities on this trip would have equaled one of Harold Lloyd's comedies. Each of us had seen him do some remarkably ludicrous thing. Unfortunately, we had all been so personally set on our own activities that we had little time to observe others.

Takahashi was not casting. He was letting his fly float down on the current and remain for moments in a place where obviously he believed there were fish. His patience was something to marvel at, to awaken acute envy.

Finally he got up to start downstream. Now that side of the river was what my old bear-hunter guide would have called "thicker'n blazes." Heavy brush overhung the steep bank, and the water was deep and swift right along the edge of the rocks. R. C. had gone down that shore once, making for an open point which no doubt now attracted George, and he had worked round behind this most difficult place. So, indeed, I would have done. Not so George Takahashi! On our hunting trips he had always been noted for his wonderful climbing abilities. He would not go round any place. George climbed up or down, always straight.

Here, however, he was attempting something new and difficult. I believe George would have tackled anything. He stooped and crawled under the leaning brush, holding on to branches, stepping on little edges of rock, sometimes beneath the water, worming around places where a full-sized man never would have gotten. George was little of body, mighty of arm, and unquenchable in spirit. Naturally, he had a good deal of trouble with his rod, catching the line on snags. I had tried to teach him always to carry it butt first, but he would not do this. He performed miracles of muscular feats, and at length came to a place where I was positive he would be halted.

A narrow cut in the rocky bank impeded his progress. The brush overhung it so that he could not stand upright. The rocky bank was almost perpendicular and the deep water ran like a mill race. I did not see that he could do anything but go back.

Nevertheless, George crouched for a leap. Like a huge frog he propelled himself across the break in the bank, and made an accurate job of it. He slipped, however, and fell face down on the steep slant. There he stuck, holding to a branch with one hand and to his rod with the other. I wanted to rush across to his assistance or to yell advice, but some peculiar confidence in him persuaded me to sit still. He did not know I was anywhere in sight.

Presently I observed that he had caught his fishing-line on another snag. Any other fisherman in the world would have jerked it loose quick, or have dropped the rod. George never wasted anything. He would not have sacrificed a leader or fly if he had stuck there for an hour. Patiently, while holding on with left hand, he extricated his line from the brush. Then he peered around to get his bearings. Next he twisted his head so that he faced me, and took his rod between his teeth. His next move was to turn over on his back, changing his handhold in a flash. With both hands free to grasp the roots and branches behind, he dragged himself along the bank until he had passed the worst part. Soon he emerged from under the brush, and waded out on a narrow ledge. Many times I had cast longing glances at that fishy spot, but they were all I did cast.

George began to try to get his fly out in the current. But always it would catch in the brush behind him. Carefully, gently he would extricate it, and try again. Always, however, it would catch. He did not seem to possess any of the temper, irritation, or discouragement most anglers are prone to. With a patience positively astounding he went on with his persistent idea of getting that fly out into the stream. Presently he hit on the plan of using a short line, flipping the fly out, and then stripping his line off the reel, so that the fly could float down to the desired spot.

Once it got there, he had a wonderful strike. I saw the swirl. George gave his rod a hard jerk. He missed the fish, and caught his fly high up on the bank in the branch of a tree. Then for a long time George cautiously and carefully tried to extricate it. In vain! Whereupon he waded back to shore, and climbing the bank and the bushy tree—a perfectly laborsome task—he broke off the branch that held his fly, and threw it down. The line caught over another branch. George could not shake it off, nor could he reach over far enough to break this offending piece. There was nothing to do save shift his position into the other part of the bushy clump. This he did. He swayed to and fro like a huge squirrel in the top of a pine. Swaying thus, by the way, in the tip of a tree was one of Takahashi's favorite outdoor sports, about which I have written elsewhere. This time he got so far out that the branch broke, letting him down with a crash, out of my sight. I heard him breaking the brush. Finally he emerged with line and fly intact. All this was accomplished slowly and thoughtfully, even seriously, as if life and liberty depended upon the outcome.

To say I was interested would have been putting it mildly. I was absorbed. Takahashi was a revelation, an education, and an inspiration at the same time he was being so funny that I nearly strangled with suppressed laughter.

Again he waded out on the point of rock; again he flipped a short line out and began to strip the reel. Breathlessly I watched him. I felt the imminence of catastrophe. But he was as grave and unsuspecting as the Sphinx. Yard after yard of line he let slip through the guides of the rod. I could not tell just where the fly was, but I imagined it was getting pretty far down.

Suddenly a heavy swirl attracted my roving gaze. At the same instant George brought up his rod hard. It bent double. Then a cracking split of the water let out a magnificent steelhead. Up he shot in a curving tussling leap! He was huge—nine pounds—ten. George had hooked him. What a splash when he went down!

This was too much for me. I jumped up out of the shade and ran to the water, thrilled beyond measure at the sight of such a wonderful fish. Then I grew horrified to see that George was pointing the rod straight in the direction of the steelhead and winding hard on the reel.

"Let him run!" I shouted. "Give him line! Hold your rod up! He'll break off!"

George looked across at me with a broad grin, not in the least surprised.

"Awful big one," he replied. But he paid not the slightest attention to my instructions.

"Hold your rod up, I tell you," I yelled, louder. "Let go your reel! You can't wind him! Give him line! . . . *Let him run!*"

Despite George's efforts to check him, the steelhead took line. He made an angry smash on the surface, and next he leaped magnificently. Oh, what a wonderful trout! I saw the silver and pink glow of him, the spotted back, the great broad tail, curved on itself. and the cruel open jaws. What would I have given to have had him at the end of my line? I grew unreasonably incensed at George's stupidity. In stentorian tones I roared at him.

"Hold your rod up! . . . Let him run!"

Perhaps the sound of my voice rather than the meaning of my words penetrated George's cranium. He yelled, "All right," across at me, a little grimly, I thought, or at least ironically. But I saw also that his failure to stop the steelhead had roused him. A Jap cannot bear either advice or defeat.

"He no come!" yelled George, piercingly. *"He stick right there! He stick right there!"*

My exasperation knew no bounds, and if George had been on my side of the river I would have committed the unpardonable sin of seizing the rod.

"Let him run, then!" I choked.

But even as I emitted this last despairing yell George's tense action ceased. The line lay limp. His rod lost its rigidity. The steelhead had escaped. When George wound in the line I saw that his leader had parted. Without so much as a word or glance in my direction, he waded out and plunged into the bush.

Some hours later, when I returned to camp, the boys had something to tell me, and they were full of glee. George had said to them: "I hook big steelhead. Mr. Grey across river. He see

me. He no like way I fish. He yell, 'Hold rod up. Let fish run.'
He holler like hell. He awful mad. So I yell back, 'All right.'
Then I pulled on fish all same like I want to. I bust leader. Shure
he get away. But I no let 'um run. I no like that way fish. I
pull hard. If break'm off, all same to me. I no care."

If there had been anyone to observe me closely during those
trying and thrilling days he would have had something to tell.
Perhaps his point of view as to what was funny would have differed
materially from mine. Tragedy and comedy in fishing are practically synonymous. It depends upon who is looking and who is
doing. To the former most incidents are funny, though to the
latter they may be supremely tragical.

Terrible things happen to even the most skilled and experienced
anglers. That is one of the fascinating mysteries of the game.
For instance, Wiborn, like most Californians, catches cold easily;
and anything like wind, or the touch of icy waters, he exercises the
most exceeding caution to avoid. Yet despite this, on the only
raw day we had on the Rogue, he slipped and fell and rolled over
and over in that ice-water. That was funny, of course, but nothing
to the sight of his face when it emerged. No words of mine could
describe it.

I saw something funny happen to Burnham, and it tickled me
so that I narrowly escaped an accident. Late one afternoon I
climbed down to my perch in the fallen tree, and expected to have
a few moments of quiet contemplation during the most beautiful
time of the day.

But no sooner had I settled myself comfortably in the leafy
covert above the murmuring water than I espied Burnham wading
down the river. He was approaching the head of the rapid, a
place where deep narrow ruts indented the ledge of rock, and
channels of dark-green water swept glancingly on into the riffles
below. This was R. C.'s favorite place, which I had heroically and
religiously avoided. No one else but he and Burnham fished it.

Burnham waded leisurely along, casting beautifully far ahead
and across. He was a picture of vigorous content. How he could
whistle and smoke at the same time was beyond my ken, but he
was accomplishing both very successfully. He was alone on the

river, indulging in his beloved pastime. Golden bars from the setting sun gleamed from the forest and divided the green shade on the murmuring river. Wild ducks winged swift arrow-like flight down the wide gorge. And there the Rogue rolled on, murmuring, roaring in an utter solitude.

I saw Burnham's fly alight like a feather at the edge of one of the dark channels. The sun shone for me right on that spot. The fly floated. Then up flashed a yard-long fish-shape, instinct with life, white and rosy in hue. There followed the most wonderful rise I had seen. But perhaps my position, high up, and scarcely fifty feet distant, accounted for this.

The rise of the steelhead, the smash on the surface, the strike by the angler, the terrific rush—these seemed almost simultaneous. Burnham's rod swept up in a graceful curve. His reel screeched above the sound of water. Then the rod jerked violently down— wagged a second rigidly—went lax. Burnham let out a mighty roar. His voice rolled like a clarion. His action then corresponded to his speech. Up swept the rod, trailing the limp line. At the same instant he threw up his free hand. Gesture of amaze, protest, grief! It was the act of a boy. All true anglers are boys. It expressed a supreme pathos. Then he swore. He passed from sublime to ridiculous so swiftly that I was convulsed with mirth and forgot where I sat. I nearly fell out of the tree.

Then Burnham stood there fumbling with a line tangled on the reel. That told the story of the tragedy. The steelhead had rushed down with the suddenness and speed of a bullet. It had overrun the reel, snarled the line, parted the leader. Here was proof of what a big fast steelhead could do to the most expert of anglers. Strangely I was not at all sorry for Burnham. That accident somehow placed me in the same piscatorial world he occupied. I had imagined he dwelt on an insurmountable height. Somehow he became more human. And his magnificent outburst— how typical of any real red-blooded angler—what a pity I cannot print his actual words!

For days I had used a five-ounce rod and a lighter reel, a cheap one that had given me trouble. It was necessary to have a reel which would hold a hundred yards of line besides the forty yards of casting-line. I had given my Hardy reel to R. C. The eight-ounce rod and heavy reel and line I had started out with had been abandoned through Burnham's advice. "You'll wear your arm out," he protested. And indeed I did.

From my collection of rods he selected a five-ounce Leonard. This I equipped with the only reel I had left, and a medium-weight line. To me that tackle appeared far too light, yet I certainly appreciated the less amount of effort required in casting. And after two weeks of constant endeavor—practice—practice—I had learned to cast very well up to sixty feet. But what had not happened to me, in the way of tantalizing opportunity and miserable misfortune, never happened to any angler on this earth.

Every angler has bad days, except those few called lucky-stab anglers, for whom the fish seem to crawl out on the bank or wrap up in the murderous airplane leaders and choke themselves to death. Some anglers have a bad season now and then. But I never have met an angler who had the same brand of misfortune that haunts me. In a way these spells resemble the batting slumps I used to get in college and professional baseball days. I would be hitting at a high clip around .400 average. Then one day I would hit the ball just as hard, but right at some fielder. The same would happen next day. That would focus my mind on the accident of bad luck. It would irritate and then worry me. I would fall off in batting until I ended in a regular slump and could not hit a ball tied on a string. Baseball slumps are common to every ball-player. They are real, and one of the peculiar weaknesses or misfortunes of the game.

My angling bad luck always seemed so singularly exasperating. At the outset of a new trip I would utterly have forgotten it. Suddenly it would rise up like a hydra-headed monster. And there I was with my old giant beside me, like a shadow. The familiar old mood would return, and following it, the ridiculous certainty that I must labor ten times as hard and ten times as long as any other fishermen, to catch the illusive fish which so willingly attached itself to his line.

Maybe this tormenting mental aberration visits all anglers. What a relieving thought! But I never can believe that.

These Rogue River steelhead must have had a council before

my arrival to decide upon the infinitely various and endless tricks they would play upon me. To be sure, they played a few upon my comrades, but the great majority, and the hopeless ones and the terrible ones, fell to my lot.

During those unforgetable ten days I kept secret and accurate account of what happened to R. C. and the boys. Some of this I saw, myself; part of it I learned at the general camp-fire narratives of the day's experience; and the rest I acquired by a casual and apparently innocent curiosity.

To some wag of a writer are credited the lines anent the universal fisherman: "he returneth in the evening smelling of vile drink, and the truth is not in him." I regard this as an injustice to many anglers. The best and finest anglers I have known did not return in the evening redolent of drink. And outside of a little exaggeration, natural to the exciting hour and the desire to excel, the tales of these fishermen could be accepted as truth.

As to R. C. and the boys, the weakness in my argument may be that they did not tell everything, or that they did not observe keenly or remember correctly. At any rate, the monstrous fact seemed to be that, during these ten days, I had as many strikes from steelhead as all of them put together.

But how vastly different the conditions of my strikes! Here was where the fiendish tricks of the steelhead began. For me the river was empty of fish at first; then suddenly they began to rise. They bewildered me. They flustered me. They baffled me.

If I made a poor cast, with a bag in my line, then a steelhead would rush the fly. Another would suck the fly in when it floated deep, and spit it out before I was aware I had a strike. Whenever I cast from an awkward or precarious position I was sure to feel a nip at my fly. And once—crowning piece of incredible bad luck of that whole trip!—when I was wading far out in the river, I had a strike on my back cast. My fly hit the water behind me and a rascally steelhead took it. I thought I was fast to the familiar willow or rock. When I turned to free myself a big broad steelhead leaped and savagely shook out my hook. I was stunned, then insulted, then furious. Could anything worse happen?

Many a rosy silvery steelhead loomed up out of the dark depths and put his game snub-nose against my fly, as if he meant to gulp it. But he did not. Many a steelhead, always choosing the inevitable and unaccountable instant when I was not ready, would strike my fly hard and jerk the slack line out of my hand. Faithfully I would cast for a whole hour, on the *qui vive* every instant, then just as I relaxed, or looked away from my leader, or lifted my foot to step—smash!

Along with all these dreadful happenings occasionally I would hook a steelhead or he would obligingly do it for me. Then he would proceed to show me how quickly he could get off. The time came, however, when I held one for a long hour. I did not see this one rise. But I felt him hook himself. He was heavy. He swam upstream and stayed in the current. R. C. yelled encouragement. I replied with Takahashi's classic expression, "He stick right there!" Indeed he did. He never leaped, never made a fast run, never frightened me by a sudden move. He plugged deep. He got behind this stone and that one, and under the ledge across the river, and he stayed by each place a long time, tugging at my line. My rod nodded with his jerks. At last, after a half-hour or more, he came toward me and got behind another stone, in a deep eddy. Here he plugged slower and slower. Several attempts to lead him forth proved futile. But at last he gave up plugging and allowed himself to be led out of deep water. R. C. had decided it was a salmon. So had I. But when I led him into shoal water I saw the beautiful opalescent glow of a steelhead. When he came clearly into view and I had actual sight of his great length and depth my heart swelled in my throat. Still no angler could have handled him more gently. He rolled and twisted— rolled and twisted, and finally he twisted the slight hold loose. I saw him drift on his side, gleaming rosily, then right himself and swim off the bar into deep water. When I turned to R. C., mute and exhausted, he gave a most capital imitation of Burnham's vociferous execration.

On October 15th we were due in southeastern Oregon, to take a hunt in a new country. I had still several days to fish before we started, and I could prolong the stay a couple of days longer, if desirable. R. C. had now eighteen steelhead to his credit, taken on a fly. The boys had added several to their string. And I still cherished unquenchable hopes. Next day I actually caught a steelhead on a fly, so quickly and surprisingly that I scarcely realized it.

I went down the river later than usual, and found Ken and Ed casting from the dry rocks at the head of Rocky Riffle. R. C. was about in midstream. When I rigged up my tackle I put on an English salmon fly. It was unlike any fly the steelhead had been rising to, and I meant to try it just for contrariness. Wading in fifty feet above Ken, I made a preliminary cast and let the fly float down. Tug! Splash! A steelhead hooked himself and leaped, and ran right into the water Ken was fishing. I waded out, ran below, and fought the fish in an eddy, and soon landed it, a fine plump steelhead weighing about four pounds.

"Bingo! Out goes a fly—in comes a fish!" exclaimed Ed. "Say, you're a fast worker!"

Ken cupped his hand and yelled up to R. C., "Hey, Rome, he's busted his streak of bad luck!"

R. C. waved and called back: "Good night! Lock the gate!"

I took R. C.'s good-natured slang—an intimation that they would now have to look out for me—as a happy augury for the remaining days. Next day I caught three, a small one, another around four pounds, and the third over five and a half.

"Too late, old boy!" quoth R. C. "I have you trimmed. Nineteen to date, and the biggest seven three-quarters."

"Heavens!" I replied. "Can't you recognize a grateful and innocent angler? I don't dream of equaling your splendid record. Too late, indeed!"

"Well, I reckon I'd better cinch this fishing trip," he said, drily. "There's no telling how you'll finish. I'll stick on the job."

The day before our last day found me with a total of twelve steelhead, the largest weighing six pounds. I was seven behind R. C. Yet still no ambition or even dream of catching up with him crossed my mind. I was fishing desperately hard to prove something to myself, as well as for the thrill and joy of it.

That day happened to be Sunday, a still, cloudy day, threatening rain. I reached Rocky Riffle ahead of everybody, even the native fishermen that usually flocked there on this day. It was a fishy day if there ever was one. I had before me the pleasure of fishing that quarter-mile of best water all by myself. I seemed to be a different angler from the one who had first waded in there nearly three weeks before. Trial, struggle, defeat, persistence— how they change and remake a man! Defeats are stepping-stones to victory.

The water was dark, mirroring the shade of the green mountain slope opposite. It had amber shadows and gleams. Autumn leaves floated on the swift current. From upstream came the shallow music of the riffle; from below the melodious roar of the channel sliding over the rocks into the deep pool.

Wading in to my hips, I began the day with a cast far from perfect and short of record distance, but I placed it where I wanted to and softly, at the end of a straight leader. Thus I worked downstream.

Suddenly, as the current swept my line down even with me, I saw a wave, then a dim pale shape, seemingly enormous in length. Lazily this steelhead took my fly. When I struck I felt the fly rip through his hard mouth. He made an angry swirl as he disappeared. "Oh! why can't I hook one of these big fellows!" I muttered, groaning inwardly. And I went on with a grim certainty that soon I would do so. After making a few casts I waded down several yards. From the instant my fly touched the water until I withdrew it to cast again I was strung keen as a whipcord. I had paid dearly for my lesson.

My line straightened out with fly sunk. Then came a vicious tug. Quick as a flash I struck and hooked what felt like a log. Downriver he raced and my reel sang. He did not leap. With wagging rod held high—no easy task—I began to wade out and down. But I could not make fast enough time. I wallowed, plunged. Then I forgot to hold the loose click on my reel. It slipped off, releasing the drag, and the spool whizzed. I felt a hard jerk—then a slack line.

"That *was* a ten-pounder," I muttered, and then I gave vent to one of the emotion-releasing cuss words. As I pulled out the loops of the tangled line my fingers trembled. At last I got my line in, to find the leader minus a fly. Wading out, I sat down to put on

GONE OVER THE RAPIDS

PLATE LII

Not the Least Ticklish Moment

PLATE LIII

another of the Golden Grouse flies. A glance up and down stream failed to add any other fisherman to the scene.

Below the place where I had hooked that big one there was a flat submerged rock in midstream. The water swirled round it, with little eddies below. On the second cast my fly floated beyond and round it. I caught a gleam of light as if from a mirror under the surface. I sharply elevated my rod even as the steelhead struck the fly. Solidly came the weight. I knew he was hooked well. He ran upstream fifty feet, leaped prodigiously, showing himself to be a long slim male fish. He had bagged the line against the current, and when he leaped again he got some slack. But the hook held. Downstream he turned, and I was hard put to it to hold the click on my reel. Twice it slipped, but I got it pushed back before the pool overran. Meanwhile the steelhead was running and I was following as fast as possible. Far down the channel he leaped again; then he went into the rapids. When I got to shore all my line was out. I ran, splashing, scattering the gravel. But I saved the line, and in the pool below I bested this steelhead. He did not weigh much short of seven pounds.

I tied him on a string. Far upstream I made out Ken whipping his favorite hole, and in the riffle above I saw R. C.'s white hat. Rocky Riffle, wonderful to see, was still untenanted by any fisherman save myself. Too good to be true! Where were the native fishermen, all out on Sundays? It occurred to me that fishing must be too good up the river. The clouds did not break, though in places they were light. Ideal conditions improved. My day seemed to have dawned.

Beyond the flat submerged stone was a deep channel with a ragged break in the ledge. Here the water swirled smoothly. To reach it meant a long cast for me, fully sixty feet, even to the outer edge of that likely spot. Wading deeper, I performed as strenuously as possible, and missed the spot by a couple of yards. My fly alighted below. But the water exploded and the straightened rod jerked almost out of my hand.

My whoop antedated the leap of that Rogue River beauty. After I saw him high in the air, long, broad, heavy, pink as a rose, mouth gaping wide I was too paralyzed to whoop. I had established contact with another big steelhead. Like lightning he left that place. He ran up the river, making four jumps, one of them a greyhound leap, long, high, curved. I had to turn so my back was downstream, something new in even that every-varying sport. When he felt the taut line again he made such a tremendous lunge that I lost control of the click and could not prevent him from jerking my rod partly underwater. I was up to my waist, and that depth and the current augmented my difficulties. The fish changed his course, swerving back between me and the shore, and he leaped abreast of me, so close that the flying drops of water wet my face. As I saw him then I will never forget him.

The slack line did not seem to aid him in any way, for he could not shake the hook. I anticipated his downstream rush, and was wading out, all ready, when he made it. Otherwise—*good night*, as R. C. was wont to say. He leaped once more, a heavy, limber fish, tiring from the furious speed. I followed him so well that he never got more than half of the line. He took me down the channel, through the rapids, along the gravel far below, down the narrow green curve into the rough water below, where I could neither follow nor hold him.

That fight gave me more of understanding of these game fish and the marvelous sport they afford. As I wearily plodded back, nearly a half-mile, I felt sick, and yet I had to rejoice at that unconquerable fish. My tackle was too light, but I would not have exchanged it for my heavy one, with that magnificent fish again fast to my line.

Upon my return to the riffle I found Wiborn had arrived in his car and was rigging up. Ed appeared on the high rock above, and the other boys had not materially changed positions.

Wiborn waded in below me, and I went back up some distance to whip the water over again. From that start time ceased to exist for me. It sped by like a dream or else it stood still. I was hooked to steelhead almost continuously, it appeared, and whenever I thought to glance at Wiborn he was similarly engaged. Only he raised the big steelhead and I the smaller ones. He would hook a fish and go through with him, and as he was fighting it in the pool, or coming back to begin over, I would hook another. I caught three small fish while he was landing one. I freed fish under five pounds.

Only once did Wiborn and I work close together. It happened when I was wading the middle of the riffle and he had started in above. I was not aware he had hooked a fish, until suddenly feeling one bumping into my legs I looked up with a start. Wiborn was trying to make his fish run between my legs. Almost he succeeded. Even so he had fun out of the attempt.

Every time I waded through the riffle I either raised or hooked a steelhead. And when the fish ceased rising I had caught eight, four of which had been released. At that my string of trout was about all I could carry. Wiborn had four between six and seven pounds, one of them probably more.

To my great delight, R. C. had quietly stolen a march on me and had watched me for a long time. We all compared notes. Wiborn said the fishing bore out Burnham's assertion—that it was the finest ever known in the Rogue.

"Once in a lifetime," was Lone Angler's concluding remark.

"Well, I had hard work getting two," said R. C. "But I can't complain about chances. I had a lot of strikes. My bad luck has begun. . . . My score is now twenty-one."

"Only one behind you, old top," I asserted, with fiendish glee. "Eight today! But, oh! if I could just forget those that got away! . . . Why, R. C., a big one, twelve pounds if he weighed an ounce, took me way down round that bend."

But my brother was not sympathetic, or inclined to be thrilled.

"You lucky-stab fisherman!" he ejaculated. "Eight steelhead and you've got a kick! One of your fish there will go over seven pounds. . . . And I, like a chump, lay off this riffle today! Well, I'm still one ahead of you."

That evening after supper, when I happened to be sitting alone, with my back propped against an oak tree and my gaze riveted on the sunset-gilded peaks, R. C. came to find a seat beside me.

"Do you know, I believe up until the last couple of days I've been having a fool's luck," he said, thoughtfully.

"Aha! Then things have been breaking against you, lately?" I exclaimed, with swift comprehension.

R. C.'s expression grew illuminating. A half-amused, self-pitying, and wholly realizing smile crossed his tanned face. He made an eloquent little gesture with both hands, and the silence that accompanied it added singular emphasis. It was no time for me to howl with glee. He was too serious, too frankly humble, for me to feel anything but understanding and sympathy. I divined at once that some tragical, thrilling, unforgetable fishing mishaps had followed hard upon his remarkable good luck. I longed to hear them, but he did not become more explicit.

"The strange thing to me is that it took us three years to get on to the wonderful nature of this steelhead game and to learn it," he went on, meditatively.

"That's occurred to me often," I replied. "But it's easier than bonefishing, which you remember took us longer to master."

"How do you think it compares with bonefishing?" he queried.

"It's totally different, and I'm bound to say infinitely higher class. I doubt if there can be any finer sport than this fly-fishing for steelhead. We'll know for sure when we tackle the Atlantic salmon game. That has the prestige. The salmon is the aristocrat of fishes. It will be a most fascinating opportunity for comparisons, and I think we should not attempt to judge until we have caught Eastern salmon on a fly."

"Well, I'm afraid I must place this steelhead sport above that of bonefishing, which I thought would always be my favorite. And I'm wondering why?"

"I'll tell you. Bonefishing is a game of hard salt water, of the glaring coral shoals, open to sun and wind. It *is* grand sport when once you learn to catch those silver bullets. But we were not born and bred on the sea. We have no salt in our blood. As boys we haunted the swift, shady, babbling brooks. We loved clear, limpid, sweet water. This Rogue River magnifies the favorite places and fish of our boyhood. This river is indeed magnificent. Think. It is icy water, crystal clear. It runs between high mountain slopes of Oregon forests. And it is full of beautiful, savage, unconquerable fish."

"It'd be perfect if we could find riffles on it that were unfrequented by strings of city anglers and crowds of native fishermen —now wouldn't it?" he concluded, with an air of finality.

"I cannot conceive a more perfect river. And I believe those lonely places can be found. There's a hundred-mile stretch of the Rogue that runs down through the mountains to the sea. Only by horse and trail, or by boat, can that stretch be fished. So far as I know it has never been fished. And the prospect begins to loom up to me."

"Let's go," said R. C., his eyes lighting.

So right there under the oak tree we planned another wild trip to add to the list. How fascinating such anticipations! The world is wide and full of lonely, beautiful, unexplored places. And the only bitter drop in the cup of adventurous dreams is the sad reality that life is short—that even such a lucky man as myself can see only a few of the wild rivers of the earth, the untrodden desert wastes, the grand isolated mountain heights, and the vast uncharted areas of the sea.

Next day, which was to be our last of fishing, we were all astir early, before the sun tipped the eastern rampart. The morning was clear, without the hanging veil of mist, and fleecy clouds moved out of the west.

Rocky Riffle disappointed us that day. Half a dozen fishermen were there ahead of us, and the steelhead were not rising well. A native fisherman with a long bamboo pole had desecrated Ken's hole, to his grief and disgust. We fished and idled, fished and rested, hoping the crowd would take their Fords and Packards and go home. But they fished relentlessly and persistently. So early in the afternoon we trudged back to camp. We rested, packed a little, and then had supper. During these leisurely hours I took occasion to walk down to the bank several times to see if any fishermen were whipping the river. As luck would have it I did not espy one. Wherefore I got into my waders. When I left my tent I was not surprised to see R. C. in his angling regalia.

"I read your mind all right," he said, with a laugh.

"We'll raise a steelhead or two," I replied.

When we emerged from the woods on the bank of the river I was singularly struck with the beauty of the time and place.

Our side of the river lay in purple shadow pierced by golden shafts of sunlight. The bluff across caught the last brightness of the setting sun, and beyond, the black slopes of timber climbed to a deep-blue sky where huge white and gold clouds sailed. The glancing dark river gleamed like a moving mirror, reflecting the fringed slopes and the white sails in the sky. There was promise of unusual color in the clouds. R. C. paused a moment to take in the growing beauty, and then he said:

"If we happen to raise a couple of fish this evening it will put us on the bum for keeps."

This remark did not appear to be an elegant one, yet I had to admit its utter felicity. We went down the sandy bank and waded diagonally across to the wide gravel bar. When we reached a point opposite R. C.'s favorite water we stopped, and I sat down on a rock and laid my rod across my knees. He was looking down upon me.

"Take a crack at that place, won't you?" he asked.

"No. I'll enjoy more seeing you raise one," I replied.

"I haven't fished it for two days. And I've never failed to get a strike there. Let's see. I've caught five there, hooked three that got away, and raised some I missed. It's the greatest place on this river."

And we fell to arguing as to who should fish it this last evening. Finally I had to refuse positively and remind him of the passing time. At that he waded in.

The river was wide here, swift and smooth, quickening its current for the incline below. The water was flecked by spots of sunlight. The sharp-toothed ledge of rock gleamed like bronze under the water, and the deep dark channels opened alluring mouths to the current. R. C. waded out until he was up to his waist, and perhaps fifty feet above the tempting break in the level surface. He made several casts before he got his fly in line with the desired channel. Then he let it float down. I could see his leader shine.

He was elevating his rod, preparatory to making another cast, when it was bent double and pulled down straight. His reel screeched. Then a big steelhead came out so fast and so high that we both yelled. I got up and ran into the water. Where was my camera? He leaped again, prodigiously, shooting up out of the first broken water, and this time in the sunlight. He shone black and white. I had seen bigger steelhead, but not one such a jumper.

"Pile out and chase him," I yelled to R. C. "He's going through."

"I'll say he is," shouted my brother, surging toward shore. . . . "Oh! look at him jump!"

Indeed I was looking. In fact, I was spellbound. My delight at his marvelous exhibition was embittered by the thought of my neglect in not bringing my camera. Four times more the steelhead sprang convulsively into the air, the last two leaps being out of the white water of the rapids. He had taken a hundred yards of line while executing those pyrotechnics. But R. C. had a large reel and a long line. He ran along the shore and I kept pace with him. The steelhead went over both the falls before R. C. could wind back a yard of line. Below the rapids the river swept to the right and presently opened out wide, with a deep cove running into the gravel bar. Here R. C. had it out with the fish. He made five more leaps before he yielded to the rod. Then R. C. drew him into shallow water where the bottom was clean sand. The steelhead began that peculiar twisting, gyrating work which nine times out of ten tore out the hook. R. C. seemed divided by anxiety and caution. I was afraid to make a suggestion, for I saw the fish was far larger than any R. C. had landed.

"Wade in behind him," called R. C., sharply, to me. "I'll try to beach him. If he breaks off pitch him out."

That looked to me a very wise move, and I quickly waded to a point outside the fish. Not until R. C. had dragged him on his side in a few inches of water did I appreciate the size of that steelhead. He was so big that R. C. could scarcely budge him. Suddenly the hook tore out. I sprang to scoop the fish up on the bar. But it was not necessary. He only gaped with wide jaws and curled up his broad tail.

"Ten pounds!" I yelled, with wild enthusiasm, and picking up the steelhead I carried him to a safe distance up the bank. There R. C. weighed him on the little scales. An ounce or so over nine pounds! R. C. was too elated to talk. Not for long years had I seen his face alight like it was then. Not even when he landed his four-hundred-pound broadbill swordfish had he looked so happy.

The steelhead lay flat on the gravel. I stared, longing for the art of the painter, so as to perpetuate the exquisite hues and contours of that fish. All trout are beautiful. But this one of sea species seemed more than beautiful. He gaped, he quivered. What a long broad shape! He was all muscle. He looked exactly what he was, a fish-spirit incarnate, fresh run from the sea, with opal and pearl hues of such delicate loveliness that no pen or brush could portray them. He brought the sea with him and had taken on the beauty of the river. He had a wild savage head, game as that of an eagle, jaws of a wolf, eyes of black jewel, full of mystic fire.

"Well!" breathed R. C. at last. "That'll be about all for me. . . . I've a notion to let this fish go. I hate to kill him."

R. C. dispatched him finally, and then accompanied me back up to the head of the rapids. There, while he watched, I had my first try at his favorite water. On my second cast I turned a fish over, saw him flash gold, and leave a swirl. That was the best I could do there, so we reluctantly moved down. I fished through the upper rapids with no better luck. Next came the heavy white water, roaring and tumbling, and that led into a wide reach where the current slowed to slide over a beveled ledge into the last pool. Here between two currents was a dark swirling spot with a sunken rock in the center. It was a beautiful nook for a steelhead to lurk, and many a time I had tried to raise one there.

I had to wade far out and cast my hardest to reach the desired water. I covered it from every angle, and finally abandoned hope. But R. C. was watching, and I was casting wonderfully for me, so I thought vainly to try one more cast, right in the center of that dark water, close to the rock. So I did. The feathered fly fell and floated. A lazy golden shadow soared out of the depths, turned pink and white, and appropriated my fly. I hooked a fine steelhead. He ran up current into the deep water of the rapid, and sulked there. I pulled on him. When he turned he came down with a rush, made a tumbling leap, and dashed on over the last fall. In the pool below, where R. C. had landed his, I finally beached a plump rosy five-pounder.

"Still one behind me," jibed R. C., smiling.

We started to walk below to the next riffle; and it seemed then

Some Rainbow Colored Beauties

PLATE LIV

Zane Grey Shooting Rapids

PLATE LV

Captain Mitchell in Bad at Lower Tyee Falls

PLATE LVI

we were stopped and waylaid by the gorgeous color effects of river, cloud, and sky. The sun had set behind the mountain, yet it still shone on the clouds. They had turned deep rose and intense gold. The valley seemed full of a supernatural light, a glory too great for land or sea. Purple shadow invested the steep forest slope to the west, and opposite the mountain climbed out of shade into the warm rich hues of the afterglow. The river, however, took on the most transcendent beauty. It was a living medium of color, a moving ribbon of rose with rocks of gold, reflecting the slopes and clouds and sky. Every second the transfiguration went on, and not until we reached the head of the riffle did the vividness begin to pale.

Wading in at the head of this rose-flushed riffle, I began to cast, and worked down rather fast, till I came to the swift ruffled water at the foot. Here was another fine place, where R. C. had taken several good fish and I had lost some. The water rippled out of the shallow rapids, gradually deepening.

I had not waded a dozen steps, nor made half so many casts, when something heavy and slow took my fly. I struck, and came up hard against a strong fish. He did not make even a swirl and ran off deep. I hurriedly waded to shore, where, with R. C. beside me, I watched a run that gathered proportions and at last beat any other I had experienced. R. C. and I looked for a leap, but none came.

"Reckon you'll have to beat it after that bird," advised R. C.

So I ran a hundred paces down the rocky shore, getting back a proportionate amount of line. Here I tried to hold the steel-head. The strain angered him and he took another long, hard, deep run. I had to follow. Again I wound back half my line. Only to lose it again! Plunging, jumping, slipping, running where I could, I caught up with this stubborn fish the third time. R. C. advised great caution. He thought I had hooked a salmon or a very heavy steelhead. The uncertainty was most exciting. And the work of running, holding up my rod, and winding the reel began to tire me. Two more hundred-yard dashes this fish gave me, which brought me to deep water along the shore and im-passable brush out on the bank.

"You can't go any farther," said R. C. "Get out on the point of ledge and hand it to him."

My fish, feeling the hard strain again, started off on his determined downstream course. I let him go, but gradually tightened my hold of the line as it slipped through my left hand. I had to hold him or lose him. How he fought! He never ceased tugging until he had most of my line out. Then began the slow work of drawing him back foot by foot. It took so long that dusk had fallen by the time we got our first glimpse of his color. He bored deep under the ledge and gave ground but slowly. The time came when he rose to the surface, and I saw clearly a bigger steelhead than any I had landed. The luck of it! I felt sure of him. I had no torturing doubts or fears. And I gave him the strain of the rod until he was beaten. When I slid him into a little cove R. C. took him by the gills and lifted him up.

"He's a peach," averred my brother, putting the fish on the little scales while I stood by, panting and glowing, and wet with sweat. "Eight pounds! I thought he'd go more. . . . Well, darn if you didn't tie me! What do you know about that? I'm glad. It's something never to forget. After all my good luck and all your bad we split even—twenty-two steelhead each!"

We walked back in the dusk, with the last pale rose fading out of the sky. The river glanced darkly, swiftly flowing by. From above came the murmuring melody of the falls, and through the black wall of trees glinted a bright speck of camp fire. Lastly we had the thrill and excitement of fording the Rogue at night, marking our course by sound of the rapids, and current and depth, and the black mountain peak with its crown of white stars.

In due time our hunting trip ended and we reached Altadena. What was my amaze to find a letter from Burnham awaiting me. Among other things he said: "A week after you left I raised thirty-two steelhead. Another fresh run! They were bigger and faster. Nine of those I hooked cleaned me out."

As I read and reread that, how the roar of the Rogue filled my ears! It was as if I had been suddenly transported back to the riffles with their amber depths. Nine! . . . Burnham meant nine steelhead had run off, breaking line or leader. Bigger and faster fish!

Exclamations or thoughts were futile to relieve me. I had to rush to tell the news to those who had shared my wonderful days on the Rogue. Somehow I instinctively felt that they would answer to this stunning information with sanity and reason. So I collected them and read Burnham's letter. Then I stared, awaiting their verdicts.

The cool, practical, ironical Ken did not seem in the least staggered.

"Why, there's nothing extraordinary about that!" he said. "Not in the Rogue River!"

"Bingo!" burst out Ed.

Takahashi's brown visage wreathed in a pleasant grin. "My graceness! We awful lucky to come 'way."

My brother sagged in his chair. Like me, he had been struck deep. He saw pictures of the past and visions of the future. "Fresh run of steelhead! . . . Bigger and faster!" he whispered, weakly. *"Good night!"*

DOWN RIVER

ALL winter we talked of the plan to make a trip down the Rogue River, Oregon, from below Grants Pass to the Pacific. None but market fishermen and lumbermen were familiar with the hundred miles of wild river that bisects the Cascade Range. Therefore, naturally, the more we planned and learned the greater became the thrill and excitement.

While R. C. and I, who had such wonderful fishing on the Rogue in October, 1924, were on our voyage in the South Pacific during the winter of 1925, we thought and spoke many times of the green-and-white Rogue River, with its high slopes of pine and fir and its iron-colored canyon walls. And while at Avalon during July and August, when the glare of the sea grew so unbearable and only swordfishing could have kept us there, the thought of the cool green forests, the dark shade, the thundering rapids, and the wonderful steelhead trout of the Rogue finally decided us to make the trip. But it turned out that R. C. stayed at Avalon in quest of the record broadbill swordfish and my boy Romer went in his place.

We reached Grants Pass on September 3rd, where we outfitted at Wharton's and the general stores. Wharton had secured the services of a guide and market fisherman, Claude Bardon, who was born on the Rogue and depended upon it for his livelihood. He had a helper named Van Dorn, nicknamed Debb, who, though a much younger man, had also put in a good deal of his life on this salmon river.

Bardon said he had obtained four of the Rogue River boats, and that he did not think much of the eighteen-foot skiffs Wharton had built for me. The probability was that they would not last out the trip. For that matter, Bardon averred none of the boats would be any good when we landed at Gold Beach. Indeed, he

Singing Waters (Plates lvii to lx)

Plate LVII

PLATE LVIII

PLATE LIX

Plate LX

was not optimistic about the trip, and his rather blunt evasions about the Rogue were conducive to thought. I began to get an inkling why no anglers had ever shot the river. Wharton and Adair confessed to have entertained longings for years to make the trip, but they had never attempted it. Burnham said it no doubt would afford marvelous sport. Wiborn vowed this adventure would be great.

But Wiborn knew me and how to inspire and help me. "Great idea!" he exclaimed, enthusiastically. "Only you would undertake it. You'll make it like a breeze, and get some story. All us guys will want to follow then."

Wharton and Adair both strongly recommended Bardon, and said he was the only man to whom they would have intrusted their lives. So altogether I had ample encouragement and help.

The automobile ride down to Lewis's Ranch below Galice, where my boats had been taken, rather gained than lost from the fact that I remembered the deep gorges, the steep verdant slopes of green, and the beautiful river with its white lacy rapids far below. Captain Mitchell, one of my guests, was in raptures over the scenery. He lives in Nova Scotia, which is comparatively flat, and though green and picturesque, and wild, too, in spots, it lacks utterly the grandeur and ruggedness of our Western states.

We arrived at the Lewis Ranch to be welcomed by Wiborn and his wife, and the Lewises, who assured us our old camp ground near the forest on the bank of the river was ready for us. A few steelhead had been caught by native fishermen.

"The big run of steelhead has not reached here," said Wiborn. "You'll meet them down the river."

"We need a good rain," added Harry Lewis. "Usually we get a storm here early in September, and that starts the fish upriver."

We unloaded cars and truck and proceeded to pitch camp. Ken and Ed then departed, to run the truck and Lincoln back to Grants Pass, then to Crescent City, and on up the coast to Gold Beach, at the mouth of the Rogue. Here they were to leave the cars and return to us.

I did not have time that day to look at Bardon's boats, or the ones I had had built. Work kept me busy till dark. Then to sit before a camp fire, after almost a year, was pure bliss. The

mountain air was cool and tangy, the river roared low and melodiously, the breeze rustled the tall firs, and the melancholy crickets
began to chirp of the coming of autumn. When I went to bed
that night I did not lie awake long.

Next morning Captain Mitchell, Romer, Ken and Ed, and even
George, just about deserted the work and hurried down to the
river. Wiborn and I went with Bardon to look over the boats.
I found the skiffs quite different from what I had ordered, and
probably the better for that. They were canoe shaped, with narrow blunt stern and sharp bow, high out of the water, with two
seats, and watertight compartments at each end.

The four boats Bardon had secured for me were of a type new
to me, and certainly unique. They were about twenty-three feet
long, sharp fore and aft, rising out of the water, very wide and
deep, with the gunwales having a marked flare, twelve inches
to the foot. They looked heavy and clumsy to me, but upon trying one I found, to my amaze, that, empty, it rowed remarkably
easily, turned round as on a pivot, and altogether delighted me.
Each boat was equipped with two sets of oars, a hundred feet
of rope, and a sixteen-foot pole with iron-spiked end. In these
seven boats we aimed to transport our large outfit and ten persons.
Bardon, to my satisfaction, proved to be one guide who did not
object to what perhaps was considerably more of an outfit than
was necessary. There are so many things I like to take outside of
food and blankets—tackle, cameras and films, books, different kinds
of kits, several changes of clothes, and numerous odds and ends.

The second day at Lewis's the wished-for rainstorm set in, beginning with a drizzle, then a fine pattering that was music on the
tents. We fished up and down the river, early and late, with fly
and spinner, all to no avail. There appeared to be no steelhead.
Romer took to light trout tackle, tiny flies, and invisible leaders,
and he interested us with his proficiency in catching small trout.
He caught a mess of fine little rainbows and cutthroats, running
from a half to a pound in weight. Then the rain ceased and we
fished a whole day under a cloudy sky. I confined my efforts to
the great riffle, where I did not see a sign of a fish. Captain
Mitchell reported hooking a steelhead that broke his line. This
occasioned me great glee. The genial captain was an old salmon

fisherman, and took some of my steelhead stories with a grain of salt, especially those pertaining to light fish making off with tackle.

George Takahashi had a hard strike on a spinner; I'd reported a rise from a steelhead that failed to hook; Ken had no luck; and Romer saw several steelhead, one of which came for his tiny trout fly. The discovery of several salmon created interest.

Bardon said the steelhead were down the river, lying below the cold brooks that flowed into the Rogue.

"Last week I was at Gold Beach," he said. "Big run of steelhead, and the biggest run of salmon into the river for years. Some of us market fishermen earned as much as nine hundred dollars a night." Bardon said he had one net-haul of forty fish weighing over fourteen hundred pounds. A few fishermen netted as much as five tons of salmon. "Course they killed a lot of steelhead that got strangled in the haul. The nets must have an eight-and-a-half-inch mesh, or steelhead can go through. But sometimes on a run a good many steelhead get caught."

We arrived at the conclusion that the lower Rogue was full of salmon and steelhead, on their way up. Romer was the most impatient one of us to be on our way down. I confessed to myself that, though the prospect was more thrilling than ever, it had begun to rouse qualms in my breast. It was one of those trips I never should have planned. But there was no turning back now.

On the following day we fished awhile, with no better results, and spent the rest of the time packing. Next morning we were up at five o'clock. A gray fog curtain obscured the mountains. We had something of a task to pack those boats. Bardon gave me the longest and the best boat, he said. The only name it had was Number 76. My credulity was to be taxed again when that boat took all my luggage and more besides. It sank six inches in the water.

By nine o'clock we were all packed and ready to start, with the Wiborns, the Lewises, and others wishing us a safe voyage. We embarked and trusted ourselves to the eleven-mile current of the Rogue. Our friends cheered us and waved good-by till we passed round a bend of the river.

As most guides are apt to be, Bardon was loquacious. Moreover, he evinced a propensity for bewildering statements. One remark of his had lodged disastrously in Ken's mind.

I had told Ken that I would consign two of the small light skiffs to him and Ed, and upon this occasion Romer had inquired of Bardon, "Do you think we'll go through safely?"

"Everything will go through, I guess, except those small light skiffs," replied Bardon.

"Holy cats!" yelled Ken, who had heard. "Ed, what do you think of that? We have to go in those light skiffs! . . . It's murder or suicide, I don't know which."

"Aw, there'll be nothin' to it," replied Ed. "We'll go right through those rapids. Bingo!"

"Sure!" scoffed Ken. "Bingo! Down goes a skiff! Bingo! Up come boards. But not *me!*"

Bardon appeared to enjoy this byplay of words, and he repeated a remark I had often heard him make. "Shore this is gettin' better an' better. Soon I won't be able to stand such funny stuff."

Bardon shot the curved rapid in the bend of the river below camp. Debb followed with another heavy boat, then Captain Mitchell with the third light skiff. Romer and the others had waded down, and with their cameras were waiting below for me to come. My big boat sailed down and around that curve so easily and gracefully and exhilaratingly that I was delighted. Number 76 handled as easily as a canoe, apparently.

There was little need to row down the riffles, for the current was swift and carried us rapidly. We drifted over the famous Chair Riffle where the year before we had fished with such incredibly bad luck and good luck. Below this, the valley opened wide for a mile, and the river swept swirling on, with most of the water close to the right bank. There was a great charm in gliding along with the beautiful shore passing, and the dark-timbered mountains changing every moment. But this Rogue River did not afford many long safe stretches. Soon I heard another rapid, louder and deeper. Bardon and Debb were waiting round a corner. The river disappeared below. I saw some white water flashing up. I rowed ashore to a bar, and went below

ZANE GREY TRYING TO BEACH A STUBBORN STEELHEAD

PLATE LXI

MITCHELL, THE PATIENT!

PLATE LXII

to see Bardon shoot this one. It proved to be straight, with all the heavy current and the back-lashing waves in the middle. The boatman and then Captain Mitchell ran it in succession. When my turn came I could not see them below me. I backed the boat into the current, picked out the right glancing dip, and sailed over to swoop down, pounding and bumping the waves. It was fascinating. I began to thrill with memories of other rivers I had navigated. The only difficulty I experienced here was in rowing out of the swift current below. Almost it carried me too far.

The other boats were lined through from the left shore. Below were several rifts, and at the end of this rapid a short fall that took nerve to shoot, but appeared easy after it had been overcome.

Then we rowed and drifted, the seven boats strung out in line, until we reached the head of the Alameda Rapid. Here was the end of the road. There used to be a bridge at this point, but last winter it went out with a flood. On both sides of the river people were waiting to watch us shoot the rapids, and especially what appeared to me to be a big drop in the river. At any rate, I could not see the water below.

I watched the boatmen go down and over. Captain Mitchell followed in his light skiff, and when he reached the big drop his boat appeared to tilt up backward and shoot out of sight. I did not like the idea of running this place below, when I had not investigated it, but I pushed off and went at it. The Alameda Rapid was easy and safe and afforded good sport, but the drop between the gateway of rocky banks, where the bridge had once spanned the river, raised more than excitement in my breast. Still, I knew where to go, and as the current between rapids and falls was not too swift, I maneuvered my boat directly into the center. As I saw the deep slant and heard the roar of water, I had only a vague perception of the crowd of people ashore on the bank. My boat swept on, dipped, and plunged down, to bob like a cork on the big waves below. I drifted into the eddy and rowed ashore, where again the Wiborns met me, with felicitations and cheers. Mrs. Wiborn said, "My heart was in my throat when you went over the fall."

"So was mine!" I replied, grimly.

While the boatmen went back to run the other boats down we

waited there, and I endeavored to take no notice of the numerous cameras ashore on the bank. Our venture had caused considerable interest along the river and this was the last place where we could be observed. Wiborn, Lewis, and others had driven down in their cars.

Soon we were drifting on the river again, waving our good-bys for the last time. The gold-green bend took us into the wilderness.

The river narrowed, and so did the canyon, and the mountain slopes swept up ragged and dark to the fringed summits. A half-mile below Alameda we encountered a bad rapid with a large rock in the middle of the lower end.

Captain Mitchell successfully shot this behind the boatmen, a very creditable performance; but I decided I could not be sure of managing my heavy boat there, so Bardon had to come and take it through. We boys lined the other boats down.

We proceeded then to the Argo Mine Rapids, another bad one, though I was not so fearful of it as of the one above. I did not attempt to run it. Captain Mitchell, however, was second through, and below the fall he ran head on into the cliff, smashing the bow of the light skiff quite badly. Work was required to get the other boats down.

"Say, Bardon," inquired Romer, while we were resting, "are there any rapids more dangerous than this?"

"There ain't nothin' dangerous till we get to Graves Creek Rapids an' then there ain't nothin' dangerous," replied the boat-man, enigmatically.

"Ah-huh!" ejaculated Romer, nonplused.

Rapid number eight appeared to be a comparatively easy one for me to run. Bardon went through without effort. It was long, with an abrupt turn at the lower end, where ugly rocks made sharp hard work imperative. I attempted it, without any worry, and got halfway through when the current swept me to the left shore. I saw my danger and plunged strenuously with the oars, but could not avert disaster. The boat got out of line, the bow turned in, and then the current swept me up on a rock. Smash! I heard the crack of wood and the shifting of cargo. For a second I feared the boat would swamp, but it went up high and stuck fast, shipping only a little water. The boatmen waded into the river and Bardon

leaped in while I leaped out. It took four of us to push her off.
Bardon went through safely.

I was considerably taken aback and discomfited, and viewed
with dismay the leak in my boat.

"Wal, there was two men drowned here," said Bardon, cheerfully, "an' another fellar lost his boat. It's worse than it looks!"

We had smooth river and easy going for a long distance, winding round the bends, all the time getting into more beautiful and
picturesque scenery. Soon we drifted into a high-walled canyon
where the river ran still and deep and silence enwrapped us. The
walls were gray and yellow, extending far up, and cut into all
kinds of shelves and ledges with green growths fringing them. Far
above towered the timbered peaks.

The Rogue here was slow, placid, eddying and drifting, meandering under gleaming walls and through silent passes, almost
gloomy in the narrowest places. Somehow, a feeling took hold of
me that the river was gathering force for a mighty expenditure of
effort. We would have to pay for this gliding between enchanted
walls.

We passed the first intersecting canyon, opening on the right
side. Here Graves Creek rushed in. We had long heard of it,
and we looked and listened apprehensively for the great rapids
named for it. Soon a sullen roar greeted my ears. That sound
recalled the roar of the jungle river I had once navigated from
mountain plateau to the jungle level. My hair stiffened on my
head, as it had many times on that wild trip.

Rounding a point, we found Bardon ashore, walking down to
look over Graves Rapid. He returned to say we would have to
line the boats through. This was difficult, slow work, and by the
time the last boat had been lowered it was midafternoon. Next
we came to lower Graves Rapid. The whole volume of water
churned through a thirty-foot gap between the black walls and slid
down a chute that was almost a sheer drop.

Bardon shot it, then the Captain, and finally Debb. While they
were returning along the rocky shore to fetch the other boats
through, some of us clambered below the fall to see them nego-
tiate it. I would not have been greatly afraid to attempt it in a
light skiff. Bardon came through in my boat, and the sight was so

thrilling I forgot to photograph it. Then Debb followed. While the boatmen were going back again, I watched that gleaming, glancing waterfall. It changed continually. It rustled, widened, hollowed, flared, and ran in a groove. Always I could see the ragged rock jaws, sharp on each side, one a little below the other. They were the teeth that had torn many boats. Sometimes they were a foot underwater, and again clear to the surface. The peril, of course, was when the swell of water subsided so that a boat could strike. It was impossible for the best of rivermen to know just when the safest moment offered.

Bardon appeared above the fall, standing to the oars. He was in the blue boat, which was full of heavy supplies. Just as he reached the brink I saw him take two powerful strokes. The boat started over differently, it seemed to me. He struck the jagged rock on our side a glancing blow, swerved and dipped, but shot down upright. When he reached shore below, the boat was full of water. He had ripped open the bottom. We beached the boat, packed its cargo in the other boats, and went on.

Reamy Falls was the last bad water between us and Whisky Creek, our first camp. This fall was one of the heaviest in the river. It took its name from an old prospector who had been killed near there.

We arrived at the head of this rapid about five o'clock. Bardon advised camping there, but as there was no fit place to camp, I thought we had better try to get through. The river was wide and full of boulders. On the right side, where we landed, the slippery rocks were almost impossible to stand upon, yet we had to carry our luggage fully three hundred yards to get around the falls. The river thundered like Niagara, and most of the water disappeared in a frothy abyss.

After we had packed most of our luggage around, at the cost of extreme labor, we were faced with the greater difficulty of lining the boats down the narrow tortuous channel that had been blasted for the fish to come up. It was a fish ladder, and some of the steps were high.

Several forest rangers happened along and lent us a hand, otherwise we would have been stuck indefinitely, certainly until the next day. We all toiled ceaselessly. I had several bad falls that took a good deal out of me. Romer was in his element. He hauled and pulled like a young giant. He fell in, floundered over rocks, lay back mightly on the lines, yelled instructions, and altogether enlightened me to the fact that he was a grown boy, and a husky one at that.

"Where'd he ever get so much pep?" complained Ken. "I'm darn near dead, and there he is yellin' for more."

My boat was the fifth in line to go down the chute. I waded along the rocky channel, holding hard. There was no one to help at the moment, and I imagined I could do it alone. When my heavy boat turned into that pitway it shot down like a flash. I could not hold the rope. My feet were jerked from under me and went aloft, while the back of my neck, my shoulder and right elbow crashed down on the rock. I was almost knocked out. Fortunately, the boat lodged below, and soon the men got to it.

I had all I could do for the time being to drag myself out of the water to a safe place. I thought my arm was broken, but, fortunately, I had sustained only severe bruises. My heavy shoes were studded with hobnails, yet were as slippery on those infernal rocks as if they had been ice. All the boys had hard falls. Romer was covered with lumps and he did not have a dry stitch on him.

By the time our entire fleet had been coaxed below the falls, I was sufficiently recovered to continue the voyage. But I felt I would not soon forget that formidable place where the river thundered down into a terrific white caldron.

Darkness had fallen when we reached a widening of the river gorge and the streams that marked our camp ground. It was a sandy shore, but steep, and to pack our belongings up to a level was a staggering task in our state of fatigue. I could do no less than the others because all of my comrades were worn out. Bardon was all in, and Debb was crippled. Captain Mitchell and Romer were the strongest, and I certainly had to admire them. Also I vowed I never again would undertake a hard trip with a lot of useless baggage. My duffle-bag weighed a ton; my several grips were as heavy as lead; and finally when they were all up on the bank there remained the further task of putting up tents, unrolling beds, and making ready for the night. But at last, how sweet it was to rest! What a terrible day!

Reamy Falls had been the seventeenth rapid we had passed. All in ten miles of the Rogue! And one boat left on the way!

We sat and lay round George Takahashi's camp fire, a starved, exhausted, silent group, wet to the skin and suffering from bruises, rope burns, and aches. How welcome the fire! And the wonderful Jap was as cheerful and deft as if he had not partaken of our labors.

"Hoo-ooh! All ready! Come an' get!" he sang out. "Nice hot soup an' lots good things!"

Eyes that fell shut as if weighted, and dead slumber, were our reward for that strenuous day. Morning disclosed a bunch of cripples, several lost articles of baggage, two leaky boats, and various other things that might have been expected.

It also disclosed our camp site, which was an ideal one for a lover of the wilds. A high sandy beach, overgrown with ferns and blooming goldenrod, with several flowering maples, some live oaks, and a single great yellow pine, stood out on a point between the Rogue and its tributary, Whisky Creek. The elevation was perhaps sixty feet. Behind opened the canyon where the creek flowed down from the green mountains; a thousand-foot slide where an avalanche had defaced the slope showed its gray rocky face and brown earth on the north.

There was a superb view down the river—a shallow bar leading to a white rift, and then a gleaming curve of river passing out of sight down the V-shaped notch. Directly across from camp roared Rum Creek, tumbling down from a timber-choked gorge, and leading the eye up to a magnificent steep peak, fringed with lofty firs and pines.

We were told that down the river a little way, Booze Creek came in. The Rogue Valley had first been opened up by prospectors, and prospectors still worked claims there. They were responsible for the queer names.

It developed presently that one of the red-shirted men who had helped us over Reamy Falls lived up Whisky Creek, where he had a gold mine. His name was Whiteneck, but it would better have been Whiteman, for he certainly was one of the kindest and most genial men I had ever met in the woods. He tried to give us everything but his gold mine, and entreated us to shoot the deer that robbed his garden patch every night. He brought us some jerked venison, dried deer meat, which is something I especially like. He wanted to lend his horses to us, or take us hunting; and in short he was a good Samaritan of the Rogue. He had lived there alone in his log cabin for over ten years, and had no neighbors. Lonely solitude suited him. The news that a so-called military road was to be cut down the Rogue did not please him in the least. He entertained some of the same ideas I have had about the fire roads and military roads cut by the Forest Service through the National Forests. I never could see the military need of them, and as for fire, I absolutely know that automobile roads cause ten times more fires than there used to be. The Forest Service want new roads for reasons of their own. They probably like the tourist travel through their domain. But all wilderness dwellers, hunters and fishermen, and lovers of the forest, hate automobile roads, and know they are one great cause, probably the greatest, of our vanishing America. The quail and the trout have vanished from California, and the forests are following. I am glad Romer can still see something of wild America, but I fear his son never will.

It consumed half a day to fix up camp, but at that Romer and Ken and Ed left off work and rest to go fishing. No small steelhead were caught. Captain Mitchell and I, during the late afternoon, spent an hour on the river, without any luck. But that did not matter. The sunset was beautiful, resembling ships of silver clouds with rosy sails that crossed the lilac sea of sky in the west.

At this camp I experienced a familiar and welcome sensation— the sloughing off of the scales of civilized life, the press of many people, the raucous sounds and vile smells of the city, the ceaseless movement and hurry, the dust and heat, the ever-present rush and honk of automobiles.

Dusk fell here sweetly, to the murmur of the river, the babble of the brook, the breaking of the sunset. The air was laden with the fragrance of the primeval forests. The place was restful, lonely. Slowly something banal oozed out of me, as it were, and I began to feel the encroachment of the strange joys of the wilderness.

Next morning Romer and I walked up the river to Reamy

Falls. We saw a few big salmon, but there was no run on, so we could not secure any pictures of leaping fish. The river did not yield any signs of steelhead. In fact the water was slightly discol· ored, to the extent that we believed the irrigation dam along Grants Pass had been opened. This had spoiled fishing for several days last season. On our way back we met George Takahashi *en route* to the falls. Later when he returned to camp he had a good deal to relate to us.

"Pretty soon salmon begin jump," he said. "One jump awful high. I want take picture. So I loose drag in reel and lay rod down. Then when I get camera ready for picture, fish grab my spoon and almost jerk rod in river. He run way down river and get round rock. I run awful hard, but fish get away."

Takahashi never failed to furnish some humorous or exciting incident for me. He was both lucky and unlucky. I think if I had some good luck once in a while, I could be philosophical about my enormous bad luck.

It annoys me at times that my son Romer, and R. C., and my friends Wiborn and Mitchell, cannot see that I am the most un-lucky of anglers. Just to prove it, the thousandth time I went out that evening and cast faithfully for two hours, with never a rise. Captain Mitchell caught his first steelhead, a small one of three pounds. His comments pleased me.

"This steelhead is evidently a hard striker. He hooks himself and is very fast and game."

Mitchell had fished the trout and salmon streams of England, Scotland, and Norway; and he knows every river in Canada. More-over, he was a great fly-caster, having made a record of something beyond a hundred feet at one of the Madison Square Garden Tour-naments. I was particularly keen to have him get into the steel-head fishing as R. C. and I had experienced it last fall. It would be fun to see him lose some tackle and fine to watch him exercise his skill. Mitchell used the English style of casting a fly. I did not think it so beautiful and graceful a method as practiced by Burnham and Carlon, but he got the fly far out and lightly upon the water.

Romer again resorted to his light trout rod and tiny flies, with such good result that I resolved to learn how he did it. The same

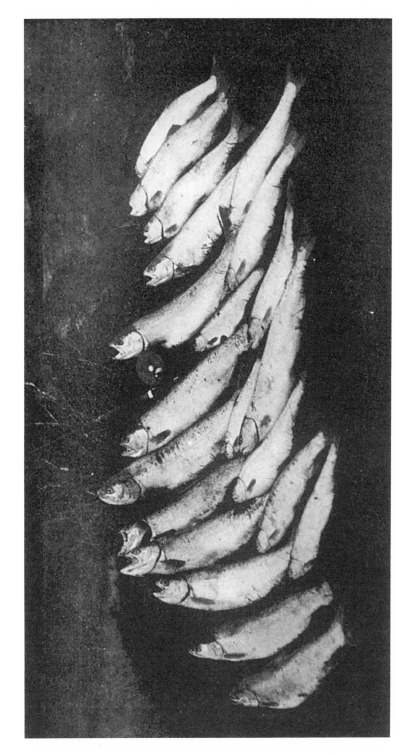

For the Frying Pan

PLATE LXIII

"Dad, I Saw That Steelhead Clean You out of Line and Leader"

PLATE LXIV

day the boatmen walked up the river and repaired the boat left at Graves Creek Rapid and came down in it. That evening Ken and Ed went deer-hunting. Captain Mitchell cast from a boat immediately below camp, and just about dark he had a smart tug at his fly.

Round the camp fire we indulged in too much speculation about the lower Rogue and too much reminiscence about the rapids we had passed.

Romer was hard to quench. He had to talk about these things. "Say, Ken, that was sure a miraculous escape you had. Didn't you see that rock?"

The incident he referred to was one that had caused me considerable concern. Ken had hung too far in the rear, so far that he could not see what we were doing. I kept calling to him, but to no purpose. I saw him drift right upon a submerged rock that we had all avoided at the expense of considerable effort. It looked to me as if Ken had not seen the obstruction.

"Oh, I saw it all right," Ken averred. "But I just couldn't make the boat keep away from it."

"Were you scared?" asked Romer.

"Listen, boy," went on Ken, earnestly. "When I saw that black rock coming up to meet me I was so scared I meant to jump, but before I could jump the boat heaved over it. You know it takes a good boatman to go over a rock like that."

Later at that session round the camp fire Ken had some more pertinent things to say about the Rogue.

"Rapids! They're not rapids," he declared. "They're falls, every last one of them, and I think the State of Oregon should make use of them. It'd be a good idea for the government to put their criminals in boats and send them down to Rogue to shoot the falls. If any of them got to Gold Beach alive they'd deserve to be set free."

One of the rangers informed us that the river was in poor condition owing to the outflow of the dam above Grants Pass. No steelhead were rising up the river. Nevertheless, we whipped the riffles industriously. Our last day at Whisky Creek was cool and partly cloudy, ideal for fishing. Captain Mitchell and I were the only anglers to go out in the face of conditions. I worked down clear to Tyee Bar, catching my first steelhead for 1925, one about two pounds and the other around four. Both rose to a spinner. I worked all the water with our favorite flies, without a strike. Captain Mitchell, however, caught one small steelhead on a fly and lost another.

Upon getting back to camp, I was well-nigh exhausted—proof anew that I had not fully recovered from the operation for removal of tonsils, done in July. I had forgotten this in the enthusiasm of starting out.

The boatmen returned this day with two deer, one a four-point buck, and the other a three, fine fat "black tails," one of which would weigh two hundred pounds, which is around the limit for Pacific-coast deer. In the interior the "black tails" weigh much more. On my tramp downriver I saw deer tracks too numerous to count, also signs of three different bear. A very curious little mink came out on the bank to watch me cast. From the expression of his lean, sly, sleek-brown face, I gathered that he thought I was far from being an expert caster. I told the little rascal that I could appreciate him and his wild environment as well as the most skillful rodman in all the world. Also I saw a ribbon snake, a very beautiful creature scintillating with bright colors. Everywhere down the river on the south side were signs of prospectors who had toiled and passed on, leaving the evidences of their dream of gold. I have a great sympathy for prospectors. Their search and mine have been much the same—for the treasure at the foot of the rainbow.

The night before we left Whisky Creek we were somewhat disconcerted to find a rattlesnake right in camp. It was remarkable that nobody stepped on him, as he was either crossing the trail or lying in it. When disturbed in the twilight, he buzzed loudly, and then slowly made for the brush. I must confess he acted very much like a gentleman and did not deserve to be killed. But Ed, who is something of a snake-killer, dispatched him with an ax. He proved to be of a barred variety, about four feet long, and had eight rattles.

We had been led to believe the season was too late for rattlesnakes; hence we had run around camp unprotected by boots, in the dark as well as by day. The incident warned us not to trust to reports, but to take caution for ourselves.

We were up at dawn—a cloudy, cool morning promising rain —and by seven-thirty had all the boats packed. Mr. Whiteneck came down to say good-by to us, and emphasized again the hazard of our adventure by assuring us he thought we would get through all right.

We ran two rapids, one a short dip, and the second a long shallow curve full of rocks, before we came to Tyee Bar Rapid. This was a zigzag aberration of the river, and not even Bardon had a notion of running it. We shoved, waded, pulled, and lined the boats over Tyee, with an amount of labor that gave us a fore-taste of the day ahead.

Tyee Bar was once a famous gold diggings. In the early days three hundred Chinamen took a million dollars in gold dust off this bar. I walked over part of it, out of curiosity, and found it a low flat of boulders. Not at first did I appreciate what the bar had once been. Presently, however, I saw a straight-sided eminence of sand and gravel standing at the edge of the river. Trees and brush and grass covered the top. Then I made out a rude cross, marking a grave, and remembered Bardon's referring to the grave at Tyee Bar. This burial spot was fully twenty feet above the rocky floor of the bar. During the gold strike a miner had been buried there, and the gold-bearing sand and gravel had been washed away, leaving his resting-place high and undisturbed. It was a monument to the spirit of the Chinamen and the succeeding generation of prospectors.

Lower Tyee Falls was a sticker. It was almost impossible to run and very difficult to line. But it had to be passed. Bardon shot it successfully, and to see him go through made the performance look easy. The long swift channel terminated in a chute scarcely twenty feet wide, through which the current roared in white maelstroms. About a hundred feet above the termination an ugly rock stuck out. It looked impossible to avoid. With the second boat, Bardon struck it squarely, stern first, but the circumstance rather helped him than otherwise.

Then Captain Mitchell, against my advice, undertook to run this rapid in one of the small boats. I went below to the foot of the fall to watch and photograph him. He started all right, but just above the dangerous rock he slid in line with it and could not pull out. When he struck hard his boat jumped up and turned bow downstream. One oar flew out into the current; the other was knocked out of his hand. My heart stood still. I could not even yell. Mitchell stood up, hurriedly picked up the oar, and as he raced down the chute was just in time to ward the boat off the cliff. Then it bounced down bow first into the white waves. He was thrown into the bottom of the boat, but got up again in time to save the skiff from the threatening rocks below.

Mitchell took this mishap coolly, and gave me the impression that he got a thrill out of it. But it surely frightened me. Bardon said Mitchell showed quick wit and cool nerve in what was a dangerous predicament.

We lined the rest of the boats through, a two-hour job that wet us thoroughly and broke us in to the knocks and strains incident upon such progress down the river.

Russian Bar Rapids was beautiful to look at, but not safe to even old boatmen. Bardon said he hated to run it. The river slanted down into a gorge of bronzed rocks, narrowed to a matter of twenty yards, and raced so swiftly and fell so precipitously that it raised enormous white and green waves. There were no rocks to hit. The danger lay in having a boat turn broadside and fill with water. We lined the small boats through, and the boatmen ran the others without any mishap aside from shipping water.

Below Russian Bar we encountered three steep falls, close together, all of which were run by the boatmen and Captain Mitchell. They were steep drops in the river, where the water slanted through gaps in swift V-shaped current terminating in the white-crested, back-curling waves. We climbed round the rocks and bailed out the boats as they were brought to shore. The blue boat, loaded heavily, took on about forty gallons at every fall. My big red boat, being so high astern, shipped comparatively little water. However, I accomplished a prodigious amount of bailing.

We came at length to a constriction in the river, with high cliffs on each side, and a fall called Plowshare.

"Shore you all got to shoot this one," urged Bardon. "Nothin'

The Roaring Gateway into Mule Creek Canyon

PLATE LXV

Debb and Ed, with Sinking Boat, Make for the Cliff

PLATE LXVI

to hit if you keep in the middle! Easy if you stay with the current!"

From where we had left the boats the Plowshare was not in view. You had to push off and go round a corner. I was the last to start. When I rounded the bluff, I espied the narrow gateway where the river dropped. I kept in the current without difficulty, and went over in fine style, but the tremendous force carried my boat straight for the cliff a hundred feet below. I strove with might and main to pull out of the current. It was not a happy moment. Luckily I averted collision, but my left oar hit the cliff and, flying out of my hand, struck my companion a solid thump that elicited a cry I heard above the roar of waters.

"Accident number two!" ejaculated Ken, pessimistically. "Wonder who's going to be next."

Following that, we had a succession of river rapids which brought us to Kelsey Canyon. What I wanted most was to be able to watch the magnificent panorama instead of the deceitful river. We had, however, quite a long stretch of deep water and gentle rifts through which the boats glided as if into an enchanted land. Loftier grew the green slopes until we had to crane our necks to see the fringed summits. Great white cumulus clouds sailed over the green horizon line into the blue sea of sky. The soft breeze was laden with spicy fragrance. Brooks flowed down over the cliffs, in lacy sheets and broken torrents; eagles soared above the gray crags. Every turn in the river opened up another and more beautiful vista of steep slopes and rugged walls.

Here in Kelsey Canyon we saw some large steelhead, the first since we had reached the Rogue. Naturally that gave us fishermen a keen satisfaction and we wanted Horseshoe Bend, our next camp, to come quickly. But though the river hurried onward, we were not able to keep pace. We met with obstacles in Kelsey Canyon. And toil! My hands felt as if I had been fighting a broadbill swordfish.

Boulder Rapids was a bad one. If I had been fresh I might have tackled it in one of the small skiffs. Bardon and Debb, then the Captain, ran it in succession. That inspired Romer to emulation. He started to follow, alone in his boat, as George refused to go. I called Romer to come back. He seemed keenly resentful.

"Why, I could shoot that one with one hand tied," he exploded. "It's easy. Bardon showed me where to go. Then I watched. . . . Please let me go, dad!"

The glow in his face, the fire in his eye, the eloquence of his voice—all so poignantly significant of my own youth—operated against my better judgment.

"All right, son. Go ahead," I replied. "Try to do as Bardon did."

Then I hurried to an eminence on the ragged rock cliff to watch him. This rapid was the kind I especially feared, because it had the features that made risk. A heavy current, running into choppy waves, broke on a submerged rock, split and swept to each side. Below at the foot were other bad rocks, with channels between. It was not one of the swiftest, roaring kind of rapids, but it was quite bad enough, and I felt misgivings. Still, Romer had to shoot his first bad one sometime. Why not now? I let him go and somehow trusted the lad's daring and strength.

By the time he had reached the head of the rapid we were all on the cliff.

"He doesn't estimate the current," said Bardon. "Ought to be closer to this side or farther over."

I thought, myself, that Romer did not row fast or hard enough. He approached that rock too swiftly to suit me.

Bardon cupped his hands and yelled, "Go to the other side!"

Romer heard, for he began to row harder to try to pull the boat out of line with the rock. I saw that he had meant to make our side of it. But Bardon's instructions made him change his course, and too late.

"He's goin' to hit!" yelled Bardon.

My action seemed suddenly stultified. I froze. I stared. I saw him hit that rock a little aft of his left rowlock. The skiff rose, lurched, and almost turned over. Romer did not lose his seat or the oars, or apparently his self-possession. The boat slid off, luckily in good position, leaving him time to concentrate on the obstacles below. He picked the best channel and shot it perfectly.

Then I felt the need of sitting down suddenly. My frozen feelings thawed out with a vengeance. Presently I was confronted with the realization that a man suffers more poignant fears for his children than for himself. Later, when I went down to join the others below the rapids, I heard Romer declare:

"Aw, it'd been apple pie if Bardon hadn't yelled. I was going down this side of that rock, and he yelled for me to take the other side."

At six o'clock we arrived at the head of Horseshoe Bend Rapids. An old mining flume, like a picturesque suspension bridge, crossed the river. All around, the mountains stood up grandly, and some of the slopes bore grassy open patches and some gray weathered slides of rock. For the most part, however, all was green-spired firs. Oregon firs that yield the best spars for ships! Here they stood up straight and tall, by the thousands. The river took a glancing incline, swept into a white curve, and vanished in what appeared a rocky bend from which came a hollow roar.

We landed on a high sand bar, overgrown with willow and brush, and set up camp under the towering dark mountain. Tired as I was, I still had strength to carry up my bags and tackle. Everything except that which we had securely protected was wet and needed to be dried by the camp fire. One by one my weary Argonauts slipped to bed, leaving me alone with Takahashi.

"Me not tired," he said in reply to my query. "Me go ten more miles. Romer captain of our boat an' he do all rowing."

I was not the first up, but there were a good many after me. The morning was exquisite, without fog or moisture, cool, fresh, sweet with some rare fragrance of the mountains. I saw circles on the water made by rising fish, and that was the signal for me to get busy with my tackle.

After breakfast, Captain Mitchell and I crossed the river and began angling at the head of the swift incline. He hooked a steelhead on his second cast, a good-sized fish that leaped to freedom. A moment later I raised a big steelhead. He made so huge a boil on the water that I jerked the spinner away from him. On my next cast he hit it hard, and thinking I had him, I yelled lustily for everybody to look. Camp became an active place, but, unfortunately, I had no further opportunity to thrill my comrades, for the steelhead pulled free.

The boys rushed to fix up their tackle, while the Captain and I fished down round the bend. We were disappointed to find a heavy rapid and below that a deep gorge, hard to fish. Captain Mitchell caught one small steelhead and raised several others. I hooked a five-pounder, and after a short stiff battle lost him. We returned to camp hopeful that the evening fishing would bring better results.

Bardon called my attention to the singing of a bird. Its notes somewhat resembled that of a song sparrow, only they were wild.

"That's a water ousel," he said.

I was interested to inquire about this rarest of mountain birds, this dark strange haunter of the Oregon gorges. I had seen several, and much regretted my limited knowledge.

"Shore, I've knowed the ousel ever since I was a boy," said Bardon. "You don't see an ousel except in lonesome places. When he wakes up in the morning he has his bath, an' then he sings like you heard. Shore, he's a queer bird. His mate builds a nest on a rock or cliff an' you can hardly see it. She likes best a place under a waterfall, where she has to fly under or through the water to get to it. There she lays five white eggs."

This information was particularly gratifying to me, because I had already written my conjecture as to this lonely, beautiful bird and his mate and their isolated nest. It was my good fortune to see several of these rare nests. They were built under shelving rocks, high above the water, and appeared to be constructed of mud or clay, somewhat similar to that of the swallow. A small entrance showed at the apex of the cone-shaped nest. Most assuredly, when the baby water ousels reached the time of their first flight, they either took to wing at once or dropped in the water. I never saw two of these birds together. In the course of a whole day on the Rogue, I would sight three or four ousels, always alone, always flitting like a phantom under dark cliffs, or bobbing on a rock where the water flowed swiftly. Strange, wild bird, like the Indian's idea of the spirit of a river! The following day saw us on our way again. The true magnificence of the scenery at Horseshoe Bend did not fully dawn upon me until we had turned half of the curve and I could really view the bend. The first half of the rapids was bad, so that all faculties had to be set on lining our boats down safely. But once at the foot of the thundering falls, I had time to see and enjoy.

All around the mountain slopes rose precipitously, so that I received an impression of being surrounded by great green and gray slopes, insurmountable, rising to obliterate half the blue sky, and remarkable for the long slides of weathered rock, gray planes in the green incline, and the splendor of the Oregon firs, magnificent trees that rival the redwoods of California and cedars of Washington. It was good to see such standing virgin timber, untouched by the arch-fiend fire and the destructive, greedy hand of man.

The Rogue flowed round in a perfect horseshoe bend, and the ridge of land and rock that held the center of this wilderness stage was dwarfed by the lofty peaks far above. Yet, in itself it had the dignity of a low mountain. The steep rocky slopes were smooth and amber with heavy moss, over which flowering vines spread and pines and firs and oaks grew just sparsely enough. On top, a cluster of pines occupied a level stand. What a place for a cabin! A wanderer in the fields has two griefs—one that he cannot return to each and every one of the lonely beautiful places he has seen; and secondly, the realization that there are countless numbers of rare wild spots that he never will see. I do not know which is the more poignant.

We drifted into a hollow, reverberating canyon, where the river boiled and eddied in an endless solitude. Here and there we met ripples and rifts that Bardon trusted us to navigate safely. No one except myself had any trouble. My boat now seemed large and heavily laden, and in swift currents or slapping waves I could only with extreme difficulty handle her. I could go straight at the top of a rift and start down all right, but when I got through, the powerful current would carry me directly for a cliff. I hit two stern first, and rather too violently for comfort. These accidents, however, afforded the rest of my outfit considerable amusement.

"Hey, dad," Romer would yell, "what was the matter back there?"

And Ken would ask: "Say, did you hit a rock? I wonder how you ever got down that jungle Santa Rosa River you wrote about."

I wondered, myself. Youth has no thought or fear of danger. Rather a courting of peril! Manhood exercises reason, caution. At maturity a man has responsibilities. When I went down that wild jungle river of Mexico, the hot spirit of adventure had not been modified by cool reason.

We made three miles or more without mishap, encountering only one rapid of any dimension, and that we managed safely, as it was straight and clear. Then we came to one of those threatening constrictions and bends of the Rogue River Valley. Even before I heard the deep murmur of tumbling waters I knew there would be a bad rapid ahead.

Bardon waved his red flag, warning us to haul ashore at the head of this bend. Only a little white water was in sight. I got out and climbed over the huge mossy boulders and under the alders. The rapid was short, with an abrupt turn to the left, and at the foot toothed by some dangerous rocks. The current had immense volume and speed here. Bardon had already gone through. The Captain appeared next, rounding the corner, rowing hard, quarteringly into the protection of the eddy behind the point. He gained it, then straightened out and shot the narrow chute below. Debb followed, and next Bardon ran my boat through with apparent ease. Soon we had six of the boats grounded on the bar below, while Debb went back to fetch the last and heaviest one. I did not wait, but followed Bardon down to the head of the next fall. Here he motioned me ashore, and then backed over the incline.

When I had scrambled up on the rocks he was safely through a hundred yards of narrow white channel. Above me somebody yelled. I wheeled in time to see Debb thrown high upon a rock. He disappeared, and then the bow of his boat shot up. Wild yells from ashore urged me at breakneck pace over the rough rocks. When I reached the end of the long bar, I saw Ken running along, splashing in here and there to pick up floating articles. He shouted to me, "Rescue the lemons!" Soon I saw the surface of the current dotted with yellow lemons, but they were out of my reach, as were also two blue oars, sundry loaves of bread, a pair of shoes, various cans and boxes, and other articles I could not recognize.

When I got to the scene of the upset I saw the boat had lodged against two rocks and was submerged, all except the end of the bow and the one gunwale. Not ten feet from shore! It had happened that four of the boys were standing there waiting to see

Debb run this doubtful place, so that when he struck and the baggage spilled out, they rescued all but the small articles. The circumstance of their being at hand saved a valuable part of our outfit. I never got a clear idea of what had really happened. The boys all talked at once, and contradicted one another. Romer was tremendously excited and thrilled.

When Bardon returned and saw the boat, he threw up his hands and yelled, "How'n hell did Debb ever get stuck there?"

I did not voice my opinion as to that, or my belief that the boat would stay there. A tremendous current ran into it, so that it seemed as solid as the rocks. All the boys came forward with suggestions as to how to get her out, but Bardon met each and every one of them with some such remark as, "What'dye think I've learned on this river in thirty years?"

Under his instructions we set to work, and indeed we performed the labors of Hercules. We carried logs, cut huge poles, commandeered all the ropes in the other boats, and worked like Trojans. The water was cold as ice, and neck-deep at the stern of the boat, and very deep and swift under the bow. Ed, being a young contractor used to moving heavy objects, would not give up. He almost turned into a fish in his contortions to get ropes and poles under the boat. He cut and bruised his legs. All of us received sundry hard knocks.

Many funny accidents happened during our endeavor to pull this boat out.

Debb slipped off the rock and lost his straw hat in the current. It shot away from him, and his frantic efforts to catch it elicited yells from all of us. George Takahashi, as always where there was something hard to do, took a leading part in our labors. Once, while we were using a long heavy pole as a lever, George rode the lower end. It went up and up, but the nervy little Jap hung on until he was fifteen feet in the air. Then the short end of the pole slipped out from under the boat. Like a plummet George dropped, souse! into the water. He went under, but came up smiling.

"Gee! Water more cold as ice!"

Another time, the eight of us were hauling on a rope slung around the boat, with the idea of pulling her out. Captain Mitchell was

at the end of the rope up on the sand bar, while the rest of us were
in the water, some knee-deep and some deeper. I anticipated that
rope would break, but it did stand a mighty strain, so much that
we all pulled to the limit of our strength. When it broke suddenly, we went down like tenpins. I saw Captain Mitchell's feet
high above where his head should have been. We all fell hard.
Ken kicked Ed in the head. Bardon went clear under; I got
eyes and mouth full of sand; and everybody suffered in some
fashion.

Three long precious hours we toiled over that boat. It was our
largest and best one, and we needed it. But we toiled in vain.
We pulled the stern seat out; then the middle seat; then the ring-
bolt in the bow. Her seams opened up. The elbows came loose
from the sides. She cracked and groaned, and at last she crashed
to pieces. We left her remains there, ribs sticking out of the water,
tall poles propped under her.

"Bingo! There she goes!" ejaculated Ed.

Captain Mitchell laughed and said to me, "Well, there's another
Z. G. trademark left on the Rogue!"

From Rocky Rift Rapid, where this accident occurred, I could
see several miles down the river to where the mountain slope
showed patches, bare of timber, shining gold in the sunlight. These
were called "The Meadows" and promised us our next camp.

A low-walled canyon opening below Rocky Rift bend presented
a twisting rapid with huge boulders blocking the passage. Here
the boats had to be lined down on two ropes. Below we had easy
going—long deep courses and safe ripples—to our next stop. Ditch
Creek poured into the river here. A grassy slope, criss-crossed by
trails and dotted with clumps of moss-barked oaks, marked the
beginning of the meadows. They were the first meadows I ever
saw that stood on end.

We made camp along the brook, up on some high benches, back
of which ran the Rogue River Trail. Across the river lay a high
bar, called Battle Bar, where the last battle between the whites
and Indians of Oregon took place. To this day, skulls and arrow-
heads are unearthed at every freshet of the river. An old miner
lived in a shack on Battle Bar. He had been there forty years,
the last third of that period living alone, and he was now eighty-

four. His little patch of cultivated ground bore mute evidence to his meager existence. He gave us grapes and plums, and he was eager to sell me his land, a mining claim of twenty acres, which proposition I looked upon with favor at that time.

A heavy shower of rain overtook us before we had everything safe and snug in the tents, and there was a scramble to get blankets, guns, tackle, etc., in out of the wet. While this shower lasted, the sun shone on river and mountain, making glistening diamonds of the raindrops.

Steelhead and salmon were rising on the smooth water above the rapid, and the swirls and circles they made caused the Captain and me considerable perturbation. We donned waders, and hurrying through our supper, were across the river on the bar by sunset. We cast faithfully until dark—the Captain raising and catching one small steelhead, while I got nothing.

Cold and wet, I sought the camp fire and hovered around it until I was thoroughly dry and warm. During the night I was awakened by the heavy patter of rain on my tent. The time was a quarter past midnight. After that I was awake on and off until dawn, during which interval it rained steadily. The clouds cleared away somewhat after breakfast, and encouraged us to think the day might turn out well. But no sooner had we started to fish than a fine drizzle set in, and gathered strength at intervals until it was a gusty rain. I fished until noon, without result, then returned to camp.

Romer, using light tackle, had caught a number of river trout, and had lost several too heavy for the thin leaders. During the early afternoon it showered heavily. George Takahashi came in with one of his characteristic stories.

"I cast fly all way down to big bend. No luck. Cast long time in swift place where water go down, and turn round to come back. No bites. Put on little brown fly I had last year. Then I stopped casting far out across swift places to let fly float down, same way you all do. Me just cast out straight an' jerk fly back little, like bug trying jump. Something nibble at my fly. Lots of times. I keep on same way. Soon I have real bite. I hook him an' jerk him out pretty quick. Nice little steelhead. Then I go on fish same way. Git more nibbles. Then had awful strike. My line whiz. My rod bend down to water. Then big steelhead come up, crack! He jump way up high. More bigges' steelhead I ever see. He jump an' jump. He tuzzle like dog shakin' water off. Oh, awful big fish! He weigh twelve or fourteen pounds. He go down an' run up rapids. Make my line whistle in water. He jump out of white water, six feet up. Awful pretty! But I scared I no get him. Then he run downriver an' I run too. He jump more times. I count fourteen jumps. But he go faster down run than me. He take the line. I fall down. Break my tip. But steelhead still on. I get some line back. Lots big rock. Deep water. Me have to go slow. Steelhead make more faster run an' tear out hook. Then I feel awful sick. Lose 'em after long time. Make feel bad."

Takahashi exhibited a three-pound steelhead and a broken rod.

Straightway then I got into my fishing things and hied down to the lower end of this long riffle. The rain went with me and increased while I fished. The wind waxed stronger and colder until it had gained storm proportions. My hands grew numb and my body chilled through. But I never had even a nibble, though I tried George's way of casting as well as my own. By the time I was tired out the storm ceased, the clouds broke in the west, and the setting sun suddenly lit up the valley and river in a blaze of silver glory.

I trudged campward through the wet willows and under the dripping alders to end my seventh unsuccessful day of fly-fishing. Through misfortunes like this I am always sustained by an unfaltering faith, and the fisherman's fancy that sooner or later he will feel the fierce tug of a monster on his line. Captain Mitchell got as wet as I and had no better luck. The boys had spent most of the day carrying wood for the camp fire and pilfering eatables from the cook tent.

Next morning the sun shone dazzlingly on silver fog clouds that floated across the mountain slopes. I spent the morning drying out my things and doing odd jobs around camp. A forest ranger visited us and remembered Bardon from former trips. He said the big run of steelhead was not on yet. The best fishing-grounds were below camp, especially Winkle Bar, which was a mile down the trail.

Late that afternoon I tried again for a couple of hours, and just before sunset, using one of the Rogue River brown flies, named after myself, I raised and hooked my first steelhead for that trip. He was a five- or six-pounder, and tumbled over the surface at a great rate, and on his last hard run he tore loose.

When I reached the camp fire I got scant sympathy, because the other anglers had met with worse luck. Captain Mitchell had raised three steelhead and had hooked one. Ed had hooked three, one of them a heavy one, all of which had fought their way to freedom. Ken had one on in too swift water to hold. Romer told another weird tale of getting fast to steelhead when he was fishing for small trout.

Next morning I took the trail for Winkle Bar. It led round the mountain-side, through a thick forest of moss-covered oaks and under wide-spreading pines, cool, dark, and odorous of damp woods. And it came out on a bluff high above the river, from which point the wilderness scene would have been hard to rival.

Directly below, the river flowed dark and still between lofty cliffs that faced out of the dense forest. Ducks with white-barred wings floated on the light-mirroring water, and salmon breaking on the surface spread ever-widening circles. Across the river a magnificent fir forest rose out of a five-sloped canyon, rising bearded and mossy and black to the far, ragged summits.

The river widened to the open valley and spread over a large gravel bar down which it raced in glistening smooth incline to break into white water. Then it narrowed into a curving channel, rushing under a green bank, to fall over another rift and broaden again into another long twinkling riffle, which in turn repeated the fascinating vagary of the river.

Winkle Bar appeared to be a level flat of sand and gravel, dotted with clumps of small trees and sloping to a lengthy curve, along which the current glided.

I descended from my lofty perch and clambered over the boulder down to the sand. And then, up and down Winkle Bar, I fished all of one of the briefest and happiest days I ever had. I cast and rested and watched the river and the mountains, and listened to the murmur of running water. Then I cast again. Where the hours sped I never knew. Not a sign of a strike or sign of a fish did I have! But that did not matter. There was something in the lonely solitude of the great hills, something in the comradeship of the river that sufficed for me.

Toward sunset heavy clouds rolled up out of the west and billowed over the mountains. A gray mist like a veil drifted toward me, and presently I was enveloped in a fine, blowing, soft rain, sweet and wet and cold to the face. The valley filled with a gray pall. I heard the roar of a shower come toward me, pass over, and on up the river. Then I watched and listened to another storm. I grew uncomfortably cold, and after nine hours of Winkle Bar I surrendered to fatigue and failing day.

Wearily I climbed to the high trail. The falling oak leaves, and the thick carpet underfoot, reminded me that autumn was at hand, the melancholy prelude to winter. The leaves rustled; the trail was lonely. No sign of living creature, nothing to suggest the presence of man. The twilight filled the side canyons where the tinkling little streams fell to the river. And at last the flicker of a camp fire through the trees!

My angling comrades had brought in a few small trout and a two-pound steelhead.

Next day the river was five inches higher, and rising, and a little discolored. Captain Mitchell and I let the boys go down to Winkle Bar. They returned soon. Ed had a small fish, and Ken a beautiful steelhead of eight and one-half pounds.

To hear him tell of its capture was too much for me. I dare not attempt justice to that narrative. But most assuredly, if he had not shown the glistening pink-and-opal steelhead, with its grand head and leonine lines and wide tail, I never could have believed him.

I heard the boys talking about the caddis flies falling upon the water to be devoured by small trout. I had observed the same phenomenon during the last several days of our stay at the Meadows. The next time I went fishing, I took particular pains to watch for these flies, and I discovered the larvæ from which they had hatched, sticking on rocks at the river-side. Presently I found a caddis fly three-quarters out of his shell, so to speak; or for that matter, more than half born. His tail still adhered to the inside of the mysterious little shell, and when I helped him out he flew a few feet over the water and then fell. Vainly he fluttered his dark gray wings to rise. I fancied there was terror in his efforts. But though he struggled desperately and fluttered about over the surface, he did not have strength enough to get up. Suddenly a little trout snapped him in voraciously. Gone! He had vanished like a flash.

I was at once confounded by this incident. And I gave up precious moments when I might have been fishing to think about the little caddis fly, the wonder of his origin and the tragedy of his end. My aberration reminded me of a remark made by an Eastern angler, criticizing my stories about fish. He said that I never caught any fish, and all that I wrote about were pretty little birds and flowers. This, naturally, was meant to be a derogatory statement, but somehow it pleased me. And here I was at my old tricks. There is such a thing as love of nature. The fate of the caddis fly had struck me deeply.

For half a second it had enjoyed freedom from its cell-like home, and then it had fallen into the merciless current to be espied by the sharp eyes of a trout. Perhaps nature meant that fly to take its part in the furthering of its species before completing its existence by becoming food for fish. But only a very small per cent of nature's newly born creatures live long enough to propagate their kind. The life of this caddis fly, as a flying insect, was indeed brief. The facts connected with its presence there on that particular rock, however, were to my mind singularly wonderful and thought-provoking. The eggs had to be deposited in or near the river; the larvæ had to go through a long period, perhaps months, of incubation; they had to crawl out on the rocks into the heat of the sun, where the caddis flies were born. What was the instinct behind this living organism? Who propelled it? Why were the caddis flies born just when the steelhead were coming up the river to spawn? Where did this great moving spirit of living organism originate?

Well, I never arrived any nearer the truth, for all my thinking. But I question the supposition of its being a waste of time. The next two hours of patient fly-casting did not gain me as much.

On the following morning we decided the river had dropped half a foot and was clearer than it had been the day before. So we all scattered up and down the rocky shores. Romer and I tramped down to Missouri Bar, where the night before Ken and

Captain Mitchell had caught small steelhead. As usual, I did not raise a fish. But the walk along the mountain trail, six miles at least, was more than worth the effort, and it took considerable effort, walking in heavy boots and waders. What struck me most along this trail were the moss-covered oak trees. This moss was a rich golden green, and different from any I had seen. It resembled a thick covering of short lacy-leaved ferns and tiny-bladed grasses and covered the whole north side of the trees. In the sunlight, the growth absorbed an exquisite coloring of gold. I did not note that it had any ill effect upon the oaks. In the deep glens and ravines, where the shade was dense, these mossy trees strengthened the atmosphere of cool, moist, dank luxuriance.

A forest ranger told us that the moss had a practical use. In those few districts of this country where cattle were raised, during the season of drought when the grass would fail, these oak trees were cut down so that the cattle could feed on the moss. Starvation was thus often averted.

George Takahashi came proudly into camp that evening with a fine steelhead weighing five and three-quarter pounds.

"I ketch him easy," said George, with a grin. "Right by camp here. Make little cast. Up come steelhead. He jump clear out to get my fly. Gee! he hungry. He grab it an' I hook him. He run off and jump three times. But I hold him hard an' soon jerk him out on bank. My! But he little one beside that big one I had other day. That one three times as big. 'Iffteen pounds, I bet."

As we had expected, the authorities above Grants Pass opened the gates of the irrigation dam and let a flood of muddy water down to defile the clear waters of the Rogue. The river rose about a foot, dropped a little, then came up again, spoiling two days or more of fishing.

Irrigation dams are a necessity to our growing country and to the thirsty land where the famous Oregon peaches, apples, and pears are grown. Any good fisherman can spare a few days from his vacation or fishing trip for the need of the state and the farmers. However, I would like to add that irrigation above Grants Pass, as in other localities subject to the same conditions, is frightfully destructive to the young salmon and steelhead. Sometimes the farmer's land is covered with small fish to the extent of many thousands. Naturally the farmer is not going to put forward any objection to the waste of young fish, for the simple reason that they make the very best of fertilizer. Somebody, though, ought to take account of this careless, wasteful, unsportsman-like destruction of game and food fish.

Such examples are common all over the United States. That kind of thing is one of the grave defects of our federal and state governments. Who cares? Only, for instance as far as the rivers are concerned, a few sentimental fishermen? But even they should band together to protect so much of vanishing America for their children. Our country is still young; its boundless resources are not yet gutted; thousands and millions of men exploit what is not really theirs for their own selfish ends. Coal, oil, timber, minerals, the great schools of food fishes, are all natural products of our vast outdoors. I do not advocate that they should belong to the government, but the government should see to it that the men dealing with these resources should not gut them and not spoil the beauty and health-giving properties of the forests and rivers.

This Rogue River was named by the French, *Rouge*, because of the red color which it takes on at seasons when the mining is at its height.

I expected to find the Rogue, after we left Alameda, twenty miles below Grants Pass, to be one of the wildest, purest, and most beautiful of all rivers. It was certainly one of the most beautiful, but the other attributes failed. Miners, prospectors, half-breed Indians, and a few whites scattered down the valley, effectively kill any suggestion of utter solitude. There were wild stretches of the river, to be sure; but just when you imagined you were drifting into an untrodden wilderness then your dream would be dispelled.

The evening of the third day of muddy water, we decided we would pack and take to the boats next morning. This break I dreaded, for before us lay Mule Creek Canyon, which was almost impassable, owing to bad rapids, and especially at a narrow cut not more than ten feet wide through which the water rushed and the boats had to go. Bardon did not relish shooting this place, and objected to any of us attempting it. Debb actually confessed his fear. Romer asked a thousand questions about this canyon, the rapids, the narrow places, how many people had been drowned there, what it was like, how swift was the water, whether one could swim out if one's boat struck, etc., etc.

Bardon lost patience with the boy and yelled at him: "I've told you a dozen times. Pretty soon you'll be tellin' me how to shoot that canyon."

After all this preamble, Romer had the nerve to ask me, "Say, dad, if I wear a life-preserver round my neck will you let me take my boat through Mule Creek Canyon?"

The last evening before we left the Meadows camp, Captain Mitchell had his first experience with a big steelhead. About sundown he began fishing at the upper end of Winkle Bar. He is a very careful angler, fishing downstream slowly and covering every foot of water. He fished through the riffle with a Golden Grouse fly, and went back to repeat this. Two more trips he made through Winkle Bar, using the same fly. Then he changed to a Royal Coachman, and waded down once with this one. For some reason or other he changed back to the Grouse, and about the middle of the riffle he raised an enormous steelhead.

He saw the fish come from the middle of the stream, saw at least two feet of broad pink-and-white side, saw the deep swirl in the water, and lastly saw the steelhead follow the fly downstream, take it, and hook himself. He made a fierce run clear across the river, and then started upstream. Captain Mitchell said he felt as if he were hooked to a heavy salmon. The fish plunged up against the strong current, dashed back across the river, then came toward the angler. Slack line gave the steelhead freedom. The Captain found the barb of his hook broken. It might have been lost on the stones at a back cast, and again it might have been broken by the fish. Captain Mitchell inclined to the former idea.

"Wonderful fast game fish," he said to me. "But he never jumped once or ran downstream."

His experience illustrates several facts regarding the Rogue steelhead. It acts like an Atlantic salmon at times. On the other hand, there are times when steelhead will rise to anything and a whole school of them can be hooked in one pool.

The Thrill and Pleasure of a Fine Long Cast

PLATE LXVII

Solitude—the Sliding River—and a Rising Trout

PLATE LXVIII

We were up at five o'clock next morning, getting ready for the long-dreaded encounter with Mule Creek Canyon. At seven o'clock, before the sun had pierced through the gray shroud of cloud over the mountains, we were on our way. Shallow rapids, rifts, and bars alternated with an occasional deep channel, overshadowed by mossy and lichened cliffs, where wild ducks whirred by before us and the water ousel uttered his plaintive protest at our approach. I was sorry to see the last of Winkle Bar, and resolved to get possession of that particular strip of sand and rock if such were possible.

From that point we had a fine pleasant run to the mouth of Mule Creek. It appeared to be a goodly sized brook of crystal water, flowing down from out of a rugged iron-walled gorge into a wide, still pool. At the sand bar at the mouth I saw a long pole armed with a huge hook like a gaff; and this, Bardon explained, was used by natives to jerk out the salmon. A deep roar swelled up from the canyon below. I caught a glimpse of white water turning out of sight round a dark corner of rock wall.

We left the boats at the sand bar above the canyon, and while Bardon took Debb, the Captain, and Ed across the river to look over the bad places below, the rest of us climbed prodigiously in and out of old placer-mining holes up to the trail. It was more than a relief to reach the level, shaded path along the timbered mountain-side. We passed the sullen roaring rapids and went on half a mile, to emerge into the open sunlight, along a bluff slope where we could look down into Mule Creek Canyon. It did not appear very deep or dangerous. At the first available descent, Romer and I and Takahashi clambered down to points of vantage along the rim.

From there I could see the white seething river, perhaps forty feet wide, swirling and boiling along at swift pace. Up the canyon I caught glimpses of several sharp rapids from which came the ear-filling roar. The Narrows, which was the most dangerous place, was some distance below me, and I aimed to photograph the boats from my position and then hurry down river.

Bardon soon appeared in his long green boat, heavily laden. He did not seem to be having a particularly hard time of it. He disappeared, came into sight again, passed on under me round the bend. Next came the Captain in his small boat. He was not making the speed I had noted in Bardon. I saw him working hard at the oars. His boat acted queerly, swerving this way and then the other, which movements, I grasped, were owing to peculiarities in the current. But he slid by in good shape and vanished round the corner of the canyon. I was glad I could not see him run The Narrows. I had asked him not to, but he had expressed no concern as to the outcome.

Soon Debb's blue boat showed sharp against the white water of the canyon. Ed was with him in the stern, with a pike pole ready. The heavily laden boat, full of our food supplies and utensils, came along at express speed. When they hit the lower end of the first fall, the stern went out of sight in the white water. So did Ed. The boat bobbed up, and came on rather low down, I thought. Debb was working strenuously at the oars. Ed was poking at the cliffs with his pole. The canyon up there appeared to be about forty feet wide. Then the boat disappeared under the bulge of rim, and soon emerged to run down the white-green slant of river nearest my position. This time the whole stern end of the boat went under. When she came out of that she was almost full of water. Debb endeavored to pull toward the cliff.

The boat rolled in the current, and as it got directly under me I saw the water run over one gunwale and fill her. I was struck cold and numb. She was plainly sinking. Ed threw things overboard and, grasping one of Takahashi's buckets, he bailed frantically. The removal of half a dozen bucketfuls buoyed her a bit. Hope that she would not sink roused in me. Debb pulled with all his might. They passed my position and I photographed them, yelling encouragement as I did so. The boat went out of my sight under the wall. I ran down the river to find a place where I could see. As good fortune had it, they had pulled round a corner into a little cove where Ed held on to the wall while Debb bailed in a haste that told much. I discovered, to my intense relief, that they had the situation in hand and were practically out of danger. Whereupon I hurried down along the rough rim to find The Narrows. A deep bellowing roar announced it around the next corner.

My first sight of the most dangerous place on the Rogue River did not fit the picture in my mind. It did not look so bad. Narrow it was, being only about ten feet wide that stage of water, but it belied its real peril.

Two low points of rock, one slanting down from the opposite side, and the other, a ledge of cliff on my side, reached out diagonally toward each other across the stream. All the tremendous volume of the Rogue River had to pass between them at sharp speed.

Takahashi held a position below me, almost level with the river, and when he became aware of my presence he pointed to an oar he had manifestly salvaged out of the notch in the cliff where the water eddied in and out of the swirling current. This place was thirty or forty feet below The Narrows. I recognized the oar as belonging to Captain Mitchell's boat, and momentarily my blood ran cold. But he had started with four oars, and loss of one did not necessarily spell disaster. Nevertheless, I was at once uneasy, and found it hard to remain there to watch the other boats come through.

The more I studied the current of the river at this place, the more I began to appreciate its menace. It changed every moment in volume, action, and sound.

Along the dark wall above The Narrows the seething water rose in a bulge, pushing up a foot higher than the center of the river. It came from some subterranean force not visible on the surface. Manifestly the canyon here was very deep. Then at The Narrows two currents shot down, deflected from each cliff to meet in a V-shaped point that suddenly took on a circular motion, very swift. Deep suck-holes opened and whirled downstream. Whirlpools! Below the constriction in the canyon the river was indeed a maelstrom. Next the deep holes filled up, smoothed out, but the swirl of the current in no wise lessened. There was no regularity about the appearance of these whirlpools. They came at the fancy of this ruthless river. Some were deep, four feet and more, and others were shallow. I noted that where the deep whirlpools formed and swirled down, the roar of water took on a hollow sound. It was like demoniac laughter.

Suddenly I saw Debb's blue boat sweep into sight, flying as if down a mill race. It had the middle of the narrow channel. Ed knelt in front, pole in hand. Down they shot, and at a moment when the whirlpools were full. But for Ed's violent thrust and shove with his pole, the boat would have struck the lower jaw of the narrow gate. At that, it just missed the projecting black rock. They passed safely, and went on swiftly out of range of my vision.

Only then did I become conscious of the strain I had been under. I breathed fully once more, and gradually relaxed to a study of the changing moods of this strange river. Nevertheless, I anxiously waited for the next boat, which I expected would be mine, with Bardon at the oars.

Half an hour passed. The delay began to get on my nerves. My boat was the largest of all, and had the greatest beam and perhaps the heaviest load. Not a good boat to take through The Narrows! In swift currents I had not been able to budge her an inch. All my tackle, films, camera, etc., were in this boat. It was impossible to pack our outfit around Mule Creek Canyon. Not few had been my qualms about the safety of things that on a trip like this were precious.

Then all at once my red skiff swept round the corner of wall. I saw it with tingling trepidation. Bardon had the oars poised, dropped one, then the other. Ken crouched in the front. As I had anticipated, my heavy boat came with greater speed than any of the others. My skin began to stretch and prickle; my heart throbbed; I felt curiously cold all over. But I did not forget to use my camera.

Bardon shot the narrow gap perfectly, but as he slid through the great whirlpools opened, and they threw the front of the boat into the lower bulging jaw of rock. He struck hard, and a second later the other end hit the cliff opposite. The vessel jammed, and careened upstream, so that the furious water began to pour in.

Above the roar of waters I heard Ken's shrill yell. His face was white as a sheet. Bardon showed his self-possession and knowledge. Before it was too late he threw his weight over on the downstream gunwale of the boat and careened her over on that side. Then leaping like a tiger to the bow he shoved away from the wall. That released the stern end, and away she swept like a live thing. And as quickly he leaped back to the oars. As the boat passed out of my sight, I crouched there, realizing how narrowly the loss of boat and outfit, perhaps life, had been averted.

I scrambled out, having seen all of the Rogue River Narrows that I wanted. It took me an hour of climbing and descending to reach the point below where our flotilla was moored in smooth water. The boys had passed above me on the trail on their way back up the canyon to fetch the small skiffs through.

"Most infernal place I ever saw," exclaimed Captain Mitchell. "Right off I felt a strangeness in that current. It dragged at my boat and oars. In one place it whirled me round and round. By golly! I was stumped. At The Narrows I hit the right-hand wall and lost an oar. I saw that oar stand up straight out of a whirlpool and go down, down, down out of sight, standing straight up all the time. Below I warded off collision by using my other oar and got out. Believe me, I was lucky. It's a hundred times worse than it looks, and I don't want any more of that."

Debb and Ed ran the gorge in a small boat without mishap, but Bardon, in Romer's skiff, which was sharp fore and aft like a canoe, had a hair-raising experience.

"Shore, Romer's boat ought to be called Suicide Jane!" he ranted. "I got drawn in that whirlpool below The Narrows, an' I'll be damned if I could pull out. Went round an' round a dozen times. I thought once we'd be sucked under, but the hole filled up an' then I pulled out. . . . Thank God we're by that place."

The Rogue below Mule Creek Canyon became once more a gliding, eddying, murmuring river, with long ripply bars and shallow rifts and winding lanes between dark-faced cliffs, where moss and flowers and vines and green trees took precarious root; and where white water like lace fell off the cliffs, and the water ousels flitted from ledge to ledge. A warm fragrant breeze moved up the stream, promising us the sun-flooded valley below. Again the sweet silence grew marked, and the splashing of an oar seemed desecration. We floated and glided and rowed several miles between green-gray, craggy peaks mounting ever higher and higher; and the wilderness and solemnity of the mountains grew ever more thrilling.

Then from round a bend came a strange deep roar! It changed all the scene, all the meaning of the wilderness. Menace! This river was indeed a rogue. That roar filled out, expanded, gathered volume, and swelled until it was thunder. A towering slope of rough rock hid whatever lay beyond, and when we turned that corner the river appeared to fall into an abyss whence pealed the mighty volume of sound. I thought of the Athabasca, God-forsaken river of the north, which the Indians believed was the spirit of thunder. We went deep down between giant mountains that hid the sun. Bardon led us almost to the very edge of the falls, into a cove under bulging rock walls.

"Blossom Bar!" he yelled to us. "An' she's a wolf—she's a bear cub! It'll take all day tomorrow to drag an' line an' skid the boats round here."

To a worn-out group of weary fishermen this was not a felicitous time to announce such an obstacle. What a task to pack up what few belongings we could dispense with for the night! All save tents, bedding, food, and utensils we left in the boats. I was utterly exhausted when my own tasks were done, too weary to eat, too tired almost to watch the gold sunset on the crags, too worn out to appreciate the wild grandeur of this spot. Blossom Bar thundered out of sight under us so that we had to shout to hear one another.

Our camp was high up above the river in the woods where the remains of early-day mining camps were still in evidence. Two ice-cold crystal streams poured down from the timber-and-crag-choked gorge opening into the river valley. Their music was drowned by the roar of the river. Twilight passed swiftly into night. The sweet air grew cold. How warm and cheerful the blazing camp fire! Then further reward for that terrifying, fatiguing day was the bed of warm blankets spread on the odorous springy fir boughs. How the tumbling waters dinned in my ears! And rolled on sonorously, thunderously, into my dreams.

The sunlight and the silver fog were contending for right over the valley next morning when I crawled out lame, humpbacked, and sore. The strain in my side appeared to be wearing away, though it hurt me to bend. It afforded me considerable satisfaction to see all of the outfit the worse for wear. Captain Mitchell had a sprained ankle; Romer's hands were blistered and cut, and his legs were bruised; Bardon and Debb had been badly battered by boats and oars; and the others were correspondingly crippled. Under such conditions the hardest day dawned!

After breakfast, Captain Mitchell and I climbed to the top of the rocky rim above the river and looked down into what they called Blossom Bar. It should have been called Boulder Bar, for the river was choked with boulders, some as large as houses, all worn round and scalloped by the action of water. Between them rushed and raced the white seething torrents and cascades. A tremendous tumult roared up at us, making conversation useless. We had to make signs to each other. The worst of the raging waters passed close to the cliff under us and between that and the largest rock, fully sixty feet high. A boat trusted to that current would instantly be destroyed. There did not appear to be any other channel wide enough to pass a boat. I thought I descried a place somewhat closer to the other shore, where a slant of green water poured between a round boulder and a flat one, almost submerged. It seemed hardly wide enough, and besides that, the drop was considerable. Below this first series of irregular falls the river widened into a white bubbling level, broken by several huge boulders, and rushed on to its numerous channels in the second series of falls. Then farther below ran swift current with high waves and hidden rocks for several hundred yards. Blossom Bar certainly was what the Captain called it—one hell of a rapid.

We broke camp, packed our stuff down to the boats, and loading them rowed across to the other side where a shallow cove afforded us a place to unload.

Bardon, after removing most of his freight, took Ed and Debb out in his boat and left them each on a rock above where the water began its green slant. They lowered him by his boat line. Bardon stood in the stern, using his pike pole to shove out of the way of rocks and passages upon which he did not want to descend. They lowered him right through the worst part of that side of the falls, down to the narrow chute Captain Mitchell and I had marked. Here the intrepid Bardon dropped the pike pole and stepped out on the flat rock. Then he edged his boat into that chute and waved to Ed and Debb to drop the rope. As they did so, he powerfully heaved on the boat, tilting it somewhat, and then he let go. Flash! The big boat slipped over and down out of sight, to reappear riding the white waters below. Bardon reached for the line. It was flying down. Once he nearly toppled over into that caldron. What nerve he had! But he could not catch the rope. Suddenly he straddled the chute, in an action as astounding as swift, and reached down to catch the line, just in the nick of time. But he faced upstream and the line was between his legs, while the boat was swerving down behind him. I held my breath. What would he do? I forgot my camera. But difficult as the position was, Bardon met it. He whirled his left leg over the rope back to the flat rock, and turned to face downstream just as the rope straightened. Then he held hard. The big boat swerved round behind a rock out of the press of current. Next Bardon leaped prodigiously to a lower boulder, then to another and another, like a mountain goat. And lastly he reached a string of boulders over which he stepped to haul the boat into a comparatively quiet and protected place where he moored it fast.

"Pack down the stuff," he yelled to us. "We'll reload here, an' I'll run the rest of the rapids."

While he scrambled over the rocks on shore and the slippery ledges and through the water back to the boats, evidently to repeat that wonderful performance, we began to portage our belongings and the supplies down below. We knew before we started what a stupendous job we had on hand. Debb and Ed were marooned on their two rocks at the head of the rapids, there to line Bardon down with the next boat. I could not see as I packed things down, for then I had all I could do to stand upright, but on the return trip I had time to watch Bardon.

He went out the second time in the blue boat, which had been almost emptied of our food supplies, and performed precisely as before up to a certain point. As the blue boat slid into the chute, Bardon did not succeed in tilting it, and it shot half through, then stuck with bow ten feet in the air. Bardon could not budge it. But the quick-witted boatman grasped an oar, and using it as a lever he pried the boat up until it loosened and slid on through. We greeted this performance with yells, all of which were drowned by the roar of the falls.

Ken, Romer, George, and I carried boxes, bags, bales, grips, making veritable pack animals of ourselves. Yet there was a zest,

an excitement in this that had been wanting in other labors up
the river. We went at that Blossom Bar obstacle with all the vim
and vigor possible. Romer had several hard falls on the rocks.
He was strong and impatient. I had to work slowly on account
of my back. I sweat my upper garments as wet as those in which
I waded. Finally Bardon signed for George and Captain Mitchell
to take positions on the rocks below to help him, and that left the
rest of the packing to the three of us. We became toiling galley
slaves.

Still, I took time to look occasionally and snap a picture.

Bardon lowered two of the small boats with an ease and dexterity that amazed me. Then he followed with my heavy red
boat, Old 76, as we called her. I had removed most of my
belongings, so felt no concern on their account, but I did not want
to lose the boat. She had more beam than any of the others.

This beam, however, did not even check her at the narrow chute.
Bardon gave her a tilt and she glided over and down like a swan.
A moment later we saw that the line was too short. It got away
from Ed, then Debb. Bardon risked his life bending over the chute
to try to grasp the rope. The red boat swerved down free, and as
if to tantalize us, drifted behind a submerged rock and floated back.
We saw then that the rope had caught in the rocks. The boat
drifted off, and swung into the current and dragged at the rope.
Bardon could not reach it. But Captain Mitchell, on the rock
farthest out in the rapid, lay down, and with hands gripping the
stone he let himself down, down, down, until I could see only his
head and shoulders. He reached for the rope with his foot. What
a daring act that was! Twice he failed, and I expected to see him
slide into the white water. On the third attempt he got his foot
under that light line and drew it up, while at the same time he
hunched himself inch by inch back on the rock. His difficulties
were not over even after he stood upright, rope in hand. Bardon,
seeing he had the line, leaped again from rock to rock, a marvelous
feat, considering the distance, the wet surfaces, and the roaring
channels between. But he reached Captain Mitchell in time to
save Old 76.

The remaining boat, which happened to be the small eighteen-
foot skiff fondly appropriated by Romer, was the double-ender,

sharp fore and aft, and very treacherous because too narrow. It was, however, the easiest boat to get over that particular fall.

With the boats all down over at least the worst part of Blossom Bar, no one except myself happened to remember Ed and Debb marooned out on their respective rocks at the head of the rapids. I saw Ed cup his hands at his mouth and yell, no doubt for help, or at least in protest against this ignominious neglect. He and Debb exchanged signs and shouts, and manifestly decided to escape from their position without aid. Debb still had a piece of rope. He tied this round his boulder and let himself down to another rock, from which, by violent exertions, he reached a second, and from that a place of safety.

Ed had a different problem. He possessed no rope and his rock was the last upstream above the rapid. It was a large high boulder, and the nearest one to it looked fully fifteen feet distant. But Ed took off in a running leap, and alighted half on the rock and half in the water. He held on and scrambled up, and sat down a moment as if to recover from his exertions. The next rock took a lesser jump, and from that one he gained shallow water.

Another hour was consumed in packing the outfit down to where the boats were moored. This brought us to afternoon, and there was the rest of the rapid below. Bardon knew what we did not know—that once we had reloaded the boats, we would soon see the end of Blossom Bar. He guided his own skiff through and had a hard struggle with the rushing currents. The smaller vessels were, however, easy to run. With Old 76 and the food-supply boat Debb helped Bardon at the oars, and they came through successfully.

At the foot of Blossom Bar we rested and ate a belated lunch. A little below roared two narrow rapids, straight and steep, over which we lined all the boats on long ropes, with several men holding and one to run ahead. Captain Mitchell's boat broke away, but, fortunately, drifted in close to shore, where it lodged momentarily. We secured it, though not any too soon.

"Now you can all throw up your hats," shouted Bardon. "We've got four miles of nice water, all the way to Solitude."

Personally, I was too weary to throw up my hat, but I rejoiced, nevertheless. And in spite of my waning physical endurance I managed to hang to the oars of my barge all the way to our next camping-ground. And what a beautiful ride it was! We had but little still water, and many long ripples where the river swept murmuringly over gravelly bars, and the boats made fifteen miles an hour.

The long shallow riffle above Solitude struck me immediately as a wonderful ground for steelhead. It was half a mile and more in length, flowing through a wide valley, with high colored banks, and the mountains somewhat back, and it had three breaks where the current hurried round and over rocks. At the lower end, ledges with deep channels between and flat-topped rocks just under the surface, appeared to be alluring places to fish. A wide gravel bar paralleled the river.

Below this bar the river turned abruptly to the left, forming two swift white narrow rapids, which we negotiated safely, though not without qualms as well as thrills. And round this turn stretched Solitude. It was a riffle and a bar, a most beautiful place and well named. The bar was a quarter of a mile long, slightly curved, and its gravel and sand sloped up gradually to fine wooded benches under the lofty mountain. Clean, lonely, sweet-smelling place, with the gliding river below; and across it the green-and-yellow timbered mountain rising splendidly, with gray crags touching the skies.

Sunset caught us in camp again, where we demonstrated the marvelous reserve force in man by putting up tents, cutting boughs of fragrant fir for beds, and eating prodigiously before we fell like logs into the deep slumber of exhaustion.

Next day we made the camp the pleasantest and most comfortable of our trip thus far. That left some hours for fishing. I rested most of this time, and watched the big steelhead rise on the river, and the little trout splash after flies. The caddis fly was here much in evidence. That evening I saw deer, mink, flocks of ducks, and a sea gull, from in front of my tent. Romer caught some small trout, and George and Captain Mitchell brought in small steelhead.

Above Solitude a native named Billings had settled in the woods to homestead a place. He knew the river, and assured us it was full of steelhead. The night before he had caught five, one weighing seven pounds, off the bar where we were camped. As the water had cleared again, the fishing ought to be good, he said, especially if a little rain came.

The third day of our stay at Solitude was an ideal one for fly-fishing. It was cloudy, dark, and cool, but not too cool. I started out with great hopes of catching my first steelhead on a fly for this trip. I angled along the upper shore of the bar, which Billings said was a good water for steelhead. The other fellows scattered up and down the river.

Romer, after an exhaustive search among his tackle—and mine—finally decided on a two-and-one-half-ounce Leonard rod with reel and line to suit, and waded the riffle above the rapid. I could just see him as from time to time I glanced in his direction. He liked light tackle and he liked to catch small trout.

By and bye a faint yell pealed above the low roar of the water. I wheeled to see Romer running for dear life along the head of the rapid, with a bending buggy-whip of a rod telling what had happened to him. I feared he would break his neck. Romer is fast on his feet; he runs the hundred in ten and one half seconds, which is swift for a boy. Well, he was then doing a hundred in less than ten flat, to my notion. He beckoned frantically for me, so I laid down my rod and ran up the bar. I nearly fell, myself. Those smooth marble boulders were like ice. When I got to the head of the bar, Romer was halfway down the long rapid, and he was traveling like a whirlwind. Of course the steelhead had taken out all his line, which accounted for his haste.

Suddenly Romer slipped and plunged headlong, face down, into the water. He went almost out of sight, but he kept his rod up. Then he leaped erect as swiftly as he had fallen, and came tearing down through the shallow water to the bar.

"Look!—dad!" he panted, exhibiting his reel, which had about a quarter inch of line left on the spool.

"Better reel some in quick!" I replied.

In the still water below the rapid he had a chance with the steelhead, and after a quarter of an hour he beached a beauty of about four pounds. I complimented Romer on so creditable a performance with a flimsy light tackle, and I advised against further use of it where he might hook a big steelhead.

He was wringing wet all over, with bruised and bloody elbow and various other lacerations he failed to note on the moment. His dark eyes beamed, his face glowed, and he actually stuttered as he told the story of that fight. I lived over again the thrill of wild sweet youth, of adventure in its incipiency.

I fished long that day, without any kind of a rise, and could not account for my persistent bad luck.

Romer hooked several other steelhead, only to lose them; Takahashi caught a small one, as did Ed. Captain Mitchell had a fine day, taking nine steelhead, the largest three pounds. He used a small English salmon fly, invented by himself and manufactured by Hardy Brothers of London. The steelhead rose voraciously for this little double hook called Dusty something.

Bardon and Debb returned to camp with a fine four-point buck deer, which they had killed and packed down the mountain. They reported all kinds of deer sign on the high ridges above, where the acorns were abundant. So all together this day was a capital one for everybody. I had to take my sport out of the achievements of my comrades, but this was easy for a story-teller.

Every lane has an end, and every trail, and even every period of bad luck. On the thirteenth day of my protracted spell of unrewarded fishing, late in the afternoon, I caught my first steelhead on a fly.

The day had been cloudy and fish were rising. I had cast until I was weary, and had made several visits to the river, both up and down. I was fishing in front of the camp, more as a matter of perseverance than anything else, using an English salmon fly, a Golden Grouse. I felt a vicious tug on my line and thought, of course, I was snagged on a rock. But my rod dipped and my reel shrieked—then a fine plump steelhead leaped in midstream. In the sudden excitement, the realization that I really had a steelhead, I handled him rather stupidly; but he was well hooked and eventually I got him.

Later I caught two small ones in the same place. My largest weighed three pounds, a fresh-run fish, all opal and pink and shimmering silver. He was indeed a delight to my eye, and furthermore I had very hungry intentions toward him. These fresh-run steelhead, right from salt water, were delicious.

In camp that night there was much merriment at my expense. George said: "My goodnish! Now you be good humor!"

Romer remarked: "Well, dad, you've busted your slump and now you ought to hit about four hundred."

Captain Mitchell added: "Fine, Doc. The first hundred fish are always the hardest to catch!"

Ken queried, suspiciously: "Are you sure you didn't catch that steelhead on a spinner?"

I had already taken five fish on a spinner, but we did not count any except those caught on a fly. Captain Mitchell had twenty-five to his credit, George twelve, and the other boys several each, including Ken's big one of eight and a half. We had fried trout and broiled trout and smoked trout. Bardon screwed up his face at the sight of fish for food, but we excused him, as he was a market fisherman.

Billings called at our camp and said the river was getting in good condition again. One of the packers coming up the trail from Illahe reported a run of steelhead at Agness. A native named Briggs, a good fisherman according to Bardon, caught a twelve-pound steelhead on a Royal Coachman. Later I met this fellow Briggs, and he verified the statement. "Gave me a 'tarnal tussel ketchin' him," he told me. "Lots of big steelhead in the river, but they ain't risin' good." He said it took a good while to learn where the steelhead were in the habit of lying along the riffles. Most of the fly-fishing could be accomplished from shore. They did not rise readily to a submerged fly. The best way was to cast near shore, along the bars, or outside rocks and ledges, and then drag the fly across the surface in little jerks, imitating the motions of a fly or bug endeavoring to escape from the water.

This method, in fact, was very much like that used by Captain Mitchell and perhaps accounted for his success. I had noted, too, that the Captain would cast a long while over one spot, especially if he saw fish rising. This was not the way I had learned to fish for steelhead. Burnham, Wharton, Adair, all expert fly-fishermen, the best perhaps on the upper Rogue, had all taken pains to instruct me and teach me their best methods. I had gained something of proficiency in them, but evidently they were not so well suited to the lower Rogue. I held, however, that the most important thing of all was to find where the fish lay. The native fishermen along the river claimed that steelhead would not rise when the sun was on the water. This rule hardly held good in our case, though early morning and evening were the most favorable time, and a cloudy day was desirable.

Next morning I was up at daylight. The mountain tops were not obscured by fog, which fact proclaimed a cloudy day. When it was fully light, I saw that the clouds were broken, showing blue sky between. Soon rosy tones tinged the eastern summits. Solitude at that hour was exquisitely beautiful, lonely, and wild. A little while after I began to fish the steelhead started to rise here and there across the river, under the gray cliff, and down the smooth end of the bar above the rapids. I changed my fly to a Professor with a jungle wing. And on my second cast I saw a curling hole break on the surface, then the gleam of pink and white. Thump! He hit my fly, and with a surge under, he rushed across the river, then out into the air. I gasped. He was as long as my arm—a glistening broad steelhead, furious in his action. I reeled in, somewhat dazed, and forgot for the time being to bemoan my miserable fate as a fisherman. I cast over the same place. Then again, and swash! I saw and felt another steelhead hook himself. When he leaped he looked small compared with the first one, but he was vicious and strong. He ran off my line, and buzzed out high into the air, then raced upstream, while I followed along the bank. Turning, he shot down, went high into the air again, and next surged deep, giving me time to regain line. He plunged low for ten minutes or more, after which he made an amazing leap, fully six feet out of the water. How thrilling to see him! Then he worked downstream, finally into a cove behind a gravelly bar, where I beached him. My left arm was tired and I certainly was glowing with excitement. It was a little after six o'clock and only George appeared to be up. He said: "Nice fat fish. More bigger than other one you get."

I was amazed to find that steelhead weighed only three and a half pounds. I think I had estimated his weight by his quality of gameness. After all, the morning turned out to be sunny.

Captain Mitchell and Ken, fishing the opposite shore, had shade for a considerably longer period than the rest of us. The Captain had a fine time all by himself, casting from a high bank and getting his fly caught on branches. I saw him climb one tree, and I yelled, "Hey, Captain, are you fishing for eagles?"

He had a pool over there that must have been full of small steelhead, because I saw a rise every cast he made, and he caught three small ones while I watched.

Romer quit fishing and appeared to be taken with a sudden longing for work. He rowed across the river and collected a boatload of old lumber from a deserted mining camp. This he brought back and packed up to his tent, a prodigious feat. He spent the morning with ax, hammer, saw, and nails, and erected the weirdest sort of table, bench, seat, and fly that I ever saw in any camp. He was having fun in the way of a boy. If I had given him such a morning task, all that hard labor, likely he would have made the valley resound with his yell, "Aw, I want to fish!"

Ken returned at noon. He had a dejected air.

"Had two big ones on and lost them both. Fished in the darndest holes—up high, and I saw steelhead rise, lots of them, big and little. They didn't want any flies, or I didn't know how to make them strike. Guess I'm a punk fisherman."

We had another rain, which Billings predicted would be fine for the river. "But there won't be any big steelhead until around October fourth," he added. "On October first, the salmon cannery at Gold Beach closes down and the market fishermen haul in their nets. Then the big fish get a chance to run up the river. It takes about four days for the first of the run to reach here."

This was news relative to the significance of the taking or killing of large steelhead by the net fishermen. Bardon declared the large mesh of the nets permitted the steelhead to swim through, though some were killed in the haul. My own opinion was that nets of any mesh would not only block a run of steelhead, but cause the loss of many, entirely aside from the doubtful fact of market fishermen and canneries not taking steelhead found in the nets. We met an old native who lived somewhere between Solitude and Illahe, and he declared he never caught any fish until October. At Grants Pass the best fishing is always in October.

DOWN THE ROGUE TOLD IN PICTURES (Plates lxix to xcii)

PLATE LXIX

Plate LXX

PLATE LXXI

Plate LXXII

PLATE LXXIII

PLATE LXXIV

PLATE LXXV

PLATE LXXVI

PLATE LXXVII

Plate LXXVIII

PLATE LXXIX

Plate LXXX

Plate LXXXI

PLATE LXXXII

Plate LXXXIII

PLATE LXXXIV

PLATE LXXXV

Plate LXXXVI

Plate LXXXVII

PLATE LXXXVIII

PLATE LXXXIX

PLATE XC

Plate XCI

PLATE XCII

It rained all night on the particular date mentioned above, sometimes pattering lightly on the tent, and again in a steady downpour. To lie snug in warm blankets and listen to the rain on roof or canvas is one of the many joys of outdoor life. Morning disclosed shrouded mountain tops and broken clouds. The rain came in showers, and during the intervals blue sky sometimes peeped through.

I elected to follow Captain Mitchell this day, but when we got a mile up the river, at the top of the riffles, he made me fish ahead of him. Not two minutes after we started, he raised a nice steelhead right behind me.

That day, under the Captain's tutorage, I had about ten rises and caught six steelhead, all small. But then, size did not spoil the enjoyment. The electrifying churn of the water and tug on the line were thrill-provoking, irrespective of size. We did not see anything like a large fish all day. Part of the time when it rained I was wet and cold, and then when the sun came out I was hot and uncomfortable.

Probably a great deal can be learned in a whole day by an angler who is ever athirst for new ideas and methods and experience. Captain Mitchell was a very slow and careful fisherman. His style differed entirely from that of the experts I had watched on the Rogue River. He waded seldom, and then not far in. He did not disturb the water. If a long cast was needed to cover a likely place, he surely could make it. Eighty feet with a light fly and leader required no effort. Watching him closely, I found that what he had told me he practiced faithfully, and that was to fish all water carefully and stay casting over the places where he thought a steelhead lay. He was dainty and deft in the manipulation of a Hardy rod; he liked the ledges of rock under whose shelving sides a steelhead might lurk, and he showed almost as much faith in submerged rocks behind which a fish could lie, to rest in the aërated water. Boiling water he passed by with scant consideration, as also currents of riffles that were swift and heavy. But he favored the sides of low riffles, especially if the break came from a hidden rock. The way he cast, and drew his fly across the surface, never letting it sink, and when the line straightened out below, the way he would gradually draw it, were certainly not lost upon me.

"These steelhead act precisely like our Canadian salmon," he said. "What they may do when a big run of fish is on is, of course, something I have yet to learn. But these steelhead here now are finicky, particular fish. Light leaders and small flies are best."

The following day, during the evening fishing, I crossed the river at the camp and cast from the opposite shore into the slow-gliding shallow water just above where the current began to narrow and slant into a rapid. I raised four steelhead and hooked the last one, which got away. It was beautiful to see them shine like silver, and curl up to the fly, refuse it, and turn down to make a swirl on the surface. These steelhead were all under three pounds.

It was after dark when Captain Mitchell returned, wearing what was for him a very long face.

"By Jove! I lost a walloper!" he declared. "Ten pounds if an ounce! I was casting from a high ledge of rock down into a still, deep pool. This big fellow came wagging up to my fly, took it, hooked himself and went down. Oh, he was a beauty! I gave him a smart jerk to set the hooks—I was using a number ten English fly—and he came up to thresh on the surface. He shook his head like a dog. Then he went down and sulked. I was trying to coax him up when the hook tore out. By Gad! I'll bet he'd have made things lively when he waked up."

On the next morning, which I had selected to go hunting with Debb, Romer accompanied Captain Mitchell up the river. They fished all day. Romer kept close behind the Captain, hoping to photograph a leaping steelhead, while at the same time he profited by watching this expert salmon fisherman. They caught, in all, nine small steelhead, and did not see anything that looked like a big one. Upon their return to camp they found Bardon back from Illahe, and they all decided the fair-sized steelhead that had been in the river along this stretch had gone on. According to reports from down river, there were none coming.

Then, just to prove what little we all knew about steelhead, Captain Mitchell, fishing after sunset over his favorite place half a mile below camp, raised five steelhead, two of which were large, and hooked three of them, losing them all. This haunt of his

was one I would not attempt to fish, owing to the high rocks and
bad water below. He had lost two large steelhead there. It
was my opinion he would catch one sooner or later. This experience of his upset our calculations again. There seemed nothing
to do but keep on fishing. A golden rule for angling, and one
safe to follow, is, "Keep your bait in the water."

Behind our camp at Solitude, an oak-thicketed ridge led up at
a rather steep ascent toward the gray crags and giant firs that were
shrouded in the morning fog.

I had not climbed, packing a rifle, since the deer drive in the
Grand Canyon Forest the previous December, and I soon found
myself scant of breath. But taking it by easy stages, I gradually
wore into the strenuous labor of mountain-climbing. My legs had
at first that dead, numb sensation, almost an ache, which told of
strong blood circulation after a long period of inaction. If it
were possible, a man should walk, climb, ride, swim, row, at all
seasons; then he would not be put to the pains of breaking in
when a particular exercise was in order.

To see Debb panting and sweating afforded me some satisfaction. Gradually the gray fog bank above dissolved, and at the
same time the roar of the rapids below grew gentler. We climbed
an old deer trail that was not wanting in fresh tracks, mostly of
does and fawns. We passed the disused flume of the Solitude gold
mine, high up on the mountain-side, and could discern where it
wound to the west, marked plainly on the slope by sections of
wooden flume alternating with a ditch dug into the steep slant.
This brought water from a canyon we could see, and had once
enabled the miners to work at their placer-mining for gold. Far
down below, great gaps in the slope, where red and yellow banks
of earth showed, told of the washing for gold, the enormous labor
of a few men for the precious metal. We were told, too, by an
old native, that very little gold had ever been mined at Solitude.
Most of the miners had passed on. I would have liked to talk
to one of those now living, to have heard of his experience in that
lonely Rogue Valley fastness they had named Solitude.

By the time Debb and I had reached the bluff under the first
summit, the clouds had rolled away and we could see the green

river far below, winding down its canyon from one white rapid to another. Range after range of ragged black mountains rose higher to the west. We were only part way up the slope on our side of the river, and this first view impressed me with its wild splendor and gave me an intimation of the magnificent outlook from above.

The Rogue flowed through a deep canyon, cutting through the Siskiyou Range, and then farther toward the Pacific, piercing the higher Coast Range. Nothing of these wonderful ranges, however, could be seen or even guessed at from the river shores below.

From my vantage-point I could already begin to see and appreciate the bigness and ruggedness of this Oregon wilderness. It was a mountain stronghold such as I had never before looked into. The green ridges rose on all sides, irregular, sharp on top, with no levels anywhere. Already I could have counted a hundred ridges and canyons. Up and down, up and down, lay this mountain world! All the hunters in the United States could not kill the game here. There never will come a time when bear, deer, cougar, wildcats, and foxes will be scarce in this part of the west.

We were rounding the base of a bluff when Debb suddenly halted.

"Isn't that a deer?" he asked, pointing across the gap below to a rock-tipped slope that rose to meet the one we were mounting.

On a promontory I espied a blue-gray color that was neither stone nor foliage. "It sure is, Debb," I whispered, slowly sinking to one knee. Debb followed suit a little in advance of my position.

"Big buck," I whispered, raising my rifle.

"Gee! look at them horns!" replied Debb.

I had seen them and realized I was looking at a great stag. He lay on his side, head and antlers erect. The distance was scarcely a hundred yards, and I thought we were sure of venison for camp. But I happened to discover that I was going to shoot almost over Debb's head, a needless risk to take with a high-power rifle; and as I cautioned Debb to get back, he rose hurriedly, rustling the brush. That frightened or at least started the buck, and he rose. Debb called hurriedly for me to shoot, so I had to act hastily, and as the big blue shape slid over the rock I missed it. Debb did not have time to follow with another shot.

"Well!" I ejaculated, amazed.

"He was an eight-pointer," said Debb. "Never saw such horns, an' I thought we had him!"

"So did I," I replied, with a laugh. "But there's always one consolation for me when I miss a deer. I'm always glad. I like venison meat in camp, but I hate to do the killing. Don't you wait for me the next time."

We crossed round and went down, but as there was thick brush on the other side, we found no trace of the buck. From there we climbed to the top of the ridge and followed it until it led down into an open saddle connecting it with the next mountain top, rising half a thousand feet above us. This open swale or slope was grassy and gold, dotted with oak trees, brilliant with amber moss and colored leaves. It was like a park standing almost on end. Deer trails zigzagged it up and down.

To our right the ridge dropped off into a canyon, so that it seemed as if I could jump down into the Rogue, a gleaming green ribbon far below. Northward the ragged country of sharp peaks, black timbered ridges, green range on range, blue canyons, staggered me with its wildness and vastness. I saw the meadows on the mountain slopes above where we had pitched our third camp; and a spear-pointed peak of stone that had towered above us during one whole day of travel down the river.

At length we attained the next summit, and I found that the ridge on the other side sloped less abruptly and was covered by a wonderful growth of Oregon fir trees. We rested on the rim, and while Debb searched the open slopes and the oak thickets below for deer, I delighted in this virgin forest of noble trees.

Near at hand were firs six feet thick at the base, straight as arrows, brown and gray of bark, covered with a light-green waving moss, and without a branch up to at least two hundred feet of their grand height. No wonder Oregon firs make the finest masts for ships that go down to the sea under sails! It was a silent forest. I did not see a living creature, nor did I hear a sound of one. The slanting rays of gold sunshine alternated with the green shadows, and both merged at length into the somber blackness of impenetrable forest. The air was cool up there, pregnant with the breath of fir, and singularly, sweetly pure.

We followed along that ridge until it led to the base of another slope, bold and rock-faced, rising sheer to a timber-fringed peak far above. As the day was far advanced we abandoned the idea of attempting that farther height, and turned down into the forest.

I found the travel easy, considering the thick woods. Deer trails led down. Soon we were in the thick of a silent enveloping forest. We jumped deer out of their beds and heard them rustling away from us, just out of sight. Whenever we stopped to rest we heard the snap of twigs, the click of hard hoof on stone, or the ring of an antler on wood. Some of the leafy beds were warm to the hand.

Gradually the character of the forest changed as we descended from the heights. The firs no longer dominated. Balsam and sugar pine, maples and oaks, lent variety and changing color to the woodland scene. The solemn stately forest had changed to one more open, colorful, musical with bird and insect life. Brooks trickled down the densely leaf-choked ravines; ferns of exquisite delicacy and enormous reach nodded from the slopes; no boulder or cliff showed a foot of stone face, for all was moss-covered, amber-gold, green; oak trees had a thick blanket of a different kind of moss, a leafy, ferny species, most beautiful to behold.

Deer kept rising just ahead of us, just out of sight. We seemed to be playing a game with them, and I forgot that I carried a deadly rifle. At last, however, Debb gave me a quick nudge, and I peeped through the foliage to espy the blue coats of deer. But as I could not discover any sign of horns I refrained from shooting. Likewise did my companion. Pretty soon the incident repeated itself, and from that time we caught frequent glimpses of shadowy forms gliding through the green shadows and down the silent aisles of the forest. They were not wild as I knew wild deer. Not one rose with a crash and tore through the brush. We could have shot deer after deer, had we been able to distinguish bucks from does.

We found at last that we had headed down into the great canyon which came in from the west. The low roar of running water acquainted us with our whereabouts in short order. We had to follow the deer trails, which, though precipitous at times, al-

ways led down at an angle that was possible for a man to descend.
Yet it hardly seemed true that we had really climbed so high.
The farther down we traveled the steeper the descent, until we
had to slide, holding to roots, trees, and even moss. There were
no bare surfaces; all parts of the forest were damp and green.
From the slope of firs we descended to the slope of oaks, and this
was even more beautiful than the upper forest. For the most part,
however, I had not much opportunity to study the woodland.
What I saw was just in the way of passing, or sliding down.

We never reached the murmuring creek, however, nor even had
a glimpse of it through the massed green foliage, for we emerged
upon an open grassy yellow slope, dotted with huge gray rocks
like prehistoric monsters browsing, and made more picturesque by
an occasional low oak tree with colored leaves.

Debb saw some more deer and worked ahead and above me.
I had had quite enough climbing for one day. I wanted to go
down. Once Debb whistled. I looked up to see him point at a
high mound above him, where at the edge of an oak thicket two
blue does stood with long ears erect, watching us. I went on and
soon lost sight of Debb.

When I saw the river again it was none too soon for me, but I
seemed a very long way above it still. The declivity below was too
rough and too rock-strewn and oak-thicketed for me to find a way
down, so I proceeded along the edge of the open slope, resting now
and then. The sun was warm here and very welcome. Lizards
rustled to and fro out of my way. Far down the valley I dis-
cerned a rough white rapid in the river, and that I knew was the
next bad one below camp. The setting sun shone out of broken
rosy clouds, casting a light upon the Rogue. In one place the
river trail wound along like a yellow thread in the green. A golden
eagle soared across the valley, huge of wing, with all that wilderness beneath his keen eye. I was startled by a rifle-shot above me.
It cracked sharply, then bellowed in echo from the high walls. I
went on, and presently espied Debb above me, standing on a high
point.

"Meat for camp!" he yelled down.

I waved my hand to him and wished him luck in the toilsome
job of packing a deer down from that height.

Not much later I came to the old flume built by the miners along the slope. It afforded level and easy walking, except over the dangerous wooden structures bridging ravines and gullies. I kept to it, however, until I found a comparatively easy place to start down toward the valley. The way I chose developed into as difficult and tortuous a descent as I had experienced that day. Hot, wet, torn, I finally reached the river trail. The mellow roar of the rapid just below camp made music for my ears. And the twilight was pierced by a welcome flicker of camp fire. The melancholy mountain night was about to embrace Solitude, the old forgotten mining claim.

Days passed swiftly, glidingly on, like the river. Every morning the mountain slopes across the river from camp flaunted more autumn colors. Every afternoon, when toward evening the breeze came up from the sea and blew for a little while, the yellow leaves of the alders went sailing, fluttering, rustling down to alight on the river and float away. Every night the air grew colder, and every dawn the silver fog hung lower and longer over the peaks.

We had another night rain, slow, steady, soft, that ceased toward morning and then showered mistily all day long. It turned out to be the best fishing day so far, for we caught twenty steelhead. Billings had been correct in his predictions. On October 5th, steelhead began to arrive in considerable numbers, and after that the run increased. On another fine cloudy day we caught twenty-two steelhead, seventeen of which fell to Captain Mitchell, Romer, and me. Captain beached a six-pounder, and Romer one over five. These fish were extraordinary fighters.

Romer's fish, upon being hooked, bounced out high into the air, tumbling and wrestling, and made the boy yell lustily. "Look, dad! Oh, look!" he kept repeating, as if I was not all excitement and eyes. The steelhead pulled off all of Romer's line, and we had to call on Billings, who was near at hand in his little flat boat. Romer got in with him just in time to save the fish, and after a hard battle he finally captured it.

That day I had no luck until late in the afternoon. I cast for hours without avail. I would rest and cast again, change flies, and go on. Then, as always, I favored the Professor with jungle wing, which fly had ever brought me the best results. About four o'clock I started in again, on the last lap, and raised a fish at once. Thus encouraged, I cast my longest and best, in the particular, swift place below ledges of rock, and soon was rewarded by the bright silver flash of a steelhead and the swirl on the water. Then the strong tug and screeching reel!

That fish actually tired out my left arm. It took a good while to subdue him in the swift current, yet he weighed only four pounds. Another steelhead, almost the same size, dragged me down along shore clear to the foot of the next rapid. I kept returning to this place, and wading out as far as possible over the slippery rounded ridges of rock, and casting seventy feet or eighty. It was hard work, and the water was like ice. Steelhead were thick in that channel. They would rise to any fly, show color, and refuse it several times. Then suddenly one would nail my lure. What an electrifying tug! Zee! Zee! went the reel, and Romer's yell would peal out.

When I was not battling a fish, either he or Captain Mitchell was, so there was always excitement. Before dark I had taken six steelhead out of that one hole, and had had two on, besides, one of which was a lunker.

Once during that enthralling period I looked across and up the river where Captain Mitchell was fishing. I did not see him at first, but presently I made out a swinging of the branches of a tree. All that shore was brushy. He had caught his favorite fly far up on a limb and was climbing for it. Presently he appeared hanging by arm's length from a branch that was slowly swinging down with him. Evidently he had calculated that it would lower him clear to the rock. But ten feet up it broke and let him down hard, half in the water and half out. To such extremes will ardent fishermen go!

Another day at Solitude was remarkable for several things. A little shower of rain hatched out flocks of caddis flies. The sun broke through the clouds and shone warm for a brief period. Then how the trout rose! Everywhere I looked I saw the small river trout feeding upon caddis flies. They would jump half a foot up into the air after a fly and sometimes get it. I came upon a small island of gravel and rocks along the shores on which six sea gulls, one white and the others gray, were regaling themselves. They ate caddis flies with a capacity that emulated the trout. Moreover, they dove at the leaping, rising little fish. The big white gull appeared to be a ringleader of this group. He swam and waded along the edge of the water and when he was not picking caddis flies off the rocks he was diving after the hungry trout. This comedy-tragedy of nature did not last long, perhaps half an hour, but it was certainly long enough to show the interdependence of live things upon one another.

This fact was further illustrated on my walk up the river trail back to camp that day. I happened upon Ken, who was so intensely interested in something in the path that he did not hear my approach.

A ribbon snake scarcely a foot long had coiled its beautiful slender body about a lizard, and had the fore foot and shoulder of the lizard already swallowed. The lizard on his part was biting the snake, and stretching its skin at least a couple of inches in its frantic attempt to escape the coils of the serpent. Plain it was that the lizard was weakening. Ken took a stick and released the lizard from the snake. There were then no further hostilities or gastronomic exertions. The lizard lay still, panting heavily, while the beautiful little ribbon snake, with its lines of yellow and black and green, made off into the rocks. Such is the story of nature. Creatures of marvelous structure and appalling beauty prey upon the flesh and blood of each other!

For several days I observed the many small trout leaping in the middle of the river during the noon hours and later. I remarked about the regularity of this and Bardon said: "Huh! Sure it's regular. That's a school of young salmon goin' back to the sea. Goin' home!"

It was indeed a profound circumstance, once it became clear to me. I was humiliated that I had not figured this out for myself. Thereafter I watched and saw that a very large school of young Chinook were swimming down the turbulent Rogue to the calm Pacific. Then where they would go no man could tell; nor when they would return, grown to maturity, to spawn once in their lives and die.

At the head of Solitude a bar reached around the corner of the mountain, and at its upper end, where the water was swift and shallow, I observed several spawning beds just made. They could be distinguished by the blue-gray color of the gravel freshly stirred and dug into, as contrasted with the customary yellow of the river bottom. I saw fish upon these beds, and Romer and I watched. We saw two steelhead about four or five pounds in weight wavering and rising and working over this bed. One would glide ahead a little, turn on his side, showing his pink and silver, and then he would dig with his tail into the gravel. A cloud of roily water would rise and float down. We watched this performance fully a dozen times. Upon our return to camp, Bardon claimed these fish were not steelhead, but blue-back salmon. With all due respect to the native riverman, I say these fish were steelhead. Next day I looked for them again, to find they were gone.

Another rise in the river and a discoloration of the water prompted me to move camp down to Shasta Costa, ten miles below, or some other place where we might find a likely camp site and fishing-ground.

"Gee whiz!" said Romer to me, with his eyes shining. "I hate to leave this place, Solitude. Just suits me, and in a week there'll be some ten-pound steelhead coming along. . . . I want to come back here. I want three extra tips for all my rods, and lots of lines, and a million flies. I'm going to save my money and buy English flies, Norwegian flies, American flies. I like the small flies best, but I want strong hooks. Also, I'm going to get silk and feathers to tie my own flies. These steelhead like brown and black with a little white and red. . . . I'm already making out a list of fishing things you can get me for Christmas. . . ."

And so Romer rattled on, enthusiastic and eager, living so much as I lived—in anticipation, and in the dream of the future. Like father, like son!

That evening I noticed that the water had risen several inches. Next morning it was almost a foot higher. Then it began to discolor and presently grew quite muddy. Bardon declared placer mining had begun, but most of us inclined to the opinion that the gates of the dam above Grants Pass had been opened, or that a heavy rain had fallen up the river. Anyway, it looked as if the fishing had been spoiled, if not permanently, at least for some days, and I decided to break camp and move down river next day.

In consequence, we packed most of the afternoon. Toward evening the river suddenly dropped five or six inches, and the muddy water began to clear. This was disconcerting, and I began to waver in my determination to leave Solitude. Romer helped me in my wavering. While we were at supper, steelhead broke water up and down the river.

Lastly Billings and Andy Huggins, another hunter and guide, visited us, and were strong in voicing their disappointment at our leaving. The river would run low and clear in another day, and the big fish were sure to come. Whereupon I changed my mind and we unpacked and got ready for an even longer sojourn at Solitude. Romer in his delight and enthusiasm performed Herculean tasks, gathering firewood, and dragging a great lot of old mining lumber down to camp, for apparently no good reason at all, unless he wanted to build a cabin to stay all winter.

"Aw, fine!" declared George Takahashi, who kept a keen eye on the lad. "Work awful hard for fish now. Then after be glad."

George had the philosophy of it. The greatest joy of any fishing experience is in remembering that which was most trying and difficult.

Huggins had spent most of his life on the Rogue, and knew the mountain country. He was a bear- and lion-hunter. He told us of two occasions when he had happened right upon sleeping mountain lions—panthers he called them. It is singular how many names this animal possesses. Fenimore Cooper called him a painter. Some naturalists call him puma. In Colorado and Arizona he is a cougar. I never considered the name lion a felicitous one, because it confuses the mountain lion with the African lion. Huggins confirmed my opinion that this species of cat was abundant in the Siskiyous. Deer were especially plentiful in these mountains, but of late years the coyotes, coming in strong, had destroyed 90 per cent of the fawns. The does would take to the high valley during winter, where the snows were not deep, and there it was easy for the coyotes to prey upon the little ones. The gray timber wolf ranged there, too.   Bears were very numerous in Curry County, the brown and black species, but the grizzly was scarce.

What Huggins had to say about Rogue River fish was even more interesting to us.   Right in front of our camp he had angled many times, and as far back as fifteen years.   He said he had caught forty steelhead at a time, and these were not the big heavy ones.   When fishing for steelhead to smoke for winter use, he did not want the large ones, and had no time to fight them, so when he hooked a fish he would jerk him right out or break him off. Often along this Solitude bar he had lost all the tackle he had. He preferred to trail a fly on the surface close to the shore, and he kept his fly moving all the time.   When he saw a steelhead flash white he drew his fly all the faster, and almost invariably hooked that fish.

Steelhead would rise to a floating or dead fly, and refuse it, but to a naturally moving fly they came up with a rush.   Wading was not the best way along the lower Rogue.   Steelhead usually lay in close to the shore, and they would move out when the water grew discolored or the gravel disturbed.   Huggins preferred a short line and small fly.   His idea appeared to be similar to that of Billings and the other native fishermen we had met up at Winkle Bar. Naturally we wished to profit by the experience of men who lived along the river, and carefully considered all they were so good as to tell us.

The river played tricks on us.   We fondly trusted to apparent conditions and made all preparations for a great day's fishing. Next morning the river was lower than ever, and scarcely as clear as the evening before.   Steelhead would not rise.   Right on top of this the river rose again several inches, some degrees milkier than at daybreak.   The hot sun hatched out hundreds of caddis flies, and they flew out over the stream, shining in the light.   But trout did not appear to be feeding.   That might have been because the caddis flies did not happen to be falling in the water.

I came upon George Takahashi sprawled upon a rock catching caddis flies and throwing them into the river.   Manifestly this had become a favorite pastime, judging from his dexterity and obsession.

"Sons-um-guns!" he ejaculated. "Last time I throw bugs in, steelhead come up bingo! Now darn fools won't eat."

We saw new fish in the river all along the bar before camp. Silversides of fifteen pounds and more, and salmon up to forty pounds. These were the first salmon sighted for ten days. George said he had a hard strike on a spinner, and that he had also had a rise from a big steelhead to a fly. Captain Mitchell declared the river was full of fish. Billings believed fishing would be fine that evening or next day. Romer had a relapse from his fiery impetuosity, and lost some of his enthusiasm. As for myself, I did not entertain very optimistic convictions for the time being. I had been through too many hard campaigns. To be sure, I possessed an infinite capacity for the romance and hope characteristic of a fisherman, but I knew this was one of the times when we would have to stick to get them. It is so easy to start anything, a fishing jaunt, or a career, but it is entirely another matter to finish. The men who fail to finish in every walk of life, men who have had every opportunity, and who have even achieved success, can be numbered by the millions. One of the most splendid articles I have ever read—indeed, it is a sermon—was written by the Reverend Harry Fosdick, on the subject of finishing. I do not know if this eloquent divine has ever fished for trout—I hope he has—but as a fisher for the souls and salvation of men he is great.

We had frost. The maple leaves across the river turned gold; the oak leaves behind camp took on tinges of yellow; and the vines changed from green to red. Even a single day had its marked influence.

I spent an hour at early morning in the tan-oak grove across the river. Tan oaks were new to me, tall, slim, gray-barked, with thick shiny foliage, rising cone-shaped. This grove was surrounded by the giant firs. At that early hour the shade was dark and cool; at some points the sun gleams brightened the green, but for the most part this woodland was somber. It was also still, silent, lifeless, without movement of any kind. No leaves were falling, as in other parts of the forest. I sat on a log and absorbed the lonesomeness and tranquillity of that place. The forest neither waited nor hurried.

The six sea gulls that had become conspicuous along the bar and objects of interest to us, considering they were so far from the sea, one evening roused our deepest curiosity.

There were five gray gulls and one white in color, as I have previously mentioned. The last was the largest and evidently the leader. Just about sunset they were observed to rise from the shore and begin to circle low over the river. After they had risen a few hundred feet they left off flying and began to sail, very much like eagles do. And they continued to rise by sailing, high and higher, until they were mere dots in the sky. Long after the gold of the sunset had faded from the rocky rim above camp we could discern the white gull shining in the sunlight. At last he led off toward the west, still sailing, and his followers kept close to him. Together they disappeared toward the west, and we lost them in the afterglow of sunset. Now what did that strange flight signify? It was strange to us because we had not seen it before. Those gulls had remained with us for over two weeks. Did their departure presage a storm, or that they had depleted what store of food they had found along the river; or were they just returning to their natural habitat, the sea? They certainly did not come back the next day or the next.

On the third day of our enforced idleness, when the contrary river began again to subside toward normal conditions, we all fished until we were tired. But after supper the shade of the green slope opposite gave the river a clearer aspect and roused our hopes again. Romer went down along the near shore. Captain Mitchell finally could not longer stay idle, so he put on a light leader and began to cast from the ledge in front of his tent. On his third cast he raised a steelhead, signaling the event by a shout, and on his fourth he hooked a fine one that brought a lusty yell from him. We all ran down to see the fun.

The steelhead leaped at the narrowing head of the swift rapid and disclosed himself to be fully a six-pounder, a big fish for us at that time. He jerked off a lot of line and dashed into the rapid. The Captain began to chase him along the bank. Romer appeared with his rod and a small steelhead, and seeing the Captain's extremity he dropped both rod and fish and yelled, "I'll help you get that bird."

Together they went clambering and running over the rough rock bank, and disappeared under the trees. Presently they returned disconsolate.

"Cleaned him out!" exclaimed Romer.

"It was that darned light leader," added the Captain. "I'd got him sure but for that."

Next morning, to our dismay, the river was rising again and somewhat discolored. We did not know what to make of it, but we were perfectly cognizant that conditions were unfavorable for us; the season was growing late; any day the fall rains might begin; and it would take a week, perhaps, for the river to get right.

"Break camp and pack," I said, finally. "We'll move on."

Then everything was bustle and excitement. The long stay at Solitude had lulled our fears of the river, and all in a moment we were faced again with strain, hard work, and danger.

We gave Billings a lot of foodstuff and other things with which we could dispense. Takahashi hated to leave so much deer meat that he was sure we could eat. "How long take?" he queried. "Three days—four? Mebbe find fish down river."

"George, we're started now and we'll go a-whooping," I replied.

It hurt me to leave beautiful Solitude, and the fir-covered shade shack that I had just erected to write and loaf under. Captain Mitchell felt keenly the departure minus one of the few big steelhead we had raised. Romer forgot Solitude and his raving about staying two weeks longer, and was wild to get in his boat on the river. We were packed by eleven o'clock and on the water.

My plan was to let Debb take my boat through the long Solitude rapid below camp; and he and the others were to hold the boats back while George and I went below to photograph them and if possible get them all in the rapid in one picture.

I hurried down the long gravel bar, and climbed one of the huge boulders at the foot of the fall, where the water rushed white and swift round the bend. When I raised my handkerchief Bardon answered, and signaling to the others he backed his long boat into the head of the rapid. How swiftly he came down! The others were to follow as closely as appeared safe. But Bardon was far ahead and almost down to me when the other five vessels floated into the rapid. I could not get all six boats in the camera finder at one time, but I managed five. Romer was the last to pass me, and he looked up with unutterable delight at being on the rushing river again.

George and I clambered over the rough steep banks to a point below, where the boats waited for us. This time I took George into my boat to help me row, a circumstance he hailed with satisfaction. Evidently he remembered what a trying experience he had had in Romer's boat.

"Romer, he must be captain all time," complained George. "Me row one way—he row another. Then he say my fault when oars mix up."

We were soon committed to the swift Rogue, whirling and rolling and singing under canyon walls and great green slopes. The boys gave vent to their spirits in cheers and yells, and gay farewells to the mountain heights. Yet I knew they were all sorry to leave Solitude behind. There was, however, a relief in starting again, to face the last hard miles, and in the thought of conquering them. The dark towering walls of green once more overshadowed us, shutting in as if forbidding us to go. The wilderness and richness of Oregon's mountains, the gloomy somber forests that stood on end, the luxuriant ferns and vines and moss, the amber-colored boulders that trooped like huge beasts down to the river—all these familiar things passed us in ever-changing form and beauty. No ugliness, no scars, no ruin marred the landscape. Even the river banks were clean and polished. The few sand beaches were like gold, always reminding us that the floods of the Rogue carried fortunes in gold down to the sea.

We had several miles of this fascinating travel, swift, easy, and not hazardous if care was exercised. Then we came to a large winding lane of quiet water scarcely moving between its black granite walls. We had to row, and thus the boats gradually widened the space between them. After a few oar-clashes with George, who certainly was a weird oarsman, I yielded to his request: "You take rest. I row. More better that way. You take picture."

The boys somewhat murdered the still solemnity of that wonderful pass. Ken, in loud, deep, authoritative voice, imitated the callers on the sight-seeing busses of California. "We are now, ladies and boobs, entering upon the grand salaam of the Pacific coast. Here we enter the Stygian Cave forlorn. If you look sharp you will spy the wild woman of the Rogue. She will come out of her cave to wave to our guide Bardon."

Ed let out resonant calls at intervals as if charmed by the strange echoes, while Romer sang some riotous school song.

Soon we turned a bend and my ears filled with a low dull distant roar, growing, swelling, rolling. Again I felt the skin chill and tighten on my face. We still had bad water to contend with, and I felt that everybody was too careless and gay. So I took up my oars and lent George a hand in catching up with my comrades.

Soon I heard Bardon's shrill whistle, and turning, I saw him wave his red flag. These were signals for us to halt well back from the top of a rapid.

This could not be Clay Hill, one of the two bad falls still ahead of us, according to Bardon's statement. Presently, when I called to him, the answer was: "Reckon I forgot about this one. But it don't amount to much."

All of us, except our guide, went ashore to climb over the huge boulders and to take a look at the rapids. There was a rough bit of white water, cut up by irregular rocks, without any well-defined channel.

Bardon yelled something, just what we could not distinguish for the roar of water. Then he nonchalantly stood up at the oars, slightly bending with a cigarette in his mouth, and backed his boat into the swift green V-shaped incline that marked the gateway to the rapid.

What a magnificent boatman! He was in his element. I had to thrill while I watched him. He shot down fifty yards or more, then rowed quarteringly behind a boulder that obstructed the current, pulled across to another channel, where he floated through foamy spray and big waves from which he emerged to slow up again, avoiding rocks, at last to glide through the mill race at the foot of the rapid.

Romer and Captain Mitchell stood high on a boulder, pointing out obstructions in the rapid, yelling to each other, and making signs. I knew what that meant. Soberly I clambered back to my boat, where soon the others joined me.

"It's not bad, Doc," said Captain Mitchell. "I'll shoot it all right." He shoved his boat off and backed into the current. I walked forward a little to watch him. At the head of the incline he rowed hard, holding back to enter the rapid at an angle and place that suited him. Then he went over and out of sight. Presently I spied him again in good position, rowing hard to cross the current.

When I returned to my boat I knew what to expect from Romer. He was already in his skiff alone, face glowing, eyes flashing, his oars gripped in strong brown hands.

"Dad, I can shoot this one," he called, in a tone slightly defiant and willful.

What could I say? I had gotten the boy into this game. I knew the danger was considerable. The wiser course would have been to line the boats through. I did not have to be told that if I tried that rapid in my big, heavy, twenty-four-foot boat I would surely come to grief. There was nothing to do but swallow my fears.

"Do what Bardon did!" I yelled to Romer.

His brown face flashed light at me. Then slowly and cautiously he backed away for the incline. The desire to watch him was irresistible, and I had to do it until he disappeared round the corner of the white water.

"I'm going to shoot it, too," shouted Ed grimly to Ken.

I left them there and wormed my way by short cuts round the rapids. It took considerable time, during which my thoughts were not happy ones, and fears played havoc with the consideration that youth and daring must be served. Beautiful, bright, alluring face of danger! I recalled my own reckless boyhood, and wondered if my father had often felt as I felt then. Presently I emerged from the labyrinthine mass of boulders to the foot of the rapid. I saw boats. There was Bardon, and also Captain Mitchell. Then my heart gave a single leap and seemed to release the tension that had hurt me.

Romer was there, bailing out his boat and talking at a great rate.

"How much water did you ship?" I asked, trying to be natural and casual.

"Huh! Didn't ship any. This was in my boat before," he replied, in a matter-of-fact voice.

That Bardon and Debb lined my big boat through this rapid was justification for my secret misgivings. It took an hour to get all the boats down.

"Now for Clay Hill," shouted Bardon. "When we get by there I'll throw off my cap. For then we'll have the Rogue licked."

Swift water for a spell, then a series of broad eddies, and another turn brought us to a wide space with a high bare slope facing us. It was a mountain-side, grassy above and at the base steep-banked with gray and blue clay. The river sheered abruptly to the left, flowing out of sight with a hollow roar.

Bardon did not, as was his custom, look this rapid over. He went ashore, and uncoiling his line pushed the boat back into the current, stern downstream. Then he began to wade and slide over the submerged boulders. His boat shot out of sight, and the last I saw of him was a glimpse of his head and shoulders bobbing above stones and willows and moving downstream as swiftly as the water.

The rest of us lined our boats down, two men to a boat. When my turn came I saw why Bardon had run so fast. Round that corner the channel was narrow and the current very swift. To hold a boat back was undesirable, not to say impossible. When we kept pace with it all was well. But I had a beautiful fall.

"Say, you can't displace these rocks that way," protested Ken, in his mock-practical way.

"Well, I displaced something," I groaned.

Viewed from below Clay Hill was just a torrent of white water, fascinating to gaze upon. Romer looked at it with regret, as if he had missed some fun. When all the boats had been safely lowered, Bardon let out a wild yell and flung his cap out into the swift current.

"All over but Two Mile, an' I'm not afraid of her," he shouted, gayly.

My tenacious memory had recorded that Two Mile Rapid,

below Illahe, was at some stages of water one of the worst on the river. Fortunate indeed was it that I had that memory!

We embarked again, once more upon a gentle gliding river, and passed the beautiful slopes in green review. Again the valley widened and bits of pastoral scenery contrasted with the rugged mountain wildness. To have Clay Hill behind us seemed to inspirit all. We lustily rowed the still lanes and shot the swift riffles, making short work of the long miles. Before we really expected it, we turned a bend to see the cabins of Illahe high on the green slope.

The river widened there and split round an island. Bardon chose the right channel, which led into a tumultuous rapid, short and steep. While Bardon dropped his boat down into the head of it, we went ashore.

Here we met two native fishermen who informed us that fishing had been very good of late. This amazed Captain Mitchell and me. Then we discovered that we had outrun the muddy water. Here the river was clear as crystal, showing the rocks of gold and amber.

"Water was r'ily last week, but it cleared," declared our informant. "We got two six-pounders this mornin'. Got one yestiddy thet dressed eight an' a half. An' last week I ketched a ten-pounder."

This fisherman carried a long cane pole, same as the natives used at Galice and Grants Pass. But instead of a brass spinner he employed leader and a Black Gnat.

"Are the steelhead rising to that fly?" queried the Captain.

"Recken they are," replied the native, with a grin. "Last week a Tan Upright was good, but they're hittin' the Gnat now."

I traded one of my flies for one of his Black Gnats. It was a small cheap fly with double hook. Then the Captain and I remembered we were on the way out, and reluctantly returned to our boats.

"Look out fer Two Mile," warned the native. "She's roarin' these days."

"Thank you, we will," I replied. "How far below Illahe?"

"Reckon about two mile an' a half. Good fishin' all along."

It required two full and laborious hours for us to push, pull, and drag our boats round this shallow rapid. The rocks were as slippery as ice and the water was ice. Debb fell in clear to his neck on three occasions, all of which furnished the rest of us much glee. Romer, too, had a long sliding tumble, and went under. Never had I seen him pop out of the water so violently. "Wow!" he yelled. By the time we got through I had lost all feeling in my legs and had to run up and down the gravel bar to get rid of the numbness.

Below Illahe we passed some riffles, pools, and ledges that caused Captain Mitchell and me many a pang. Such places to fish! Then the water had cleared to that beautiful green hue so satisfying to the fly fisherman. I saw many pleasant camp sites where little brooks poured down into the river. Firewood was abundant. The great fir trees leaned out as if to woo us to tarry. Perhaps another mile of that bewildering allurement would have halted me. But again we turned a curve in the river to be met with the presaging roar. Two Mile Rapid! We could not stop to fish.

Strangely, the very beginning of the confines of this rapid was ugly. Somehow forbidding! Yet the green banks, the dark forests, the great mountain, had not changed. Perhaps the sinister aspect came from my feeling. At any rate, I approached this bend in the river with a cumulative restlessness and anxiety, and with some feeling quite inexplicable at the moment.

Above the rapid the river was broad, slow, with smooth surface, broken near each shore by outcropping ledges. The swelling, thundering roar came from below, from the bend into which we could not yet see.

Bardon drifted, waiting for us to catch up. And when we all got near he waved us ashore and yelled, "I'm goin' through."

This was a surprise to me, because it certainly held in my mind that he had not intended to run Two Mile Rapid.

Romer edged his boat toward the left shore, while Ed and Ken and Debb worked toward the right, all, of course, at the same time rowing somewhat downstream.

Captain Mitchell and I, being behind the others and near the center of the river, gradually drifted toward the bend. We both had the same wish—to see Bardon shoot that rapid. Possibility of

danger to ourselves did not enter our minds. Yet I seemed to
have a vague appreciation of a subtle quickening of the current.

I saw Romer land on his side of the river and hurry over the
rocks, evidently to find a place where he could watch Bardon
shoot the rapid.

I wanted to see that, too, and no doubt all of the others were of
like mind. Presently we reached a point about a hundred yards
above Bardon at the turn of the river where we had a view of the
rapid. It was a terrific-looking channel. And at that I could see
only about half of it. The descent was steep. From the name Two
Mile I had gathered that this rapid was very long. But it was
short. The name, as I learned afterward, applied to a brook
flowing in there.

Bardon, as always, stood up for a survey, plying his oars
slowly. He was, however, taking more time than usual about
going down. No wonder! It took the nerve of a dare-devil to
face that seething caldron. I called to the Captain, and he replied,
but I could not hear a word he said. The thunder of the rapid,
even so far above it, was as deafening as Reamy Falls.

My interest grew absorbing when I saw the current catch
Bardon's skiff. It was swept onward in a flash, down the green
slant, into the white ridge of black-curling waves. It disappeared,
then reappeared. The wild waters appeared to cover him, whirl
about him.

I saw his boat strike a rock and bounce high, almost tipping him
out. Then it turned clear around, bow downstream. In my excitement I leaped up so I could see better. Bardon was in a
perilous predicament. I yelled and pointed and waved my hands.
But if anyone answered me, I did not hear or see.

Bardon leaped out of the boat upon the submerged rock where
he had struck. He gave a mighty shove. The boat appeared to
leap forward, and it jerked Bardon off the rock at arm's length.
His bare head went out of sight. I thought he was lost. The
boat sped on, tossing and pitching. But Bardon reappeared,
climbed back into the boat, and leaped to his seat.

Suddenly I became aware that something was wrong with me,
with my boat, with us. George Takahashi was watching Bardon.

So was Captain Mitchell, and both of our boats had drifted close to the head of the rapid. We were not fifty feet from the gliding green slant that sped so swiftly down into leaping-tongued waves.

With a fierce yell to warn my companions, I sprang back to my oars. George did the same, and Captain Mitchell began to row frantically.

But pull as I would, I could not move my boat. I strained every muscle. We kept drifting down, faster and faster. George's oars locked momentarily with mine, increasing our peril. We were not far from a ledge of rock on our right, toward which I labored spasmodically to row.

In another instant I discovered that the ring-bolt on the Captain's skiff had hooked fast over my stern. Our boats were locked together. Mitchell could not see it, for he was rowing desperately with his back upstream. My boat, broadside in the river, was merely gliding with Mitchell's toward the head of the rapid, now not many yards below. In one swift glance I could now see the whole of Two Mile Rapid. A long narrow channel where the riffling white water, violent, contrary, proved the presence of hidden rocks! One boat might, with luck, win through there. But two boats fast together! It seemed sure death. I grasped that, and terror struck me. But it also roused a fury in me.

Dropping my oars, I leaned far to one side and gave the boat a tremendous lurch. It broke loose from the Captain's. George, rowing powerfully, stayed the motion downstream. Then when I resumed my oars, we bested the current and soon reached the sunken ledge where, the instant we struck, I leaped out to hold the boat. Captain Mitchell, whose skiff was small and light, got safely to another rock just below me. Then George jumped out to help me pull our boat to anchorage on the ledge.

And there we were, marooned on narrow rocks, with deep swift water on each side, at the head of Two Mile Rapid, not the length of our boats from the brink of the thunderous maelstrom.

Bardon soon appeared on our side of the river, and to effect our rescue he had the boys let him down in a boat, using a rope. We pulled our boats around on the other side of the ledge, and from there safely made the shore.

Our guide had some very forceful and unprintable things to say to Captain Mitchell and me, which we took meekly.

Romer, who had rowed back from the other side, confronted me with white face and glaring eyes.

"What're you trying to do?" he bellowed, fiercely. "Scare me to death?"

There were times when my son was unanswerable. This was one of the occasions.

We set to work lining the boats down the right side of Two Mile, a task for which, at the moment, I was not of much service. It came to me after a while that there had been a reason for my singular dread of the river. I had known that in spite of eternal vigilance things can happen.

Two Mile Rapid was indeed the climax of our struggle with the devilish Rogue, and the end of our perils. Below, the river widened and lost its fierce impetuosity.

We traveled on to Shasta Costa Creek, across from which, on a wide gravel bar, we established camp. We were indeed a tired, hungry group of voyagers.

Romer was the only one of us with energy and will enough to have another and last try for steelhead. After the labor of pitching tents, toting bags and firewood, he changed his wet clothes for dry ones and hied himself to the head of Shasta Costa riffle.

From my seat by the camp fire I watched him begin to cast. His figure added a final vital touch to the beautiful scene. Shasta Costa Creek poured out of a green-foliaged ravine into the wide swift shallow river. Bare grassy slopes mounted up to forested mountains, the peaks of which were shrouded in a sunset-flushed bank of fog.

Romer, careless and violent as always, and no doubt fatigued from the exertions of the day, fell off a rock and got soaking wet. He came tramping back to the camp fire complaining about "the darndest cold river in the world."

We enjoyed a bountiful supper, an abundance of firewood, and comfortable beds. The night was like a moment in passing. Morning dawned cold, gray, foggy, showing the influence of the sea. We had rested, and eager and active, were ready to leave

Shasta Costa by the time the pale sun and blue sky shone wanly through the fog.

Romer invited himself to my boat and generously proclaimed that he would guide it down the remaining rapids and row the rest of the way to Gold Beach.

"Thirty-three miles!" I exclaimed. "Say, boy, you must feel strong this morning."

"I sure do," he replied, gayly.

I imagined I might save him some humiliation, so I replied that I believed it would not be fair for him to do all the work. I really did not think we would make more than twenty miles.

Thus began what was destined to be our last day on the Rogue. The fast-running river bore our boats as if to make up for the labor and pain it had given us. We had miles of swift water between dark walls of forests and silent canyons of mossy rock, but no more troublesome rapids.

What delight there was to glide down the hurrying stream, where cool breezes fanned our faces and our ears were filled with the low melody of riffles! We passed out of the Siskiyous into the Coast Range, round-topped green mountains that loomed high. The Rogue grew ever wider and shallower, running clear over gravel bars where often our oars touched. Gradually the riffles grew shorter and less numerous, and the wide stretches of quiet water longer.

Agness, the mouth of the Illinois River, Lobster Creek, and many places with which we had become expectantly familiar, all passed behind us. No more overhanging mountains! They sloped back gently from the wide valley, dressed in autumn hues of gold and red and purple, lending contrast to the green.

Early in the afternoon Romer manifested signs of tiring. I had expected that. When we got by the long swift mill-race channels he began to lose interest. First he found fault with my rowing along with slow steady stroke; then he wanted to row alone; next he was hungry and ate the remains of our lunch; after that he rowed awhile, until he found another excuse to rest. He complained of sore hands, and exposed to my gaze sundry blisters and cuts.

"What could you expect?" I asked. "And didn't you want this last long hard day?"

"Sure. But they hurt like the dickens."

As he weakened further it plainly worried and annoyed him that I had kept steadily rowing for hours. He tried his best to break my long drill, even at the last asking me to take a rest. My back ached, my hands hurt, but I did not let him know. And finally he burst out plaintively: "Dad, I've always noticed how you get a second wind—or spirit—or something—and keep on going at the last when everybody else has quit or is half dead."

That was the finest compliment he ever paid me, and I took advantage of the moment to give him a little talk, which ended somewhat in this wise:

" . . . So it is in life, my boy. On fishing and hunting trips, on exploring adventures, in baseball and tennis, in your school studies. It will be so in your chosen career. Anyone can start well. You can start with enthusiasm and joy and ambition. But it is the *finish* that counts. All else is in vain if you do not finish. The great thing is to know that."

He took that talk so seriously that he never answered a word—which silence was most unusual with him. And he took up the oars and never flagged again, though plain it was what the effort cost him. And he was the first to discover the ferry above Gold Beach, which sight he announced to us with his lusty yell.

It was indeed true. We shot the last shallow riffle, and rowed down to the ferry, where we beached our skiffs and got out to stretch weary, aching limbs. Over thirty miles in nine hours! We had finished early and strong.

After unloading our baggage we sat down to rest while Ken and Ed went into town for the truck and car. It was about all I could do to straighten my back, and I found a seat on the bags wonderfully restful. From the position of my companions I judged I was not alone in my appreciation of comfort. Romer was the only one who talked much and I heard him say to Debb, "Wouldn't be afraid to shoot Two Mile if I had a good empty boat!"

Presently my half-drowsy memories of the Argo Mine Rapid

and Whisky Creek and Horseshoe Bend and Winkle Bar and Solitude were dispelled by a familiar yet strange sound. It was a low distant pounding of the surf. Over the bare wind-swept hills lay the sea. We had indeed trailed the wild Rogue, shot and lined its rapids, rowed its canyon-walled lanes, and glided down its innumerable riffles to its home in the Pacific.

WINKLE BAR—1926

ON MY never-to-be-forgotten trip down the Rogue we had camped in the canyon above Winkle Bar, and I had reveled in my first sight of this beautiful isolated spot.

The rushing river at this point makes a deep bend round a long oval bar, with rocky banks and high level benches above, and both wooded and open land. Here it flows through a lonely valley set down amid the lofty green mountain slopes. A government forest trail leads up and down the river, not close; and another trail winds out some twenty miles to the nearest settlement. Far indeed is it across the dark Oregon peaks to railroad or automobile road!

We tarried at Winkle Bar a few days, far too long if one ever hoped to be free again of its beauty and solitude and its wonderful fishing. But I rather invited being chained by that memory. And this summer I had bought Winkle Bar from the native prospector who held it on a mining claim; and all through the long restless days of our swordfishing on the Pacific I had dreamed of the verdant green, the murmuring river, the stillness and sweetness of that Oregon fastness.

My younger son, Loren, earned his first distinction this summer at the boys' camp on Catalina Island. He won the prize for fishing and his comrades bestowed upon him the name "Big Fish." So I thought Loren had earned his first trip with me. I had my misgivings, for he was a gentle, dreamy lad of nine, with a habit of self-forgetfulness and abstraction that was something to be feared in the woods. He was wholly unlike his brother Romer, whom I had taken to the Tonto Basin on a bear hunt at the same age. But once having hinted of the trip to Loren, I was lost. I had to take him.

In due time we arrived at West Fork, an isolated railroad station in the mountains west of Grants Pass, where we were to meet our pack outfit. All supplies going in to Winkle Bar have to be packed. There are no roads, and only one trail.

Charles Pettinger, of Illahe, was the guide I had engaged; and he was on hand with sixteen pack mules and eight saddle horses. I had a pretty heavy load of bags, tents, supplies, etc., not to mention tackle; and I rather feared sixteen pack animals would not suffice. Pettinger had three boys with him, but he preferred to do the packing himself. I saw that he certainly knew his business, but I began to worry over what must be a late start. I did not want to have to ride down into that Rogue River mountain fastness after dark. But they all assured me we would get to Winkle Bar by sunset.

We left West Fork at twelve-thirty, with twenty miles of mountain travel ahead of us. Before we had gone far I knew we would never make Winkle Bar during daylight, and that caused me concern. The trail, however, was fine and broad, with only a gradual ascent; the horses were gentle and easy-gaited; the scenery grew more wildly beautiful as we climbed up the mountain.

It took us three hours to make the top of the mountain, nine miles; and I began to hope we would, after all, see the river before dark. But the packs began to slip, the mules to make trouble, and so we lost time.

Sunset overtook us while we were still on top. I had to halt my horse to gaze across the innumerable blue peaks and purple ranges, across the hazed canyons, black and wild with dense forest, to the gold and creamy clouds behind which the sun was sinking.

Darkness fell on us at the beginning of the descent down to the Rogue, five miles and more of zigzag trail through the forest. We got along surprisingly well clear down to where we could hear the river. What a low mellow roar! I could see down into the black depths.

Pettinger and his men became separated, one to the front with a few mules, the others behind. We tried to follow the former, but lost him, and soon we found ourselves on an unknown trail which ran at points into so pitch-black a forest that we actually could not see a hand before our faces.

R. C. and I got Loren between us, and did our best to warn

him of obstructing branches and bad places in the trail. The lad kept calling to me, and then to his uncle, every moment. Luckily we had good horses, and by letting them have their heads we kept from becoming separated and lost in the woods.

Our situation presently became quite serious because eight or ten of the pack mules caught up with us and stuck to us. If we turned they would do likewise. More than once a pack animal bumped my horse off the trail, in darkness so dense that I did not know the mule was there until he hit me. It was impossible to keep close to Loren, and only by calling and hearing him could we keep him located.

We should have stopped at one of the clearings we crossed, and have waited there, until morning if necessary. But we did not do this when the chance afforded; and we found no more clearings. Once when Loren yelled I had a bad scare, but he was all right and said he only wanted to know where we were.

We wandered around over these trails for two hours, lost and hungry and saddle-sore from the long ride. At last I espied a camp fire far below and knew that it was burning on Winkle Bar as a signal for us. Heartening as this was, we had yet another half-hour of penetrating black thickets and ebony jungles before we got down to the open bar.

Loren, I believed, stood that hard ride better than any of us. When I asked him if he was tired he answered, "No, not much— I guess—a little."

Captain Mitchell fell off, rather than dismounted, catching his shirt over the pommel of the stock saddle, which he had anathematized all day long, and then he used surprising language, such as I did not know he was familiar with. We extricated him from his tangle and had our laugh at his expense. He could just about walk. R. C. expressed himself in this wise: "Well, Cap, this little Z. G. jaunt wasn't anything Wait till we strike the Tonto Basin and the bear hunt."

"By Gad! you'll have to bury me if you ever put me on another saddle like that," declared Captain Mitchell.

Supperless we went to bed, at eleven o'clock; and I lay under a pine, wondering how many of the pack mules were lost. I fell asleep before Pettinger got in. And I never moved till sunrise;

and then, when I did move, it was to groan. We were all more or less knocked out by the last few hours of that ride. The mules were all located early, and we gathered our duffle together, minus some of the food supplies and the Dutch ovens and a few other things. Fortunately our tackle had arrived intact.

It took us all day, on and off, to pitch camp. I spent about as much time looking at the dark green, rushing Rogue, and the magnificent fir forests that towered above the bar, as I did working over camp tasks.

Eight months of the sea had almost burned my eyes out, it seemed; and this soft green wall all around me was so soothing, so restful and refreshing, that I was like an Indian with an eye medicine.

Bardon, his father, and Debb were at the Bar, where they had been at work for over a month on the flume that brought water from the mountains down to my place. They reported very fine steelhead-fishing for the last ten days. There had been a rain and the fish had risen voraciously at any kind of a fly. One forest ranger had caught thirty. Three natives, one of them a woman, had caught a tubful of steelhead in a few hours. Seven- and eight-pounders were common. More common had been the big ones that had "cleaned out" the fishermen. At Illahe hundreds of steelhead were being caught. We certainly heard enough to give us the fishing fever.

Before that day was ended I had succumbed to the reaction which had set in, and I was hardly able to drag one foot after the other or to lift my hand. More than half a year of strenuous travel, writing, and fishing had worn me out. I did not realize until then my enormous expenditure of energy.

But I had considerable consolation in observing the others of my party. Little Loren, strange to say, had suffered least of all from that strenuous ride. The Captain, and Ken and Ed, who had neglected to bring riding boots, chaps, etc., bore sundry bruises and raw spots on their legs. R. C. was crippled in one leg and lame in the other. Takahashi had not escaped and he hobbled about his tasks. "Long ride first day orful bad!" he said, with a grin.

Nevertheless, everyone except myself rigged up tackle that evening and went fishing. I was content to walk around under the oaks and pines, to breathe the fragrance of the forest once more, to listen to the singing river, to watch the flight of wild fowl and hawks, and to gaze long at the sunset-flushed clouds above the lofty peaks in the west.

One by one the anglers tramped back to the camp fire, all weary, yet glowing with importance or chagrined with loss. Romer had a six-and-three-quarter-pound steelhead, which he had caught on a fly and a five-ounce rod; and the story he told warned me that some day I must look to my laurels. He had the enthusiasm, the fire, the imagination, and the creative power of the born writer. This creative faculty of his manifests itself most remarkably in relation to a fish story. He raised big steelhead that would not take a fly; he saw the broad silver sides of large steelhead, that to judge from the spread of his hands were three feet long; he hooked a huge one that went over the rapids and took him tearing down shore in hopeless, frantic zeal.

Captain Mitchell had a couple of mishaps—to wit, the hooking and losing of a big fish, and then slipping off the rock into the icy water, to go clear under. "By Gad! I had to scramble!" he ejaculated. Ken and Ed reported various adventures with trout, large and small, the honors evidently going to the fish. And Takahashi, the patient, the ever-fishing fisherman, said with his broad grin: "All same like last year! Me hook steelhead. He jump high, then run under rock and stick there!"

Loren, whom I had let go fishing with Debb, one of the boatmen, was the last to return. In the glare of the bright camp fire my young son was a spectacle to behold. He was dirty and wet. He smelled of fish. He had four small steelhead on a string, and a broken rod. His little face beamed and his eyes held a radiance that fascinated me.

"Gee, dad, I had some time!" he exclaimed, in a high, trilling voice, and he held aloft the fish. "See! Caught four, and that puts me ahead of everybody. Had a big one on that busted my rod. Whatja want to give me a cheap rod for?"

Like father this younger son! I was somewhat appalled to see myself in that eager wild lad. Deeply thrilled, and yet somehow saddened!

"Lorry, old top, you'll have Izaak Walton skinned to a frazzle some day," observed my brother, R. C.

In this manner was ushered in our 1926 fall fishing trip on the Rogue. The camp fire crackled and blazed; the low roar of the rapids floated up from the black hollow; the wind moaned through the firs; the wild ducks whirred overhead.

During the night I awoke, restless, nervous, with aching limbs and an oppression of the chest. And I lay awake, fully aware of the warm soft bed. Yet I could not rest or lie still. I realized that I must pay for the last eight months of intense physical and mental activity. There could not be a better place to regain lost nervous energy. And as I lay awake for hours, the dead quiet of the night broke occasionally to wild sounds—the strange plaintive notes of a screech owl, the raucous croak of a heron, and the cry of some night prowler. I was conscious of solitude, but the weight of the cities, the crowds, the labor still burdened me. It was long before I went to sleep.

Four days I idled around camp, or strolled on the boulder-strewn banks of Winkle Bar, or sat in the sun, or lay under a fir tree. And at night I found rest, and sleep came back gradually to me, until it was a joy to go to bed. Pain and oppression, and the dejection sometimes attendant upon them, left me by imperceptible degrees, until once more I seemed free and energetic again.

Meanwhile my comrades had been exceedingly active, especially Captain Mitchell and Romer, who each caught a good many steelhead. The fish were hard to catch. The river was lower than in the memory of the oldest native, and in the clear water it was no easy task to fool the wary trout. The lightest of tackle was needed to get any rises at all. And naturally, with the delicate camouflaged leaders and small flies, the hooking of steelhead of any size at all resulted in disaster.

R. C. had started in with his regular steelhead tackle, suitable for heavy fish, and as luck would have it, right off he raised, hooked, and landed a seven-pounder. This gave him a bad start, for he stuck to the heavy tackle, and lured no more fish those first days.

Discussion waxed hot and heavy round the camp fire in the evenings. Any fly with a little yellow in it appeared to take well, but gradually the Captain and Romer gravitated to a No.

8 Sandy Special, or a No. 6 Carson, or Royal Coachman with a jungle cock wing.

Wading along Winkle Bar was not productive of good results. Our method up river, at places like Pierce Rapids and Chair Riffle, had been to wade in and cast quarteringly down and across stream. But these tactics would not do here. The steelhead lay close to shore on the shallow slopes of Winkle Bar, and in fact at other places. So it turned out that in these few days we surely learned what Fred Burnham, the up-river expert, had meant by saying it was pretty "sweet fishing." At any rate, we found it extremely difficult to raise trout and harder to hook them. I prayed for rain and a higher river and for a run of steelhead.

On the afternoon of the fourth day, at sunset, we observed a great cloud of swallows flying and circling high above the bar. Bardon said that was an indication of storm. During the night the air grew warmer, and at dawn the sky was overcast. Next morning near midday a misty rain began to blow down from the mountains. On and off all afternoon these light-gray clouds floated down upon us, and night brought a patter of raindrops on the tent. The wind rustled the leaves. How wonderful to lie warm and snug under the blankets and listen!

LOREN

BUT all these signs of a storm were misleading, for no storm came, and I was disappointed. I voiced my regret to the extent that I was warned not to tempt the storm gods. An Oregon storm in October was not to be desired by campers. Nevertheless, so keen was my eagerness for a run of steelhead, such as I had heard about, that I went on praying for rain.

Meanwhile we fished. Captain Mitchell roamed down the river; Ken and Ed favored Missouri Bar; Romer tramped up river to Kelsey Canyon and performed mighty tasks of wading and rock climbing; R. C. kept pretty faithfully to the long swift channel in front of Winkle Bar.

My favorite place was at the head of the rapids above the Bar. The place was difficult to fish, but it had all the other fascinating attributes of a wonderful fishing-hole.

A deep-green V-shaped gorge stretched up the river through which the water wound placid and smooth, mirroring the forest slopes and ferny cliffs. The river quickened at the turn and spread fan-shaped to circle in at both ends, and running swifter and swifter, narrowed to a glancing chute that ended in a white roaring rapids. Here was the music of the singing Rogue. At all hours of the day this place was beautiful, but most so at sunset and twilight. Still, it never seemed the same at any two times. On the side from which I cast there were rugged rocks edging off into deep water, under which the steelhead rested from their labor of buffeting the swift current. Across the stream a high gravelly island broke the current and shelved off gradually to the head of the rapid, affording a fine lingering place for fish.

The first time I fished this water it was along late in the afternoon, when the shadows were lengthening over the river, and the gold and pink of the sunset clouds showed as lovely as in a crystal

THE GREYS IN CAMP AT WINKLE BAR

PLATE XCIII

LOREN AND HIS CHUM GUS

PLATE XCIV

The Great Takahashi—the Inimitable—
the Irrepressible—the Indefatigable

PLATE XCV

Ed's 11-pound Steelhead

PLATE XCVI

mirror. Trout and steelhead were breaking everywhere. Sometimes I heard the heavy souse of a salmon coming out. The breaks on the surface spread into rippling circles and went floating and widening down the smooth incline over the rapids.

I worked out upon the farthest edge of ledge and cast quarteringly a little downstream. I was using a six-ounce Granger fly rod with as heavy a line as it would carry. And I would not like to admit the number of casts I made before I landed my fly in the exact spot that I wanted to cover. This was right in the middle of the channel, about seventy feet out, and just above where the water took its first smooth curving dip. There most of the steelhead had risen, and one of them was a "walloper," to use Captain Mitchell's favorite epithet. My fly, a Golden Grouse, floated down in plain sight and nothing happened. The tingle of thrilling expectancy passed out of my finger tips, apparently, and did not return so powerfully on my next successful cast. The steelhead continued to rise out there, but not at my fly. So I changed to a Royal Coachman. I never had caught a trout on this particular fly, though my companions had been successful with it. No good! After half a dozen casts I tried another; and in the succeeding half-hour used at least five other flies.

Then came the afterglow of sunset, that most witching hour for angling, with its lovely lights upon the water, with the sweetness of river solitude and the murmur of running water, and the low faint melody of the water ousels.

But the elusive and tantalizing steelhead would have none of my lures. Finally I tried a Carson fly, which is one that imitates a Royal Coachman and in addition has something of a dash of yellow. It did not look attractive to me, and besides, my hope of getting a rise had as nearly died as was possible. My first cast fell short, but the second, being a careless, powerful switch of the rod, was the best of all the casts I had made. It quite amazed and thrilled me. Then just a second after it fell, a broad silvery bar rose out of the dark water and a powerful fish shape swooped up at my fly. Smash! The water broke. I felt the line jerk out of my left hand, and then my rod bow and bend. Next my reel sang merrily. I hardly realized what had happened. An instant later, however, a big pink-and-white steelhead shot out of the water, quivering high into the air. He plunged back, to R. C.'s yell of delight, and then he ran upstream to the extent of all my casting line, and soon half of the backing—eighty yards—before he slowed up. My state was one of supreme excitement. What good luck that he had run upstream!

He remained up there for some time, during which he made three leaps; and then when he started downstream he was so tired that I was able to hold him from going over the rapid. Eventually I wore him out and beached him, a splendid specimen of fresh-run steelhead, a male fish, seven and one-quarter pounds. R. C. had much to say about the fight of the fish, his beauty, and also my astounding good luck. He was vastly concerned about that quarter of a pound more weight than his largest fish to date.

I could not lure another steelhead there, though I cast until after dark. Next evening, however, I raised and hooked one in precisely the same spot, and had a spirited battle with what turned out to be a smaller fish—five and one-half pounds. Once more at the twilight hour, the following day I caught another that weighed four, as game a fish for his weight as I ever hooked.

These three steelhead, with several smaller ones, were the extent of my bag for the first ten days at Winkle Bar. I did not seem to be able to connect with fish in any other spot, and only one now and then at my favorite hole.

Captain Mitchell and Romer ran their score up to the neighborhood of thirty. Romer had one six and three-quarter, one six, and three around five pounds. The Captain had raised and hooked some large steelhead only to lose them. He and Romer were partial to very fine tapered leaders and small flies, sometimes as small as No. 8. R. C. caught a good many small trout, and so did the other boys. But the big run of steelhead had not come.

During this period Loren was to me an object of endless interest, amusement, wonder, and awe. I never saw a lad like him. He was hardly a boy. He was an elf, a spirit. He spent hours watching lizards, bugs, worms—and if he could get a live trout in a little corral of rocks he was wholly content. He was not afraid to pick up anything. As for poison oak, which ran rampant, he would vigorously rub his hands with the treacherous leaves and exclaim, "Never touches me—that poison oak!"

There was a kind of yellow lizard, fortunately not very numerous, that lived in the stone-wall fences long ago erected by prospectors; and these reptiles, according to the natives, were poisonous. I rather doubted it, but as I could not classify the species I took their word for it. Loren was fond of catching these yellow lizards by the tails. As for snakes—they were his favorite dish. Many times I caught him tearing up the rocks in pursuit. It did no good to command him to leave the snakes alone, or read him a severe lecture upon possible danger. Straightway he forgot both. The only solution was to watch him, and this indeed was next to impossible. He ran here, there, everywhere. He flitted about the camp like the little Oregon junco, the snowbird that began to visit us.

Gophers and ground squirrels held irresistible fascination for Loren. Like a dog he would dig for them. He never caught any, but that made no difference. He was indefatigable in pursuit. He manifested the destructive boy's instinct in regard to the snakes and lizards, but I did not discover that he wanted to kill anything else.

The occasion arrived when I presented Loren with a fishing-rod I had bought and saved for him. It was not expensive, but a nice little rod. And when I presented it I gave him a little talk about the care of it. I was serious, and I imagined quite impressive. Taking good care of fishing-tackle was one of my hobbies. When I ended my advice and admonition Loren looked up with his impish glance and exclaimed: "Well! . . . All right, dad."

Not a quarter of an hour later I chanced to see Loren handling his new fishing-rod in a very peculiar manner. Upside down and precariously bent! I went closer. He was absorbed in his task and did not hear me. To my utter consternation I discovered that he had half of the rod stuck down in a gopher hole.

"Come out of there—you son-of-a-gun!" he was muttering.

I fled. I wanted both to rage and to yell with mirth, but did not care to let him see me do either. So I fled to a safe place and there indulged myself.

"Shades of Izaak Walton!" I declared. "What kind of a fisherman will that kid make?"

Nevertheless, Loren showed a very decided leaning toward the sport of angling. He did pretty well, fishing out of a boat, with a short rod. He really had not had any other kind of experience. On the shore, or wading with a fly-rod, he made a marvelously funny and sometimes pathetic little figure. No matter how much instruction we gave him, it did not seem possible for him to remember. He jerked his rod forward and back, trying to get his fly out. It never went far enough to suit him, so that there was little chance of a trout espying his fly. Then he was always catching the brush or himself; and his efforts to extricate himself were violent. Invariably he grew impatient and sometimes angry. When he lost his fly, which happened often, he would cry. Time and again I told him that this was nothing—that it happened to me quite often, which was a lamentable fact. But that did not console Loren.

One evening I placed him out on a log platform we had built from the bank, to facilitate casting. He made a brave picture standing out there, bareheaded, with his sunny locks disheveled, and his dirty solemn little face rendered beautiful by eyes of rapture.

While he essayed to cast, I stole glances at him. We had learned not to laugh openly at Loren's efforts. That hurt his feelings. He was in deadly earnest, and tried so desperately to switch his fly out far enough. With every cast he stuck out his tongue, and it seemed to take the direction of his fly—out—up—down—and every way. He simply was screamingly funny, but I did not dare laugh at him. And I could not look continuously, for I had my own casting to attend to—a task not any too easy.

Eventually I raised a steelhead—a wide bar of silver that flashed under my fly—and in successive endeavors to make him strike I forgot Loren.

Suddenly a shrill scream rent the air. I wheeled to see the tip of Loren's rod go under. He had actually hooked a steelhead. I yelled all the advice I could think of. But Lorry acted upon the theory that there was nothing to do put pull. He surely did that. The rod bent more than double. It went under the platform.

Then the steelhead, a small one of about fifteen inches, began to jump on the other side of the platform; in fact, behind Loren. He went through some amazing weird performances, the last of which was to turn round, straddling his rod, and then kneeling to pass the butt under the platform. All this time the little fish was leaping and tearing around frantically. When Loren got the rod and line straightened out he bounced off the platform and unceremoniously yanked that steelhead out upon the sand. He lifted the shiny wriggling fish and turned to me a face utterly glorified.

"Look, dad!" he called. "I got him. On a fly, too!"

"Son!" I whooped. "That was a grand exhibition. I hope your luck always stays with you."

Loren put his fish on a string and back into the water, where he watched it awhile before resuming his casting. When he did begin again, he was even funnier than before. He was at first vastly confident. His attempt to imitate Captain Mitchell's jerking of a fly across the water was something worth seeing. Back and forth he whipped his rod, and when at last he got his fly out a few yards he began to jiggle it. He made it dance, leap, fly, and dive. If these gyrations did not frighten a trout out of his wits they would surely irritate him to rise. But Loren soon lost his fly, and it took him a long while to put on another. Meanwhile twilight stole down from the hills. And the bats came out to flutter in their peculiar zigzag way over the water. On the next cast Loren made a bat flit after his fly. Immediately, then, Loren evolved into a fly fisherman for bats. He quite forgot about the trout, and when I hooked a small one he did not evince his usual interest. Finally he actually caught or snagged a bat and threw it far back over his head. He greeted this with a sharp cry.

"Oh, gee! he got off," he shouted.

We returned to camp in the gathering dusk, wet and tired and hungry. Loren exhibited his trout with great pride.

"My first steelhead on the fly," he said, impressively.

Romer, true to the nature of elder brothers, eyed the little fish with contempt. "I'll bet dad hooked it for you," he said.

Whereupon Loren delivered himself of a hot retort.

On the following afternoon Loren again accompanied R. C.

and me down to the river; and here he soon put the last of his tackle out of commission, a fact which he bewailed with great vehemence. R. C. hooked a small steelhead and let Loren have the rod. It was a precarious test for R. C.'s rod, but it certainly lifted Loren into the seventh heaven. He pulled the trout in, a little beauty of fifteen inches, and got the hook out without injuring it. Then Loren put the fish in a stone-fenced pond he had previously erected, and his delight was complete.

I waded on down to the break above the bar, where I raised and hooked a three-pounder, only to have it leap and leap to throw the hook. Darkness had about set in when I retraced my steps.

Lorry was sitting on a stone beside his pond, his elbows on his knees and his hands covering his face. His posture was one of extreme dejection. R. C. was standing, rod in hand, looking down at the boy.

"Lorry, what's the matter?" I inquired.

The lad flung up his hands dramatically. "Oh, my God! Oh, my God!" he cried.

"Son, I don't see any occasion for such talk," I returned, reprovingly.

"My trout jumped out of the pond. He got away," replied Loren, tragically.

"Too bad. But you'll get another tomorrow. Come, it's late. Let's go to camp," I said, consolingly.

"Don't mind, Lorry," added my brother. "If you're going to be a fisherman you must learn early that all the big ones get away."

We climbed the gravel bar and entered the oak grove, where it was quite dark. Here Loren slipped his little cold wet hand in mine and trudged to camp in eloquent silence.

Just before we reached the camp fire he whispered: "Dad, don't tell Romer about me losing the trout. He'd make fun of me."

SEPTEMBER 8, 1927

ANOTHER year! How short those words—like the thing they imply! It did not seem so very long since we had left here, a twelvemonth ago. I had spent seven months in New Zealand and among the South Sea Islands.

And, as always, the fresh green foliage of Oregon—the wall of firs and oaks and pines—proved a medicine for my tired eyes, a soothing relief, a blessed change from the vast expanse of ocean.

We arrived twelve in the party, among whom were all my family, Dolly, Romer, Betty, Loren and myself. It was not such an undertaking as I had imagined. We had never before all been in camp at once. An event! R. C. stayed on at Avalon, hoping to add another broadbill swordfish to the wonderful record of seven already accumulated this summer.

Romer brought his friends Junior, Marie, and Jeanette, and we also had Loren's pal, Gus. Ken and Ed, and of course Captain Mitchell—a gay party.

The flood of February had reached up to my cabin, nearly sixty feet above the river, and the bar had been almost wholly covered. Piles of driftwood were lodged against the trees, enough to make firewood for years. Everywhere the river bed had been changed. Old pools were gone and new ones formed. There were riffles where there had been deep holes, and *vice versa*.

I did not start in fishing very soon. I wanted to rest and watch the green hills and listen to the river. But the boys and Cappy pitched in hard. Ken got seven at Missouri Bar the first day; Romer five up river. Cappy had bad luck at first and could not appear to get started. After several days I got out my tackle and—after my Tongariro experience in 1927, when I caught eighty-seven big trout—I expected to catch all the steelhead in the Rogue. Well, in four days I never raised one single trout. The first day

I laughed and joked; the second day, I wondered, and worked harder; the third day I swore; and at the end of the fourth I began to feel badly. A fisherman cannot help this. It is in him. All the time the others were catching fish. Romer went to twenty-five, Captain to thirty, Ken to thirty-four.

Then the next day, late after dark, Ed and Ken came back with an eleven-pound steelhead which Ed had captured after a terrific fight of over an hour, in which the fish took him way down the river.

Ed was wild with excitement. "I was casting off Missouri Bar, close to shore. Bingo! Up comes a steelhead! I didn't see him, but I felt him. Nearly yanked me in. My line was whizzing out. I thought he was down river. But he jumped right upstream, and he was so big I nearly dropped the rod. Then down he went with the current, and I had to run. I came to a big rock. Couldn't get around it. Climbed up. There was Ken fishing. He yelled: 'Hell of a big trout jumping here right in front of me!' "

" 'That's my fish,' I yelled back."

" 'What! you got him on *your* line?' "

" 'Yes! Help! Help! Don't stand there yapping. Do something.' . . . After that I don't know what I said. Ken took my rod. I jumped back and ran around. All my line was off the reel. Ken said: 'Take it and run!' I did, and tore down the river. Caught up with him. Got my line back. Fought him awhile in front. He went upstream. I was beginning to feel better. Got my breath back. Then—bingo! down he went, tearing off all my line. I had to run, wade, climb rocks and ledges, walk logs. He kept going. I'd get some line back. Then he'd take it. Meanwhile it had grown dark. But I could hear him jump. Then the moon came out. He passed a big rapid and got into a still deep pool. Here I fought him for a long time. Then he took a notion to move on down toward Gold Beach. I was afraid of that light leader and had to follow. Came to a bank thick with willows. The water was deep—over my head. But I held on to the willows with my left hand and stuck my feet up under the bank. Got past somehow. Then I was all in. Made up my mind to hold him there or die. Ken came panting after me. 'Hey— I thought you'd drowned. . . . Haven't you got that fish *yet?*'

LOREN HAD A SUSPICION THAT HE WAS WATCHED

PLATE XCVII

Loren Casting

PLATE XCVIII

Loren Disconsolate

PLATE XCIX

'Got nothing,' I said. 'He isn't even tired!' But it turned out he was, and finally I got the better of him and dragged him in to shore. Ken grabbed him and carried him out. Gee! What a steelhead! Greatest time I ever had in my life!"

Ken's story differed from Ed's. "I was fishing lower Missouri. All of a sudden there was a terrible splash right in front of me. Then I saw a whale of a steelhead jump up high. I cast where he dropped back. He jumped again farther out. I thought he acted kind of funny. Then I heard Ed yell. He was up on the rock above me. His rod was bent double. His reel was screeching. 'My God! What'll I do now? I can't get down.' I asked him if that fish was on his line. Then he swore and raved at me. He had gone crazy. I took his rod so he could go round back of the rock. The trout nearly pulled me in. I tried to stop him. You can bet I was glad Ed got back to take the rod. 'Here, take it. I want to fish myself,' I said. Ed grabbed the rod and began to run down the shore, splashing, stumbling. He sure was funny. Finally he went out of sight. I hooked a nice trout myself and forgot Ed. Then I caught several small ones. Happened to think of Ed and wondered why he didn't come back. It got dark. Then the moon came out. When he had been gone over an hour I grew worried and started down to look for him, yelling all the way. I had to go a mile. And there he was still hanging on to that fish. His voice was about gone and he couldn't hold the rod up. 'Where—you—been?' he whispered. 'Hell of —a guy—you are. I darn near—drowned!' . . . Well, I stayed with him then, and it's a cinch he'd never got that steelhead if I hadn't."

The steelhead in question certainly was a magnificent fish. He was thirty-two and one-half inches long and weighed over eleven pounds, being the largest I ever saw. He was longer than Romer's fifteen-pound rainbow caught in New Zealand, but not nearly so thick or deep.

That night there was a long powwow in camp. Ken had caught seven fish, Ed six, capping his with the record, Romer five, and Captain four. There were two six-pounders and several around five in that collection. I did not join in the *mêlée*, for I had not even had a rise. Again it appeared to be a matter of very light leaders. Captain Mitchell and Romer were partial to the light Hardy leader No. 355. I could not hold a pound fish on that flimsy leader. Ed had used a No. 345, which was light enough. It was a mystery to me how he ever landed that steelhead.

Next day Betty caught a two-pound trout and was in ecstasies. Then to Loren's poignant mingled distress and delight, his pal Gus caught a fifteen-inch steelhead. After this I had no peace. The youngsters pestered me to death for leaders, flies, and everything they could beg. Loren lost his new tapered line on a snag. He said, "Romer swore it was a snag, but *I* know it was a fish!" Then Loren broke the tip of his new rod—the first really good one he had ever owned. The same day he broke the second tip. He made a thousand excuses. Then, seeing me unbelieving, he wept. Next he spent hours mending that rod. It was almost as funny as to see him cast a fly. He wanted to get out a long line, and therefore he snagged the brush and broke his flies on the rocks. Loren had grown considerably in a year. He was stronger, but he had not improved materially in his fishing. He was not in any sense practical. He could not remember—anything could distract him.

On the sixth day of our stay at Winkle Bar the sky became overcast and showers of rain fell. It looked a fine day for fishing. Dolly and I went down the river, and I had the pleasure of raising two steelhead, of seeing them snap the fly off the surface, turn and shine and, when I struck them, shoot high into the air. These two weighed four and five pounds, and were the only ones I caught on the whole trip of nine days' fishing. It was not my lucky time.

But though I did not have much luck at fishing I caught many things perhaps more profitable. I saw a rainbow shine down into the V-shaped cleft of the river canyon—a very broad, marvelously colored rainbow, so exquisite and ethereal that I could scarcely believe my eyes. The trout rose to make beautiful circles in the water, where the afterglow of sunset lingered with wonderful light. Wild ducks winged swift flight up and down the river. In the high noons buzzards soared over the crested mountain slopes.

In the gray of dawn a heron winged over my tent every morning at that hour, and croaked his dismal cry. During the day ravens flew by with a different kind of croak. At sunset the swallows appeared from somewhere and filled the sky with fluttering chaff. They were darting to and fro, feeding on the insect life, nevertheless they were flying for sheer joy. Once I saw a sparrow-hawk swoop down from a high perch and pounce upon a luckless little swallow. There was a puff of feathers. The swallow seemed enveloped by the hawk. It flew back to the dead snag of a fir tree and bent over its prey. The watcher cannot escape the tragedy of nature.

Days passed without Loren catching a single steelhead. In his desperation he went to using a spinner, and then grasshoppers. It was fun to see him chase them, but I disapproved of his bait fishing.

"But dog-gone it, dad, I read where President Coolidge fished for trout with worms!" he protested, stoutly.

"True, Loren, he did, and got himself criticized by a lot of high-brow fly fishermen who think it disgraceful to use bait. Don't misunderstand me, Loren," I replied, earnestly. "I've seldom used anything but flies here on the Rogue, but in my own brook in Sullivan County, New York, I used to fish with worms. We couldn't catch trout there with anything else. It's no disgrace to catch a fish on anything, so long as the tackle is right and you do it fairly. But in your case I want you to practice casting with a fly."

"Well, I'm not stuck on it," said Loren, glumly. "Here I've cast flies for six days. *Six days!* and no fish. . . . Then you saw me snag myself in the seat of the pants. *And you laughed!*"

"Loren, boy, I couldn't help it," I replied, apologetically. "You were so funny."

"Huh! Say, if you want me to practice casting, why don't you take me fishing?" he queried, seeing he had me in a corner.

"All right, son, I'll do it. Tomorrow! All day!"

"Down to Missouri Bar?"

"Yes. We'll start early so as to get there first."

He whooped and ran around like a lunatic, and pestered all of us for tackle.

Next morning bright and early we were off. I would have preferred it dark and lowering, for sunny days are not good on the Rogue. We climbed to the Gold Beach trail, and went down, with Loren ahead, manifestly content.

Our destination was a mile below camp. We crossed the river in our skiff, and began to fish. I let Loren go ahead. Sometimes he managed to get out a good cast. But not when he saw me looking! I simply prayed for a trout to rise to his fly. But none did. Slowly we worked down the river; and in the place where the others had had such good sport neither of us had a rise. Still there was always hope and Loren seemed happy.

When lunch time came he was hungry as a bear. I had not brought much lunch, so I saved most of mine for a later hour, when I knew he would be hungry again. We went on down the river, and Loren never showed a single sign of weariness or disgust until mid-afternoon.

"Oh, heck! Can't I get a bite?"

"Lorry, a fisherman must learn to stick," I replied.

We went on trying likely holes. Never a rise! I had gotten to the point of yearning to hook a trout and let Loren take the rod. It was a very vital occasion. I seemed to be on trial. But the lad had the true spirit of a fisherman. The rocks and river and mountains were sufficient. We plodded back, finding we had come miles over rough shore. Loren never complained, and he stayed with me without a falter. He had on heavy wading boots, too large for him. But no one would have guessed it from word or action. When we got back to Missouri Bar I was tired. The sun still shone hot. I sat down on the sand, with my back to a rock, while Loren went to fishing. He would not give up, though his arm was limp. I went to sleep.

When I awoke he was chasing grasshoppers. It was great to watch him, for he might have been stalking big game. He would talk to them in this wise: "You yellow son-of-a-gun! I'll assassinate you!" Then whack with his stick. Very often Loren would quote something from one of my books, as his brother Romer, at his age, had been wont to do.

I discovered presently that during my nap Loren had built an elaborate water corral. He had done this before on other occasions. Finally he captured a grasshopper and put it on his hook. "Now I'll ketch a trout," he averred, happily. The sun went down, and it grew time for us to start back. He fished so patiently that I hated to call him. We crossed the river and climbed the steep slope to the trail. Loren again took the lead, with a good brisk step —one I found hard to imitate. He had an eye for trees, lizards, squirrels, birds. But he did not talk. Once I said, "Lorry, I'm sorry it was such a bum day."

"It wasn't bum, dad," he said, cheerfully. "You don't have to ketch fish to have a good day!"

THE END